Queen
of the
Courtesans

Queen

of the

Courtesans

Fanny Murray

BARBARA WHITE

In memory of my parents
Thelma and David G White

First published 2014

The History Press
The Mill, Brimscombe Port
Stroud, Gloucestershire, GL5 2QG
www.thehistorypress.co.uk

© Barbara White, 2014

The right of Barbara White to be identified as the Author
of this work has been asserted in accordance with the
Copyright, Designs and Patents Act 1988.

British Library Cataloguing in Publication Data.
A catalogue record for this book is available from the British Library.

ISBN 978 0 7509 6869 3

Typesetting and origination by The History Press and Printed in Malta by Melita Press
Production managed by Jellyfish

Contents

A Note on the Text

The spelling, punctuation and capitalisation of original documents has been retained to give the reader a sense of the colour of the period, although the long 's' and other typographies have been modernised. American spelling has been anglicised. Quotations from *An Essay on Woman* have been taken from Arthur H. Cash's reconstruction of the poem. Where appropriate, page references to *The Memoirs of the Celebrated Miss Fanny M-----* (1759) are given within the text.

Square brackets around an author's name such as [John Oldmixon] denotes that the writer was the probable author even though his name does not appear on the title page. Square brackets around dates such as [1765] indicates that this is the most probable date of publication, even though it might not appear in the text.

Before 1752, according to the Julian or Old Style calendar, the New Year began on 25 March. Throughout this text, the Gregorian or New Style calendar has been adopted and the year taken to begin on 1 January.

The place of publication of books cited is London unless stated otherwise.

Pre-decimal Currency

Prices are given in the currency of the time, and the purchasing power calculator at http://www.measuringworth.com has been used to estimate modern values.

One pound was made up of 20 shillings or 240 pence, so that there were 12 pence to a shilling. A crown was 5 shillings; and half a crown, 2 shillings and sixpence – this was written as *2s 6d*. A guinea was 1 pound 1 shilling – £1 1*s* 0*d*; 2 guineas, 2 pounds 2 shillings and written as £2 2*s* 0*d*, and so on.

Glossary of Terms

Abbess, or Lady Abbess	the keeper of a high-class brothel.
Bagnio	a bathing house, but with a reputation for sexual intrigue.
Bawd	brothel-keeper.
Bawdy house	brothel.
Bon ton/haut ton	fashionable and highly fashionable society.
Demi-monde	a class of women of dubious reputation, including actresses and courtesans, who inhabited a world on the edge of respectable society.
Demi-rep	a woman of doubtful reputation including actresses and courtesans. Literally 'half reputation'.
Dirty	disreputable.
Gallantry	sexual intrigue.
Fleet marriage	until Hardwicke's Marriage Act (1753), this was a legally binding marriage which did not have to take place in church and which required neither banns nor licence.
High-keeping	the maintenance of a mistress in the greatest of luxury.
Keeper/protector	a man who keeps a mistress.
Nosegay	a posy of fragrant flowers often used to ward off evil smells.

Nunnery	a high-class brothel, run by an abbess.
Sponging/spunging house	a place of temporary confinement for debtors, normally run by the local bailiff.

Abbreviations

BCL	Bath Central Library.
Biographical Dictionary of Actors	Philip H. Highfill, Kalman A. Burnim, Edward A. Langhans (eds), *A Biographical Dictionary of Actors, Actresses, Musicians, Dancers, Managers & other Stage Personnel in London, 1660–1800*, 16 vols (Carbondale and Edwardville: Southern Illinois University Press, 1973–93).
BL	British Library, London.
BM	British Museum, London.
BRO	Bath Record Office.
LMA	London Metropolitan Archives.
NMM	Caird Library at the National Maritime Museum, London.
N&Q	*Notes and Queries*.
RCS	Library of the Royal College of Surgeons of England, London.
T&C	*Town and Country Magazine*.
WAC	City of Westminster Archive Centre.
Walpole Correspondence	Peter Cunningham (ed.), *The Letters of Horace Walpole, Earl of Orford*, 8 vols (Richard Bentley, 1857).
WNA	Woodhorn – Northumberland Archives.

Acknowledgements

Numerous individuals have been instrumental in offering advice and encouragement during the writing of this book and I would like to begin by thanking The History Press – in particular, Katharine Reeve, Gary Chapman and Stuart Biles for their belief in Fanny Murray, and for bringing this fascinating courtesan to the page. I am also grateful to Lindsey Smith for her patience and helpfulness in answering my many enquiries during the process of writing, and especially to my editors Mark Beynon and Rebecca Newton for their considerable support and advice.

I would also like to thank the staff of the following libraries and archive centres without whose kindly assistance, help and knowledge, this book would not have been possible – the Bodleian Library, the British Library, the Caird Library at the National Maritime Museum, the City of Westminster Archive Centre, the Department of Prints and Drawings at the British Museum, the Library of the Royal College of Surgeons, the London Metropolitan Archives, the National Art Library at the Victoria and Albert Museum, the National Library of Scotland, and Woodhorn Northumberland Archives. Thanks are especially due to Anne Buchanan, the local studies librarian at Bath Central Library, and also to Lucy Rutherford, the archivist at Bath Abbey; Jo Johnston, formerly archivist at Bath Preservation Trust; and Colin Johnston, the principal archivist, and the staff of Bath Record Office, all of whom were immensely helpful as I sought to confirm Fanny Murray's connections with Bath.

I am also indebted to John Montagu, 12th Earl of Sandwich, for his patience in answering my questions regarding the minute book of the Divan Club (1744–46), known as *Al Koran*, and on Murray's involvement with the club. I am equally grateful to Sir Edward Dashwood, Bt, for his clarification on the identity of the sitters for the oriental portraits at West Wycombe Park, and for his kind permission to reproduce his portrait of Fanny Murray. My thanks also go to Roderick D. Cannon and Keith Sanger who were especially helpful in sharing their considerable knowledge about eighteenth-century pibrochs as I tried to identify the addressee of the Scottish piping tune, 'Salute to Miss Fanny Murray'.

Friends and colleagues have been overwhelmingly kind in their unflagging support and encouragement, and I would particularly like to thank Martine Brant, Barbara Cheney, Graham Davis, Ian Gregson, George O'Har, Claire Pickard, and Neil Sammells for reading draft chapters – the book has profited greatly from their insightful comments and suggestions. In addition, Judi Stephenson, Michael Stewart and Martine Brant offered generous hospitality and joyful company on research trips to Buckinghamshire, Edinburgh, Oxford and Northumberland. I have also been fortunate to have a 'sisterhood' of my own to rival that of Fanny Murray (including some honorary females), all of whom have provided immense encouragement, quite often over welcome cups of coffee, lunches and dinners, and I would especially like to thank Judith Birch, June Breeze, Chris Brown, Helena and David Cook, Stephanie Fleet, Becky Gallagher, Jane Glaser, Peta Hall, Mary Hayward, Carol Jenkins, Penny Holroyd, Roy Johnson, Joyce McDonald, Elspeth Montagu, Chris Pelling, the Priory girls, Diana Rejiester, Janet Scott, Su Underwood and Joan Walker.

My greatest debt, however, is to Elaine Chalus and Ceri Sullivan for their unbounded generosity with both their time and scholarship in reading versions of the book in its entirety. They kept me focused on Murray when fascinating characters like Betsy Wemyss, the 'one-eyed squinting Venus' or the feisty Elizabeth Roach tempted me to digress, and our many lively conversations helped me enormously in my quest for the real Fanny Murray. Those errors and omissions that remain are my own.

The illustrations in this book represent the most comprehensive collection to date, of prints and portraits associated with Fanny Murray. I am indebted, therefore, to a number of institutions and individuals for their permission to reproduce these images and for their patience in answering my queries. My thanks to the Althorp Estates (and especially Sophie Slater), the Art Archive/Garrick Club (and especially Sally Paley and Cheryl Thomas), 'Bath in Time' at Bath Central Library, the Berkeley Castle Charitable Trust (and especially David Bowd-Exworth and Mr and Mrs Berkeley); the Bibliothèque Nationale de France, the British Library; the British Museum (and especially Christopher Sutherns), Sir Edward Dashwood Bt, the National Portrait Gallery, the National Trust, the Paul Mellon Centre for Studies in British Art (and especially Jenny Hill) and the Victoria and Albert Museum. I am also grateful to Jon Ryan, who assisted with images and especially to Dan Brown, the founder of 'Bath in Time' for his advice and expertise on reproducing images, and for his immense kindness in photographing mezzotints and engravings from my own collection for reproduction in this book.

Finally, I wish to express my gratitude to the late Dr Timothy C Curtis, an inspirational teacher and scholar, who first instilled in me a love of history and a deep admiration for those men and women, like Fanny Murray, who lived their lives on the edge.

Introduction

When first I took a distant view,
My fainting spirits quick withdrew;
My heart beat in a hurry.
But when I near approach'd her rays,
'Twas hard to bear the dazling [sic] blaze,
To gaze on Fanny Murray.[1]

Fanny Murray would not have approved of this biography. Even at the height of her power when she relied on publicity to oil the wheels of her fame and fortune, she recoiled from intrusions into her personal life. Yet it has only been by reading her surviving private letters, delving into the correspondence, memoirs and journals of her contemporaries – men like James Boswell (1740–95) and 'the very prince of Gossips' Horace Walpole (1717–97) – and by following her in the gossip columns of the day that new facts have emerged which allow her fascinating story to be told definitively.[2]

Hers was a classic tale of rags-to-riches that could be found in any of the prostitute narratives of the day.[3] Born Frances Rudman, into an impoverished musician's family in Bath in 1729, she rose to become a great beauty and premier courtesan of her day. At the height of her celebrity, she inhabited an elegant demi-monde of courtesans, actresses and mistresses whose lovers were drawn from elite society, from royal, aristocratic and political circles. In Murray's case, her numerous *amours* included the Hon. John Spencer (1708–46), a member of one of the wealthiest aristocratic families in England; Richard 'Beau' Nash (1674–1761), the flamboyant master of ceremonies at Bath; and the rakish John Montagu (1718–92), 4th Earl of Sandwich, who rose to become First Lord of the Admiralty. Her lovers also included a fair number of fraud-sters, rogues and ne'er-do-wells for whom Murray appears to have had a particular weakness. As with a number of other celebrated courtesans, Murray's rags-to-riches story was not a straightforward upwardly mobile trajectory but rather one of fluctuating fortunes, of immense wealth one day and near penury the next. She was often plagued by debt and, after she withdrew from the sex trade around 1755 and had settled into mar-riage with the actor David Ross (1728–90), she returned, if not to rags, then at least to a kind of genteel frugality.

Murray did not conform to today's idea of perfect beauty, being nei-ther tall nor willowy like twenty-first-century top models and style icons. Indeed, she did not fully conform to the ideals of her own day, for Murray was short and slightly overweight. The anonymous author of the two-volume *Memoirs of the Celebrated Miss Fanny M-----* (1:8) (hereafter termed the *Memoirs*) described her as 'but of the middle size, and though inclined to be plump, she had delicacy enough in her shape to make it agreeable'.[4] Ross's good friend, the journalist, editor and drama critic John Taylor (1757–1832), who described Murray in later life, was also struck by her petite build – she was, he remembered, 'short, and by no means elegant'.[5]

In her prime, however, Murray was one of the perfections of the age, and her voluptuous figure drove men wild with desire. She was especially admired for her bosoms, 'those fair hemispheres, those orbs of more than snowy whiteness, which seemed to pant for release from irksome robes' (1:70). It was her face, however, that was her undoubted fortune, and her 'apple-faced Beauty' was described admiringly by the author of the *Memoirs* (1:6–7) as:

A perfect oval, with eyes that conversed love, and every other feature in agreeable symmetry. Her dimple cheek alone might have captivated, if a smile that gave it existence, did not display such other charms as shared the conquest. Her teeth regular, small and perfectly white, coral lips and chestnut hair, soon attracted the eyes of everyone.[6]

Queen of the Courtesans: Fanny Murray is the first full-length biography of Murray since the publication of the *Memoirs* in 1758. They followed Murray's fortunes from her childhood in Bath to her retirement from prostitution, and concluded in 1756 just after she had embarked upon her twenty-two-year marriage to Ross. Understandably, subsequent attention has concentrated on Murray's promiscuous heyday, as described in the *Memoirs*, rather than on her quieter marital life, and yet the years during which she proved a devoted wife are not without their own excitements and the occasional glittering moment. Her marital years also give fascinating insights into the way the media, and her once adoring public, responded to the former 'toast of the town' in her declining years. This biography explores Murray the courtesan and Murray the wife in equal measure. It also draws on a wide range of sources, including many that have not featured before in narratives of her life, in order to disentangle the real Murray from the apocryphal anecdotes and myth-making stories that have grown up around her.

Indeed, the first biography of Murray, which preceded the *Memoirs* by ten years, was a complete invention. 'The Secret History, &c. of the Famous Miss F---y M----y' appeared in 1748 in *The Humours of Fleet-Street*, a collection of biographies of 'the most noted Ladies of Pleasure'.[7] A second volume followed in June 1749.[8] *The Humours of Fleet-Street* took the form of twenty-four letters, written principally by a character named Captain Henry Rakewell to his friend, George Bellfield, and Murray's eight-page biography appeared in the first volume as the fourth of thirteen letters. The letter was dated 20 December 1746, when Murray was 17, although she was portrayed as older in the narrative. Advertisements for the first volume, on sale at 2*s*, began to appear from mid-November. By the end of the month, and possibly to boost sales, a list of the more notorious ladies featured in the volume was also added, their names lightly disguised by a mixture of letters and dashes to avoid the possibility of libel action.[9] Aside from Murray, these included the well-known brothel-keeper Jane Douglas (*c.* 1700–61) and the actress Margaret 'Peg' Woffington (1720–60). As Stella Tillyard has noted, and as Murray would learn to her cost, this simple device for obscuring names meant that 'no slander or gossip was unprintable'.[10]

According to *The Humours of Fleet-Street*, rather than being the daughter of a musician in Bath, Murray was born into a well-connected family in the west of Scotland and became the toast of Edinburgh.

Her biographer claimed that she was seduced at the age of 18 by 'a young nobleman lately married' and made pregnant by him. Disowned by her parents, Murray was then taken 'into keeping', as it was termed, by her seducer who infected her with venereal disease and abandoned her sometime after the birth of her child. The narrative made no further mention of the infant, charting instead Murray's descent into private and then common prostitution.

According to her biographer, Murray finally ended up in a house of correction where she was indented for seven years to a merchant intent on placing her in service in Virginia. Murray escaped by means of an elaborate plan that centred on her seduction of the merchant as they travelled together to Glasgow to rendezvous with the boat bound for America. This biography of Murray only becomes at all plausible in the final paragraph, after her arrival in London, when the character Rakewell gave every appearance of actually having observed Murray 'at all publick places with as much *eclat* as any of her profession'.

Murray maintained a stoical silence when *The Humours of Fleet-Street* appeared, as she did whenever she was reported in the press, and did nothing to confirm or deny its fictions. It was the same a decade later, when the *Memoirs* were published.

Historiographically, the *Memoirs* are key to any study of Murray, as they have formed the basis of all subsequent narratives of her life in the absence of anything more reliable or substantial. The first volume, which was advertised in the newspapers from the end of November 1758, was savaged in review.[11] A writer for the *Critical Review* called it a 'miserable catchpenny book' and confidently predicted that 'nobody will throw away their money upon this collection of absurdities'.[12]

In similar tones, a critic for the *Monthly Review* dismissed the *Memoirs* as 'ill written, imperfect, and … little more than mere invention'. He also alerted his readers that 'the author promise[d] to finish [the *Memoirs*] in another volume, provided the first part meets with success'.[13] The first volume did well enough, seemingly, for an advertisement in the *Whitehall Evening Post*, dated 13 March 1759, to announce a sequel at '3*s* bound, sew'd 2*s*. 6*d*'.[14]

It was in the second volume that the anonymous author of the *Memoirs* (2:106–15) took revenge on his reviewers by imagining an episode between Mr L, an author, and 'Mr G---s's right hand', a reference to Ralph Griffiths, the Nonconformist bookseller who had founded

the *Monthly Review* in 1749. In the satirical conversation that followed
(2:113–5), the *Monthly Review* was said to sell reviews to order, while the
Critical Review was ridiculed for having 'less judgment and impartial-
ity, and greater scurrility than even the *Monthly Review*'. Despite being
goaded in this fashion, the writer for the *Critical Review* was willing to
concede 'that the second volume [was] better than the first', but insisted
that its author 'might have applied his talents to a better purpose'.[15]

Despite the reviewers' criticisms, the *Memoirs* appear to have enjoyed
popular appeal, and were still amusing readers some thirty-five years
after their publication. In 1796, *Ranger's Repository* printed a letter, osten-
sibly from a drunken 'Lover of Fun', who wrote to deliver a 'Confusion
to your books of Science, Philosophy, History and such d[amne]d dry
stuff. – Give me the Adventures of a Buck, or the History of Fanny
Murray and be hanged.'[16]

The inebriate's enjoyment of the *Memoirs* is not surprising, for the
narrative maintained a lively pace throughout and recounted its colourful version of Murray's life in entertaining fashion. For added spice, the
author of the *Memoirs* reproduced letters and papers that he claimed had
once belonged to Murray and her associates. He also included imagined
encounters with aristocratic rakes, pimps and prostitutes, and even the
King of France.

Indeed, a quarter of both volumes is taken up by five first-person
'autobiographies within a biography' of characters, both real and imagined, who purportedly told their life stories to Murray. The first volume
featured the autobiographies of a Mrs Stevens and Miss Charlotte S---,
both fictional fallen women, the Covent Garden pimp Jack Harris
(d. *c.* 1794), and the polygamist Captain Plaistow, while the lengthy
account of the life and loves of the rake Robert 'Beau' Tracy (d. 1756)
appeared at the beginning of the second volume.[17]

The fictional scenes and flights of fancy that characterise the *Memoirs*
were very much part of the biography's charm for those contemporary readers eager for gossip about Murray's private life, no matter how
inaccurate or far-fetched. Yet the *Memoirs* were more than 'mere invention', as suggested by the critic from the *Monthly Review*, and not every
episode was a fabrication.[18] In fact, the loose framework of Murray's
life that the *Memoirs* constructed for reader entertainment was largely
accurate. As a consequence, the *Memoirs* are valuable in bridging some
of the tantalising gaps in Murray's narrative, and they are often the only

source available to add flesh to the bare bones of claims and stories that circulated about her. If the broad brushstrokes are mostly accurate, it is only in the close detail, in the colourfully imagined scenes and conversations, that the reader must be *en garde*.

The same issues of verisimilitude arise with many of the other contemporary sources that are used to authenticate episodes from Murray's life. For example, Murray sometimes featured in the immensely popular 'tête-à-tête' series that was published in the *Town and Country Magazine* between 1769 and 1792. The 'tête-à-têtes' are a mine of salacious detail as, each month, the sex lives and previous *amours* of a well-known pair of lovers were served up for the prurient interest of magazine readers. As Cindy McCreery has shown, however, in her study of the genre, '*tête-à-têtes* were often only partly accurate, and occasionally completely inaccurate' so that claims for Murray as the former love interest of a number of distinguished men are also to be treated circumspectly.[19]

Inaccuracies and embellishments have also been introduced into more recent accounts of Murray's life, and repeated with such regularity that they too have become part of the Fanny Murray narrative. A case in point is an anecdote about a culinary tribute which is still credited to Murray even though it was originally intended for someone else.[20] The anecdote, in which a young gallant drank champagne from the shoe of a '*fille de joie*', was first retold in *Ladies Fair and Frail* (1909), Horace Bleackley's engaging study of eighteenth-century courtesans. Suggesting that the shoe might have possibly belonged to Murray, Bleackley described how the gallant ordered it to be prepared for supper. The French chef duly shredded the fine damask upper part of the shoe 'and tossed it up in a ragout, minced the sole, cut the wooden heel into very fine slices, fried them in butter, and placed them round the dish for garnish'.[21] What Bleackley omitted to mention, as he transcribed this anecdote from either the *Monthly Review* (1754), or possibly the *London Magazine* (1754), was that the chef named his concoction, in honour of the young lady in question, 'de soulier à la Murphy'.[22] Either by an accident of mistranscription or by design, the anecdote, which has become part of the Fanny Murray myth, does not belong to her at all.

Recovering Murray's past history is not only hindered by the unreliability of sources, but also by the fact that Murray left so few textual traces. Apart from a handful of letters to the Spencer family of Althorp, in Northamptonshire, Murray's authentic voice is rarely and only faintly heard in any of the contemporary sources where she is mentioned. She did not engage personally with the press or keep herself in the public eye by penning letters to editors or by issuing rebuttals when false claims were made about her; nor did she place advertisements to promote herself in any of the newspapers.

By contrast, Kitty Fisher (*c.* 1739–67), Murray's nearest rival from the next generation of courtesans, embraced publicity and deftly managed her own career by capitalising on every opportunity to market herself. Thus, when a fanciful memoir appeared in March 1759 entitled *The Juvenile Adventures of Miss Kitty F----r*, Fisher immediately took out an advertisement in the *Public Advertiser* to complain of her treatment in censorious terms that were guaranteed to boost both sales and her own status. Writing in the third person, Fisher described how she had been:

> abused in public Papers, exposed in Print-shops, and to wind up the Whole, some Wretches mean, ignorant, and venal, would impose upon the Public, by daring to pretend to publish her Memoirs. She hopes to prevent the Success of their Endeavours, by thus publickly declaring that nothing of that Sort has the slightest Foundation in Truth.[23]

In addition to maintaining a low profile in the press, Murray also refused to trade on her famous name and scandalous past by writing her autobiography, and she had no hand in the *Memoirs* that appeared three years after she had settled into marital respectability. Other courtesans were not so reticent, especially when a lucrative income was at stake. Laura J. Rosenthal in *Infamous Commerce*, a study of eighteenth-century prostitution, has estimated that at least two or three dozen prostitute narratives were published during the eighteenth century.[24] Constantia Phillips (1709–65), for example, was offered £1,000 for her *Apology for the Conduct of Teresia Constantia Phillips*, which was first published in instalments in 1748. She planned to earn more, however, by blackmailing former lovers, especially Lord Chesterfield, into buying annuities for her in exchange for being expunged from her narrative.[25] Harriette Wilson (1786–1845) received £400 from the sale of her memoirs in 1825 but might have received several thousand pounds more following blackmail letters to over 200 of her former lovers.[26] Arthur Wellesley, 1st Duke of Wellington was one who refused to pay up and is credited with the famous challenge to Wilson of 'publish and be damned'.

The unreliability of contemporary sources, and the paucity of detailed accounts relating to Murray is not altogether surprising, since courtesans were often regarded as little more than footnotes to the lives of famous (and infamous) men, their literary significance restricted to the light they shed on the lovers with whom they had shared an intimacy. After all, courtesans only came to prominence as a result of 'the accident of their promiscuous relations with a number of the wealthiest and most influential men of their day'.[27] As a result, references to courtesans, even those who left behind memoirs, are often sparse and spread widely but thinly across a range of ephemeral writings – in newspapers, magazines, jest books and poetry collections, and in snippets of news buried in the private letters, diaries and memoirs of society gossips.

As a consequence, Murray is often only to be glimpsed fleetingly, and nearly always from a male perspective, in the writings of the day. Only her portraits, which were reproduced in their thousands for the print-shop market, permit a longer gaze, which can linger over her beauty and distil her essence. Taken together, however, these visual and literary evidences, garnered from a multiplicity of contemporary sources, unlock a life of fascinating contradiction – of love, marriage, immense wealth, refinement and marital reputation on the one hand, and sex, debauchery, grinding poverty, vulgarity, scandal and humiliation on the other.

Bleackley's chapter-length study of Murray in *Ladies Fair and Frail* was the first serious biography of the beautiful courtesan since the *Memoirs* appeared in 1758. After her death in 1778 Murray had soon slipped from memory, and it was not until the 1850s that there were the first glimmerings of a revival of interest from a new generation of gentlemen admirers. In particular, contributors to *Notes & Queries*, among whom Bleackley was often an authoritative voice, were keen to reconstruct her life, to verify her anecdotes and establish the nature of her relationships with famous men of the eighteenth century.

These relationships were not always sexual. Murray's connection with the radical politician, John Wilkes (1725–97), for example, stemmed from the furore that surrounded *An Essay on Woman* (published 1763), a blasphemous poem credited to Wilkes and addressed to Murray. Similarly, her connection with the rakish Sir Francis Dashwood (1708–81) was largely the result of her tangential involvement with two of his gentlemen's clubs – the Divan Club and the Order of St Francis. The latter, which was founded by Dashwood, is now best remembered as the most scurrilous of the so-called hell-fire clubs.

As a result, Murray's name appeared with increasing regularity during the last century in surveys, both scholarly and popular, of 'the Wilkes affair', hell-fire clubs and biographies of (often) scandalous eighteenth-century figures. In such studies, to borrow Philip Carter's phrase, Murray was the subject of a 'gentleman's club school of biography' and interest in her was largely limited to normally unsubstantiated asides and anecdotes that accentuated both her promiscuity and her beauty.[28] Her name and the broad outline of her life, therefore, have long been familiar to those interested in the eighteenth-century demi-monde. Even so, it is surprising to find her making brief appearances in works such as Daphne du Maurier's *Mary Anne*, a novel first published in 1954 and based on the life of du Maurier's great-great-grandmother, the courtesan Mary Anne Clarke (1776–1852), who was once mistress to Frederick, Duke of York.[29]

Popular interest in Murray has increased noticeably since the beginning of the new millennium. Fanny Murray mugs are now offered for sale on a number of internet sites, and she acquired her own Wikipedia page in 2013. On a more serious note, there has been a surge of scholarly interest in libertine literature, the sexual life of Georgian England and the nature of celebrity that has made the world of the courtesan altogether more accessible.[30] In addition, several biographies of notable courtesans, including Emma Hamilton (1765–1815), Mary Robinson (1757–1800), and Harriette Wilson, have also appeared and *Whore Biographies*, Julie Peakman's eight-volume collection of often rare libertine narratives, including the *Memoirs*, is an especially valuable resource.[31] Within this canon, however, interest in Murray is still largely limited to a retelling of her colourful life.[32] Even so, some new and thought-provoking perspectives on Murray and particularly, on Murray as viewed through the *Memoirs*, have emerged.

For example, Rosenthal's study of eighteenth-century prostitution placed Murray, as portrayed in the *Memoirs*, firmly within a commercial rather than a sexual context. *Infamous Commerce* charted the development of prostitution from the seventeenth-century's emphasis on sex as gratification, to the eighteenth century, when sex became a commercial transaction, increasingly divorced from pleasure.[33] This transformation from pleasure-seeking whore to businesslike prostitute, suggested Rosenthal, was reflected in the prostitute literature of the day, which focused on 'class and economic concerns' rather than the sexual activities of its promiscuous heroines.[34]

Thus, the *Memoirs* offered little help in pinpointing what it was that made Murray quite so irresistible sexually, yet they were assiduous in describing her shifting fortunes as a marketable commodity within the sex trade. Murray was described, therefore, as she experienced immense wealth and upward mobility but also such penury that she was arrested for debt and held in a sponging house (2:184). Within this context, Rosenthal viewed Murray as someone who was 'not so different from anyone else working their way through an unpredictable commercial world'.[35] Situating Murray within Mandevillian ideas on the necessity of private vice – of luxury, vanity and covetousness – to bring about economic prosperity, Rosenthal presented Murray as one who, by partial self-objectification and self-division (i.e. the separation of her own self from her business self), successfully reconciled vice with the rewards of the commercial marketplace.

Rather than a business context, Mary Peace, in her reading of the *Memoirs* (and also of *The Uncommon Adventures of Miss Kitty F----r* (1759)), placed Murray and Fisher within contemporary discourses on luxury and moral sense ideas, to regard them as sentimental figures and exemplars of natural virtue.[36] Published at a time of national prosperity, when the tide of the Seven Years War turned in favour of Britain's territorial interests, both texts, Peace considered, were 'freighted with significance far beyond their immediate subject matter'.[37] It was a significance born of the intense intellectual debate on the relationship between luxury and virtue that Britain's increasing affluence had provoked. To the classically educated, noted Peace, Britain's prosperity invited troubling comparisons with ancient Rome, a civilisation destroyed at the very height of its prosperity by the degenerative power of luxury. It was, argued Peace, the 'prominence of this classical-republican history of the fall of Rome, in the contemporary cultural imagination, which place[d] stories about the lives of prostitutes centre stage in 1759'.[38] In such a context Fisher and Murray became 'textbook representations of the allure and dangers of luxury'.[39]

Yet, as Peace explained, neither the *Memoirs* nor *The Uncommon Adventures* portrayed their heroines as corrupted by luxury, or as avaricious and sexually rapacious. Rather, informed by theories of moral sense, most prominently expounded by the Scottish philosopher David Hume, both women were 'framed as fundamentally sentimental figures: they have natural delicacy, good sense, good taste, and compassion, which act to curb the fatal excesses of luxury'.[40] Arguing that moral sense philosophy was deeply embedded in the *Memoirs*, Peace drew particular attention to a telling description of Murray (2:190) where she was portrayed as naturally virtuous, and as:

> one, whose natural disposition was not vicious, but who, having made a false step, found many obstacles to return into the path of virtue – who was neither avaricious, luxurious, or debauched, further than necessity obliged, but animated with sentiments that would have adorned a much more worthy and exalted station.

As a consequence, Peace considered both texts to be 'consoling narratives for a luxurious society in the midst of war'; texts that offered reassurances that luxury, when tempered by moral sense, could promote national virtue.[41] Indeed, as Peace pointed out, Murray's self-improvements and her self-fashioning as a creature of refinement were 'attendant upon a life of commerce and luxury'.[42]

Peace's reading of the *Memoirs* as a text imbued with moral sense ideas was in concert with Rosenthal's, who also viewed Murray, through the *Memoirs*, as a sentimental figure, one whose virtuous nature was not undermined by the immorality of her profession. Indeed, in what Rosenthal described as a '"tail-piece" of morality', she noted how Murray's virtue, despite her previously immoral life, was rewarded in the *Memoirs* by a marital happy ending.[43] It could be argued, of course, that Murray's marriage was simply art reflecting life. As this biography of Murray intends to show, however, these benign representations of her as a model of luxurious restraint and possessed of natural virtue, are at odds with a range of contemporary sources, outside the *Memoirs*, that depicted Murray in her heyday as the antithesis of the sentimental figure, as one marked by licentiousness and covetousness. It was only after Murray had retired from prostitution and was married to Ross that her qualities of benevolence, loyalty, stoicism and decency became more apparent.

Retrieving Murray's real character from those sources that either mirror the *Memoirs*' benevolent attitude toward her or present her in altogether less flattering terms is one of the challenges of this book. During her years as a courtesan, there must indeed have been a 'peculier gaiety in her temper' and 'great felicity in her company' (1:7) for Murray to have succeeded so spectacularly as the companion of pleasure-seeking men.[44]

Yet her geniality, and indeed the natural virtue that Peace distinguished, might have been superficial – no more than the simple ploy of a good businesswoman to keep customers happy and trade booming. This is suggested in an amusing it-narrative entitled 'The Episode of the Petticoat' after the eponymous narrator had come into the possession of one of Murray's maids. Able to observe Murray at close quarters, the petticoat described her as:

> good-natured and affable; in the Exercise of which Virtues she finds her Account; for as Miss lives on the Publick, it is her immediate Business to please her Company by Blandishment and Indulgence.[45]

There was, therefore, more to Murray the courtesan than the simple 'sprightly wench' that the nineteenth-century author Fitzgerald Molloy observed and the 'gay, plump little thing' of the writer Francis Askham's imaginings.[46] Another less attractive side to Murray existed behind her professional exterior as a 'good-time girl'. It was well known, for example, that she was quick-tempered and that men quailed at her petulant outbursts. In a letter to John Russell, 4th Duke of Bedford (1710–71) his placeman Richard Rigby (1722–88) described the fallout from a row between the 23-year-old Murray and the diplomat and politician Thomas Robinson (1695–1770), afterward 1st Baron Grantham. It is unclear if Robinson was Murray's lover at the time and the row no more than a lovers' tiff, but the exchange was sufficiently heated to require an intermediary to placate matters: 'Lord Waldegrave talks of going with me [Rigby], but he is appointed plenipotentiary between Fanny Murray and Mr Robinson, in a treaty of peace that I believe will engross too much of his time to allow of any absence.'[47]

As a result, sources outside the *Memoirs* have regularly painted Murray as an egotistical and impetuous courtesan. In 1809, for example, the biographer of du Maurier's famous relative, Mary Anne Clarke, described Murray, Fisher and Lucy Cooper (d. 1772) as 'abandoned prostitutes [who] were only distinguished by their selfish extravagance'.[48] More recently, writers have variously described Murray as 'disreputable and grasping', given to 'outrageously obscene talk' and as 'one of the impulsive belles who knew no law but her own whim for the moment'.[49] This was undoubtedly true, but this study has also discovered new material to show that, while she was avaricious as a courtesan, in private she was a deeply caring and generous individual who undertook the lifelong support of her father and siblings.

These contrasting aspects of her character – her jovial cordiality and seemingly innate virtue on the one hand and her fiery-tempered covetousness on the other – have divided opinion on the extent to which Murray should be regarded as a reluctant prostitute – one who was forced into the profession following her seduction, around 1742, by the aristocratic rake, John Spencer. For example, Rakewell in *The Humours of Fleet-Street*:

> sincerely believe[d] she would abandon [prostitution], if there were any possibility of gaining some share of her former reputation, by the most hearty contrition and repentance: but that is impossible; and I am afraid she must continue what she is, while youth and health lasts, and then die miserable.[50]

In similar terms, Bleackley argued that Murray always hankered after domesticity, and would have been happier as 'the blameless helpmate of some good citizen of Bath', had Spencer not ruined her marital prospects.[51] It is certainly true that she proved an exemplary wife to Ross throughout the years of their marriage. Yet, numerous anecdotes attest to her ardent enjoyment of venal pleasure and to her vigorous pursuit of the vast wealth that prostitution could bring. Indeed, it has been suggested that Murray was very grateful to Spencer for having first set her on her scandalous path to fame and fortune.[52] It was her own drive and determination, however, that made Murray the most successful courtesan of her day.

Rosenthal's two models – of the pleasure-seeking whore and the commercially minded prostitute who sacrificed pleasure to business – are indeed helpful, but what of courtesans like Murray who were neither whores nor prostitutes, and yet both? Several studies have sought to define their often indefinable qualities. Elite courtesans were the 'it' girls of the eighteenth century, who were known variously as *impures*, demireps (literally, women of half reputations), votaries of Venus, Thaïses (after the fourth-century Greek *hetaerae*, Thaïs) and Cyprians (after Aphrodite, the Greek goddess of love, said to have been born on Cyprus).

They were exceptional women, a breed apart, at times wild and unpredictable, but always captivating, alluring and somewhat elusive – women who could be bought, at a price, but never quite possessed.

The anonymous author of *A Congratulatory Epistle from a Reformed Rake* [1758] placed courtesans second in his ten categories of whores to be found in London. Graded in descending order, he listed courtesans, whom he termed 'Demi-reps', just below 'Women of Fashion, who intrigue', but above 'Good-natured Girls, Kept Mistresses [and] Ladies of Pleasure'.[53] Such pedestrian attempts at classification, however, denied courtesans their essential uniqueness and luminosity. They were exquisite creatures, skilled at creating auras of exclusivity about themselves, and whose dazzling allure made even happily married men think twice about the nature of their domestic arrangements. Women, too, were captivated by courtesans and the world of luxurious high living, if not the assault on propriety, that they represented. As a consequence, women from all walks of life were often slavish in following the courtesans' fashionable style and taste.

The courtesan was often beautiful, but not exclusively so, and, of course, she was sexy and well versed in the arts of pleasing men. It was, however, more than just her physical attributes and sexual prowess that made a courtesan irresistible. The truly elite courtesan was possessed of a quality of mind that made her bright and mesmerising, accomplished and witty; a fitting companion for elite men in their leisured, unbuttoned hours. Yet, surprisingly, neither Murray nor Fisher had reputations for wit or for having anything other than average intelligence. Ross's friend, Taylor, noted how both women were generally regarded as intellectually inferior to their fellow courtesan, Cooper, whom Taylor judged to be 'a woman of more understanding than her fair rivals'.[54] This theme was reflected in 'The Young Coquette', a poem that appeared in *Lloyd's Evening Post* in September 1758. Having been chided for her lack of wit, Fisher:

> Flies to her Friend, and in a Pet,
> Cries she, my Dear Miss Fanny,
> The Grave will ne'er persuaded be,
> That we have as much Wit as they,
> Nay, scarce allow us any.[55]

The courtesan was also meticulous in presenting herself in public as an expensive and rarefied commodity, available exclusively to the select few who could afford her prices or the expense of taking her into protection. Only the wealthiest of men were able to provide the essential accoutrements of a courtesan in high-keeping – a lavish home complete with furnishings, servants and equipage, a box at the theatre, sumptuous clothes and jewels, and an almost limitless allowance.

Somewhat analogous to the aging millionaire who takes a trophy wife, men driven to possess such creatures were motivated by a desire for status as much as by lust. Within the realms of gallantry, taking the most expensive and coveted courtesan of the hour into keeping was a statement of a man's wealth, taste and virility. As a consequence, men vied with each other to possess premier courtesans just as energetically as harems of courtesans set luxurious honeytraps to attract the wealthiest of protectors.

Despite her wealth, elegance and cultured bearing, the courtesan occupied a nebulous position in society. Her scandalous reputation and the threat to decency that she posed, prevented admittance into respectable, elite circles, yet her lovers were invariably drawn from this class. Indeed, as Peakman has noted, the successful courtesan often 'maintained a similar social status and lifestyle to that of her clients'.[56]

Reputable women could not receive her in company yet they aped her fashion sense, and male admirers bought pin-ups of her in the form of mezzotints and engravings or tucked tiny portraits of her into their pocket watches to hold next to their hearts. There were other ambiguities too – the courtesan was both high-class prostitute and mistress, yet neither term fully embodied her. In common with high-class prostitutes, she exchanged sex for money, expensive gifts and substantial financial settlements, yet the courtesan was in the privileged position of being able to choose or reject lovers as the caprice took her.[57] Moreover, the elite courtesan did more than simply sell sex: she offered sophisticated companionship within an elegant *milieu* and conferred kudos on those she accepted into her bed. Even as mistress to a wealthy protector, the courtesan was rarely monogamous, but conducted simultaneous sexual liaisons for profit with a number of clients. In so doing, she ensured her financial and emotional independence by keeping replacement protectors in the wings, lest the eyes of her present lover should begin to stray.

Kevin Jordan Bourque, in his re-evaluation of celebrity, has taken issue with those studies (and he would include *Queen of the Courtesans: Fanny Murray*) that seek to accentuate the unique and inimitable qualities of their subjects.[58] Using Fisher as one of his case studies, Bourque has argued that rather than being exceptional and the product of 'an intense manifestation of singularity', celebrities were characterised by their 'interchangeability, commutability and disposability'.[59] Providing a wealth of supporting evidence, Bourque has demonstrated how 'texts, images, anecdotes and poses' of fading stars were recycled and repurposed to satisfy consumer demands for the latest celebrity figures, and claimed that celebrity depended upon 'substitution rather than invention'.[60]

Thus, in a portrait entitled *Miss Fanny Murray* (1754), Murray's head was copied by the engraver Richard Bennet (or Bennett) from a popular engraving after the artist Henry Robert Morland (*c.* 1716–97). Within a few years, however, when Murray was past her prime, the portrait was repurposed at least twice more – once as *Miss Fanny Murray, the Fair and Reigning Toast, in her Primitive Innocence* (*c.* 1764), by the Irish engraver James McArdell (*c.* 1728–65) and once as a portrait of Kitty Fisher.[61] This theme of substitution was commented upon in *St James's Chronicle* in 1761: 'The Galleries of Hampton-Court and Windsor afford a fine Collection of Faces, and with a little retouching may serve for Beauties not yet born; and a Fanny Murray, or a Kitty Fisher of the present Age, were formerly, perhaps, a Nell Gwyn and a Jane Shore.'[62]

Bourque's thesis is important, and this biography takes account of the way Murray's image and ephemeral materials were recycled, reassigned and recirculated, while also allowing her considerably more than her mere fifteen minutes of Warholian fame. This study also argues that in her declining years, Murray found another kind of singularity which was not at all flattering – in a number of poems, epigrams and the occasional print, Murray became the butt of pointed derision as a faded has-been whose premier position had been usurped by younger and more beautiful successors.

Throughout her career, Murray had her fair share of luck, but she also showed remarkable resilience and, in particular, a steeliness of character that enabled her to escape the poverty she had known in Bath, survive the seamiest of London's brothels and dominate the world of the courtesan. A courtesan's primacy was often short-lived, lasting no longer than her looks, her novelty value or her ability to please. Yet Murray presided as the reigning toast of the town for eight years, during which time she lived her glamorous life in a blaze of publicity, fêted by an adoring public. Her staying power within the transient world of the courtesan was extraordinary, especially given the number of fresh-faced rivals who were a constant challenge to her primacy. As a result, she has earned her place among the handful of incomparable creatures whom the biographer Katie Hickman has described as 'exceptional women: forces of nature, as rare and scintillating as their fabulous jewels'.[63]

Notes

1 Funnybus Oddibus, *A Collection of Original Comic Songs and Others* ... [1765], pp.72–3. Song lxxxiii. 'On Fanny Murray'.

2 Ronald Blythe (ed.), *William Hazlitt: Selected Writings* (Harmondsworth: Penguin Classics, 1985), p.418.

3 Laura J. Rosenthal, *Infamous Commerce: Prostitution in Eighteenth-Century British Literature and Culture* (& Ithaca: Cornell University Press, 2006), p.98.

4 This study refers throughout to *Memoirs of the Celebrated Miss Fanny M-----*, 2nd ed. (1759), vol. 1, and *Memoirs of the Celebrated Miss Fanny M-----* (1759), vol. 2. These editions are reproduced in Julie Peakman (ed.), *Whore Biographies, 1700–1825*, 8 vols (Pickering & Chatto, 2006–7), vol. 3. Peakman notes that a copy of the first edition, which was published in November 1758, is held in the library of the University of California, Los Angeles. See Peakman, *Whore Biographies* (2006), vol. 3, p.4. Another edition, entitled *Memoirs of the Celebrated Miss Fanny Murray, Interspersed with the intrigues and amours of several eminent personages*, was published in Dublin in 1759.

5 John Taylor, *Records of My Life* ..., 2 vols (Edward Bull, 1832), vol. 1, p.363.

6 *The Vis-à-Vis of Berkley-Square: or, a Wheel off Mrs W-t-n's Carriage* ... (1783), p.11 (footnote).

7 *The Humours of Fleet-Street: and the Strand; Being the Lives and Adventures of the Most Noted Ladies of Pleasure ... By an Old Sportsman* (1749), pp.17–25.

8 *The London Evening Post*, 13–15 June 1749.

9 See, for example, *The General Evening Post*, 26–29 November 1748.

10 Stella Tillyard, '"Paths of Glory": Fame and the Public in Eighteenth-Century London', in Martin Postle (ed.), *Joshua Reynolds: The Creation of Celebrity* (Tate Publishing, 2005), p.63.

11 See, for example, *The Public Advertiser*, 30 November 1758, the date on which the first edition of the *Memoirs* was published.

12 *The Critical Review: or, Annals of Literature* (January 1759 issue), vol. 7, p.87.

13 *The Monthly Review: or, Literary Journal. By Several Hands* (December 1758 issue), vol. 19, p.580.

14 *The Whitehall Evening Post: or, London Intelligencer*, 13–15 March 1759.

15 *Critical Review* (March 1759 issue), vol. 7, p.288.

16 *Ranger's Repository: or, Annual Packet, of Mirth, Whim and Humour for the year, 1796* ... (1796), p.43.

17 *Memoirs*, vol. 1 for Mrs Stevens, pp.21–36; Miss Charlotte S---, pp.116–25; Jack Harris, pp.125–37; Captain Plaistow, pp.170–88. Robert Tracy is discussed in vol. 2, pp.23–77.

18 *Monthly Review*, vol. 19, p.580.

19 Cindy McCreery, 'Keeping up with the *Bon Ton*: the '*Tête-à-Tête*' series in the *Town and Country Magazine*', in Hannah Barker and Elaine Chalus (eds), *Gender in Eighteenth-Century England: Roles, Representations and Responsibilities* (& New York: Longman, 1997), p.213.

20 See, for example, Fergus Linnane, *Madams, Bawds & Brothel-Keepers of London* (Stroud: The History Press, 2009), p.130; Ronald Webber, *Covent Garden: Mud-salad Market* (J.M. Dent & Sons Ltd, 1969), pp.74–75.

21 Horace Bleackley, *Ladies Fair and Frail: Sketches of the Demi-Monde during the Eighteenth Century* (John Lane, The Bodley Head, 1909), p.14.

22 *The London Magazine: or, Gentleman's Monthly Intelligencer* ... (June 1754 issue), vol. 23, p.270; *Monthly Review* (1754), vol. 10 (Appendix), pp.501–02.

23 *Public Advertiser*, 24 March 1759. See also, *N&Q*, 3 Ser. VIII (29 July 1865), p.82; Stella Tillyard, *A Royal Affair: George III and his Troublesome Siblings* (Chatto & Windus, 2006), pp.47–49.

24 Rosenthal, *Infamous Commerce*, p.97.

25 Teresia Constantia Muilman, *An Apology for the Conduct of Mrs Teresia Constantia Phillips...*, 2nd ed., 3 vols [1748]. See also, Lawrence Stone, *Uncertain Unions & Broken Lives: Marriage and Divorce in England 1660–1857* (Oxford & New York: Oxford University Press, 1995), pp.266–69.

26 Frances Wilson, *The Courtesan's Revenge: Harriette Wilson, the Woman who Blackmailed the King* (Faber & Faber, 2003), p.224.

27 *N&Q*, 10 Ser. XI (15 May 1909), p.398; Helena Wright, *Sex and Society* (George Allen & Unwin, 1968), p.26.

28 Philip Carter, 'Beau Nash', in H.C.G. Matthews and Brian Harrison (eds), *Oxford Dictionary of National Biography* ..., 60 vols (Oxford: Oxford University Press, 2004), vol. 40, p.231.

29 Daphne du Maurier, *Mary Anne*, with an introduction by Lisa Hilton (Virago, 2003), p.97. Murray also featured in Malcolm Bosse, *The Vast Memory of Love* (New York: Ticknor & Fields, 1992), a novel about eighteenth-century London.

30 See, for example, Dan Cruickshank, *The Secret History of Georgian London* (Windmill Books, 2010); Faramerz Dabhoiwala, *The Origins of Sex: A History of the First Sexual Revolution* (Allen Lane, 2012); Julie Peakman, *Lascivious Bodies: A Sexual History of the Eighteenth Century* (Atlantic Books, 2004); Hallie Rubenhold, *The Covent Garden Ladies: Pimp General Jack & the Extraordinary Story of Harris's List* (Stroud: Tempus, 2005).

31 Paula Byrne, *Perdita: The Life of Mary Robinson* (Harper Perennial, 2005); Lesley Blanch (ed.), *Harriette Wilson's Memoirs: The Greatest Courtesan of her Age* (Phoenix, 2003); Kate Williams, *England's Mistress: The Infamous Life of Emma Hamilton* (Hutchinson, 2006); Julie Peakman (ed.), *Whore Biographies*. See also, Katie Hickman, *Courtesans* (HarperCollins, 2003).

32 See, for example, Vic Gatrell, *The First Bohemians: Life and Art in London's Golden Age* (Allen Lane, 2013), pp.90–92; Fergus Linnane, *London, the Wicked City: A Thousand Years of Vice in the Capital* (Robson Books, 2007), pp.129–33.

33 Rosenthal, *Infamous Commerce*, p.2.

34 Rosenthal, *Infamous Commerce*, p.98.

35 Rosenthal, *Infamous Commerce*, p.109.

36 Mary Peace, "'On the soft beds of luxury most Kingdoms have expired": 1759 and the Lives of Prostitutes', in Shaun Regan (ed.), *Reading 1759: Literary Culture in Mid-Eighteenth-Century Britain and France* (Lewisburg: Bucknell University Press, 2013), pp.75–91. *The Uncommon Adventures of Miss Kitty F----r* (1759) was a shorter and expurgated version of *The Juvenile Adventures of Miss Kitty F----r*, 2 vols (1759). See, Laura J. Rosenthal (ed.), *Nightwalkers: Prostitute Narratives from the Eighteenth Century* (Peterborough, Ontario: Broadview Press, 2008), p.xxxi.

37 Peace, '1759 and the Lives of Prostitutes', p.76.

38 Peace, '1759 and the Lives of Prostitutes', p.76.

39 Peace, '1759 and the Lives of Prostitutes', p.79.

40 Peace, '1759 and the Lives of Prostitutes', p.82.

41 Peace, '1759 and the Lives of Prostitutes', p.89.

42 Peace, '1759 and the Lives of Prostitutes', p.86.

43 Rosenthal, *Infamous Commerce*, p.105.

44 *Humours of Fleet-Street*, p.25.

45 *Memoirs and Interesting Adventures of an Embroidered Waistcoat. Part II. In which is introduced, 'The Episode of a Petticoat'* (1751), p.20. It-narratives, in which inanimate objects or animals were the central character or narrator, were popular in the eighteenth century. See Mark Blackwell (gen. ed.), *British It-Narratives, 1750–1830*, 4 vols (Pickering & Chatto, 2012).

46 Joseph Fitzgerald Molloy, *The Queen's Comrade: The Life and Times of Sarah Duchess of Marlborough*, 2 vols (Hutchinson & Co., 1901), vol. 2, p.618; Francis Askham, *The Gay Delavals* (Jonathan Cape, 1955), p.75.

47 John Russell, Duke of Bedford, *Correspondence of John, Fourth Duke of Bedford: Selected from the Originals at Woburn Abbey with an introduction by Lord John Russell*, 3 vols (Longman, Brown, Green & Longmans, 1842–46), vol. 2 (1843), p.114. Letter dated 13 August 1752. See also, Ch. 6, below, pp.135 and 144 (note 49).

48 W. Clarke, *The Authentic and Impartial Life of Mrs Mary Anne Clarke … 2nd.ed.* (T. Kelly, 1809), p.7.

49 John Walters, *The Royal Griffin: Frederick Prince of Wales 1707–51* (Jarrolds, 1972), p.76; Lujo Bassermann, *The Oldest Profession: A History of Prostitution*, translated from the German by James Cleugh (Arthur Barker Ltd, 1967), p.147; Charles E. Pearce, *The Amazing Duchess, being the Romantic History of Elizabeth Chudleigh … 2 vols* (Stanley Paul & Co., 1911), vol. 1, p.197.

50 *Humours of Fleet-Street*, p.25.

51 Bleackley, *Ladies Fair and Frail*, p.40. See also, Louis C. Jones, *The Clubs of the Georgian Rakes* (New York: Columbia University Press, 1942), p.86.

52 Kinsman de Barri, *The Bucks and Bawds of London Town* (Leslie Frewin, 1974), pp.107–08.

53 *A Congratulatory Epistle from a Reformed Rake to John F-----G, Esq; Upon the New Scheme of Reclaiming Prostitutes* [1758], p.8.

54 Taylor, *Records of My Life*, vol. 1, p.51.

55 *Lloyd's Evening Post and British Chronicle*, 4–6 September 1758.

56 Peakman (ed.), *Whore Biographies* (2007), vol. 5, p.7.

57 Joanna Richardson, *The Courtesans: The Demi-Monde in 19th-Century France* (Phoenix Press, 2000), p.1.

58 Kevin Jordan Bourque, 'Blind Items: Anonymity, Notoriety, and the Making of Eighteenth-Century Celebrity' (unpublished doctoral thesis: University of Texas at Austin, 2012).

59 Bourque, 'Blind Items', p.vii.

60 Bourque, 'Blind Items', pp.vii and 2.

61 Bourque, 'Blind Items', pp.12–13.

62 *St James's Chronicle: or, the British Evening Post*, 10–12 September 1761.

63 Hickman, *Courtesans*, p.12.

I

'The Bath Goddess'

… 'tis a Valley of Pleasure, yet a sink of Iniquity; Nor is there any Intrigues or Debauch Acted at London, but is Mimick'd there.[1]

*I*n 1744, at the age of 15, Frances Rudman changed her name to Fanny Murray and took herself off to the brothels of London. The capital would make her famous, but it was Bath, the city of her birth, that shaped the course of her future life. Murray emerged from the squalor of Bath's medieval streets to become the very embodiment of fashion, beauty and pleasure. It was the claustrophobic alleyways of the old medieval city, as much as the elegant refinement of its open urban spaces and its new classically inspired squares and terraces, which moulded Murray into a premier courtesan, the most desirable woman of her day.

Bath lies at the southern extremity of the Cotswolds, some 12 miles from Bristol. Distinctively hexagonal in shape and surrounded by the River Avon's 'winding Streams', Bath is dominated by the Abbey Church of St Peter and St Paul.[2] The city, which had traditionally welcomed the sick who came in hope of a cure from the medicinal properties of its spa waters, had also benefited from royal patronage, dating back to the days of Elizabeth I.[3] In particular, it was Anne, visiting in 1692 as princess, and then as queen in 1702 and 1703, who firmly established Bath not only as a health-giving spa but more importantly as a leisure resort.

From the end of the seventeenth century, Bath's 3,000 residents found themselves increasingly outnumbered by seasonal visitors, who converged on the city and drove the development of Bath as a fashionable playground for the affluent beau monde. By 1749, the architect John Wood the Elder estimated that Bath was attracting 12,000 visitors a year, a number that rose to 40,000 by 1800.[4]

At the end of the seventeenth century, however, the city's residents and visitors were still crammed behind an encircling 20ft-high Roman defensive wall of 'Time-defying Stone'.[5] Contained within a mere 24 acres, Bath's population lived in a rabbit warren of over 600 tightly packed houses.[6] Wood, who began his recreation of Bath as a classical Roman city during the 1720s, recalled the squalor of its medieval streets in lurid and olfactory detail. His aim might well have been to overstate the foulness of the cramped, narrow lanes and darkly oppressive alleyways in order to aggrandise his own architectural achievements, but his description brings Bath old town, where Murray would have lived, vividly to life:[7]

> The Streets and publick Ways of the City were become like so many Dunghills, Slaughter-Houses, and Pig-Styes: For Soil of all sorts, and even Carrion, was cast and laid in the Streets, and the Pigs turned out by Day to feed and rout among it; Butchers killed and dressed their Cattle at their own Doors; People washed every kind of thing they had to make clean at the common Conduits in the open Streets; and nothing was more common than small Racks and Mangers at almost every Door for the baiting of Horses.[8]

The pressure on Bath was only released when the city walls were finally breached and new developments began to appear beyond the city's limits. There was Trim Street (1707) to the north, and Marchant's Passage (1709) to the south-east, while beyond the west gate, 'in comely Order, *Rows* of *Buildings* stand'.[9] Visitor entertainments were also improved, and a new Pump Room was erected adjacent to the King's Bath in 1706. This was followed in 1708 by Thomas Harrison's Assembly Rooms on the east side of Orange Grove, between Terrace Walk and the river, which provided refreshments and gaming tables. A ballroom was added in 1720. Seven years later, in 1727, Lindsey's Rooms opened for business on Terrace Walk opposite Harrison's, offering rival entertainments.

Indeed, such were the transformations at Bath that by 1724 Daniel Defoe could describe the city as 'the Resort of the Sound, rather than the Sick; the Bathing is made more a Sport and Diversion, than a Physical Prescription for Health'.[10]

By 1727, however, two years before Murray was born, Bath still 'comprised no more than fifteen streets, sixteen lanes, four inferior courts, five open areas, four terrace walks, three alleys, four throngs [narrow passageways], and a few private courts'.[11] A further phase of building in Bath would begin in earnest the following year. Most celebrated of these early developments, and which Murray would have seen under construction, were the elegant Queen Square (1728–35/36) and Royal Forum (1740–48). Wood's design for Queen Square was breathtakingly innovative, with handsome individual dwellings on the north side of the square erected behind an imposing palace frontage, decorated with Corinthian columns and pilasters, and unified under a dramatic pediment that extended across the five bays. The same unifying principle was at work in Wood's Royal Forum to the south-east of the city, which he envisaged as 'a grand Place of Assembly' although, in the event, only the dramatic Grand (later North) and South Parades, intersected by Pierrepont and Duke Streets, were completed from the original scheme.[12]

The elegance of Bath's new buildings was reflected in refined codes of conduct which were designed to promote good manners at the spa. The civilised behaviour for which Bath became famous was due largely to Richard 'Beau' Nash, the city's flamboyant master of ceremonies.[13] One of Murray's earliest lovers, their affair is discussed in the following chapter.

Henrietta, Lady Luxborough, during her 1752 visit to Bath, was impressed by the regal authority with which Nash regulated the city:

> Would you see our law-giver, Mr Nash, whose white hat commands more respect and non-resistance than the Crowns of some Kings, though now worn on a head that is in the eightieth year of its age? To promote society, good manners, and a coalition of parties and ranks; to suppress scandal and late hours, are his views; and he succeeds rather better than his brother-monarchs generally do.[14]

Born in Swansea in 1674, the son of a glass manufacturer, he had arrived in Bath around 1704 with a reputation as an adventurer-cum-gamester, and indeed, much of his subsequent wealth derived from the gaming tables. Nash, however, very quickly discovered his *métier* as a social organiser and soon made a name for himself assisting Captain Webster, the incumbent master of ceremonies, in the social organisation of the city. On Webster's death about 1705, following a duelling incident, Nash was Bath Corporation's obvious choice as successor.

During a reign that spanned over fifty years, the 'Monarch of Bath', as Nash was affectionately known, imposed 'a superior form of refined sociability' that transformed Bath into the foremost provincial city of its day, setting the standard for refined urbanity, even as far as London itself.[15] Bizarrely though, Nash's own tastes ran to the flashy and excessive. He lived in a grand mansion in St John's Court that was 'so profuse in Ornament, that none but a Mason, to shew his Art, would have gone to the Expence of those Inrichments'.[16] His dress was equally extravagant – in a letter to Henrietta, Countess of Suffolk, dated 2 November 1734, Lord Chesterfield waspishly remarked on Nash's attire at a ball to celebrate George II's birthday which had been held on 30 October. Nash wore 'his gold laced clothes on the occasion', wrote Chesterfield, 'and looked so fine, that, standing by chance in the middle of the dancers, he was taken by many at a distance for a gilt garland'.[17]

Sporting his signature white hat and long black wig, Nash was a conspicuous figure at all the city's activities and entertainments, personally welcoming the more important visitors, 'the quality', among the 'ministers of state, judges, generals, bishops, projectors, philosophers, wits, poets, players, *chemists, fiddlers*, and *buffoons*' who thronged to Bath.[18] He socialised in the coffee houses, gaming rooms and Pump Room, and presided authoritatively over the public balls and other glittering occasions. In the *Memoirs* (1:5), he was thinly disguised as 'Mr Easy', a name probably derived from his being 'if not a brilliant, at least an easy companion'.[19]

Influxes of seasonal visitors of every social class and distinction coalesced, in theory at least, under his jurisdiction into a single and homogenous group, which was known as 'the Company'. Jery Melford, a fictional visitor to Bath in Tobias Smollett's novel *The Expedition of Humphry Clinker* (1771), confirmed the Company as being 'the general mixture of all degrees assembled in our public rooms, without distinction of rank or fortune'.[20] Moreover, it was the Company that colluded in a willing suspension of the correct social hierarchies in order to submit to Nash's 'sovereignty'. There was something pleasingly novel for the quality in being commanded by Bath's very own pseudo-monarch, the son of a tradesman. Thus, Catherine, Duchess of Queensbury gracefully acquiesced to Nash removing her fashionable and expensive white apron at a ball as it was a contravention of his dress code, and Princess Amelia bowed to his immovable insistence that dancing at the Assembly Rooms on Tuesdays and Fridays ceased upon the stroke of eleven.

Bath's refinement and homogeneity was, in part, a myth, and subject to ridicule. Smollett's dislike for Bath found its expression in *Humphry Clinker* in the complaints of Jery Melford's uncle, the Welsh squire Mr Bramble. He grumbled about the Company at Bath, for example, remarking that:

> the mixture of people in the entertainments of this place was destructive of all order and urbanity; that it rendered the plebeians insufferably arrogant and troublesome, and vulgarized the deportment and sentiments of those who moved in the upper spheres of life.[21]

The city was also well known as the resort of parasites that fed off the rich pickings to be found among the quality. Rakes, prostitutes, fortune hunters gamesters, sharpers and thieves made their way to Bath just as readily as royalty, aristocracy and the political elite, who gamed and whored just as keenly. As a result, alongside its reputation for politeness and refinement, Bath was notorious as 'a licentious place, where the pretext of drinking the waters was pleaded to countenance every kind of vice and immorality'.[22]

Bath, as a centre for flirtation and intrigue, even among seemingly respectable members of the Company, 'was suffused in sexuality' and it was said to be as easy to get the pox (syphilis) in Bath as the cure.[23] Murray grew up in this sexually charged atmosphere, eavesdropping on salacious gossip and absorbing the city's loose moral codes. In her adolescence, Murray would have watched as 'Bath trulls' (prostitutes) plied their trade, but she would also have seen superior young women dangling provocatively off the arms of the rich, rakish and titled as they enjoyed the city's diversions and amusements.[24]

Sexual favours could be rewarded with fine carriages, shimmering jewels and expensive satins and silks, as happened to the actress Lavinia Fenton (1708/10–1760), the illegitimate daughter of a naval lieutenant named Beswick. Fenton became the mistress of Charles Powlett,

3rd Duke of Bolton and married to Anne, Lady Vaughan, shortly after he had seen her play Polly Peachum in John Gay's *The Beggar's Opera* (1728), at Lincoln's Inn Fields. They, and their three illegitimate children, made annual visits to Bath where, noted the author and bluestocking Mrs Elizabeth Montagu (1718–1800), the duke was very open about his liaison with 'Mrs Beswick'.[25] It would not have been lost on Murray that the seeming ease of the lives of such high-class prostitutes and mistresses contrasted strongly with her own lifetime prospects as a flower-seller on the streets of Bath.

But who was Fanny Murray? Little is known of her early life other than that she was born into poverty and probably grew up in the narrow alleyways of the old town, where her home might have been even less inviting than the visitor lodgings as described by Wood for 1727:

> The Boards of the Dining Rooms and most other Floors were made of a Brown Colour with Soot and small Beer to hide the Dirt, as well as their own Imperfections; and if the Walls of any of the Rooms were covered with Wainscot, it was with such as was mean and never Painted.[26]

Most biographers have accepted the *Memoirs'* (1:2) version of events, that she was one of triplets, born to Thomas Rudman, a Bath musician, and that her brother and sister died within three days of their birth. They have also accepted the erroneous claim, to be found in the first volume of the *Memoirs* (1:3), that she was orphaned by the age of 12, and left alone and unprotected to earn her living on the streets of Bath.[27] The second volume of the *Memoirs* (2:90–2), however, states that Murray had two surviving sisters, who were eight and ten years her junior, whom Murray supported and educated. They purportedly lived with Murray in an apartment at her house in Marlborough Street in London, and were helped by her into respectable marriages with a tradesman and a dancer. The *Memoirs'* claim is in part borne out by an obituary notice that was placed in the *Morning Chronicle and London Advertiser* on 2 April 1778, announcing Murray's death. There it was stated that she had 'brought up and set forward in the world many brothers and sisters' and that she had cared for 'an aged parent'. In addition, Murray's death-bed letter, written on 29 March, made reference to a sister, known only as Mrs Brown, who had been widowed during England's war with America.[28] The letter also confirmed that Murray was survived by her father and that she had regularly sent money to support him.

Historiographically, there has been some debate as to whether Murray was actually born in Bath. Thomas Hinde, for example, in his history of the city, claimed London, rather than Bath, as the place of her birth. His version of her story sees Murray coming to Bath as a grown woman and living with Nash 'for a number of years' before returning to the capital.[29] It is, however, an interpretation that sits uncomfortably with the chronology of her adolescence, and with the circumstantial evidence to be found in the Bath archives. While it has proved impossible to locate Murray in Bath's parish registers, they record that there had been Rudmans in Bath since at least 1605, when John Rudman married Julian (sic) Russell on 27 October in the parish of St Peter and St Paul.[30] Another branch of the family was living in the parish of St James in 1638, when Richard Rudman married Elizabeth Timdall on 12 June.[31] Rudmans were also to be found in several outlying parishes – there were, for example, Rudmans in the parish of Woolley, 9 miles from Bath, as early as 1566.[32]

By the time Murray was born in 1729, numerous families of Rudmans were firmly established across the city, and at least one member of this extended family was connected to Bath's musical life. An Isaac Rudman was a member of the Corporation's 'City Band of Musick' until he lost his position 'for his insolent bahaviour [sic] in the Town Hall' on 9 October 1755.[33] Isaac's dismissal from the orchestra might have been catastrophic financially, as an Isaac Rudman was registered in the Bath rate book as living in Lady Mead in the parish of Walcot, an impoverished district of Bath, from 1766 until 1771. He paid his 8d quarterly rates until 1771, when he was registered as too poor to pay his dues.[34] He lost his home, or died, the following year.

Other Rudmans were equally impecunious – a John Rudman died a beggar on 14 January 1705, and a Rose Rudman died in the poorhouse on 7 June 1740.[35] At least one other Rudman was distinguished by his uncouth behaviour. In 1714, a William Rudman was reprimanded, along with other parents, by members of the Board of Trustees of Bath's Blue Coat Charity School, for abusing the schoolmistress Mrs Bell 'by coming up into her School and calling her Names'.[36] Rudman's 11-year-old son, also named William, had been admitted to the school in June 1711.[37] It is clear that some of the Rudmans of Bath were a rough and ready lot.

As a musician, Thomas Rudman's livelihood probably depended as much upon the city's long-term reputation for good music as upon gratuities from the Company. Edward Ward commented in *A Step to the Bath* (1700) on the 'Consort of Delicate Musick, Vocal and Instrumental, perform'd by good Masters', to be found at Bath.[38]

The best wages were earned by Nash's own musicians in the Pump Room Orchestra, whom he had brought from London shortly after his arrival in Bath around 1704. This seven-piece orchestra played in the Pump Room every day until ten in the morning (except Sundays, of course) and at the formal twice-weekly balls. They were paid 2 guineas a week during the season.[39] EJ Burford has suggested that Murray's father was one of Nash's fiddle players, but there is no evidence for this and the *Memoirs* (1:2) merely state that he was 'a musician at B[at]h.'[40] This means that he might have been no more than a street musician who 'played in the Grove under some large trees' or entertained the Company on their promenades.[41]

If Thomas Rudman were a more accomplished musician, however, he might have been one of the 'City Waits', as Isaac Rudman had been. Independent of Nash's musicians, the City Waits were established by the Corporation in 1733, and played in venues all over Bath, both public and private, earning 4 guineas a year.[42] While *haut ton* musicians played exquisite music in the Pump Room, the Waits had a less elevated reputation. Melford, in *Humphry Clinker*, regarded them as 'noisy intruders' when they 'struck up their music (if music it may be called)' in a passageway below the family's lodgings – the cacophony was only stopped by what amounted to a bribe.[43]

Thomas Rudman's livelihood was not only tied to the generosity of the Company but also to the vicissitudes of the Bath season. Although the season had extended into both spring and autumn, and increasing visitor numbers suggested a healthy economy, there were impecunious months in the Bath year. These peaks and troughs were bemoaned in *A Step to the Bath* – 'five Months in the Year 'tis as Populous as *London*, the other seven as desolate as a Wilderness'.[44] As a result, Murray's father, like other musicians in Bath, probably supplemented his income by following another trade, anything from brush making to sign painting, and everyone in the Rudman household would have worked to help sustain the family through the leaner months of the year.[45]

According to the *Memoirs* (1:3), Murray was selling flowers and souvenir jewellery known as Bath rings from the age of 12 after she had been supposedly orphaned. More than the delicious Bath bun and Bath chaps (cooked pigs' cheeks), or Bath lace and Bath beaver (a coarse woven cloth), Bath rings were the must-have memento of the city.[46] They were made of woven hair or polished Bath stone, taken from the local quarries at Combe Down, and were sometimes decorated with mottoes. When Lady Luxborough was in Bath, she sent a Bath ring as a present to her friend, the poet William Shenstone.[47] Some twenty years later, Smollett had Lydia Melford write to her school friend Laetitia Willis in *Humphry Clinker* that she was about to send her 'two dozen of Bath rings; six of the best of which I desire you will keep for yourself'.[48]

Murray made her living by following the Company, those 'gay birds of passage', as they migrated from one venue to the next, in the highly prescribed and precisely regimented daily routines of the spa as laid down by Nash.[49] Her day might have begun at six in the morning, as the Company entered the Baths, and where the bathers stayed until nine, immersed in the restorative spa waters. There was good money to be made from selling her posies there, as it was usual for female bathers to have little 'floating *Jappan*-Bowles' in which they placed a handkerchief, nosegay and snuff box to ward off the smells of the waters.[50]

By ten, Murray might have stationed herself outside the Pump Room, or perhaps she was allowed inside to tout for trade, as the freshly bathed drank their requisite three glasses of Bath water and gossiped loudly to make themselves heard over the orchestra. Some days, she might have followed the gentlemen to their coffee houses, where they read the newspapers and breakfasted on 'Buttered Rolls, or *Bath* Buns, not to be equalled elsewhere'.[51] On others, she might have approached the ladies as they made their way to their lodgings for private breakfasts or to Mrs Bertrand's toy shop to read the news. Toy shops sold all sorts of goods and curiosities, from salves for the relief of corns, to:

Trinkets of various Size, and Sort;
Bracelets, and Combs, Bodkins, and Tweezers,
Bath-mettle Rings, and Knives, and Scissers.[52]

For the rest of the morning Murray might have tailed her potential customers to their public breakfasts in either Harrison's or Lindsay's

Assembly Rooms, or to their music concerts and morning lectures. Her opportunity for a last sale of the morning came when the Company made its way to the Abbey for the eleven o' clock service.

The Company then worked up an appetite for dinner at two by playing cards at the Assembly Rooms or by taking the air, either by carriage or on horseback, in the surrounding countryside. For those wishing to promenade, Queen Square with its elegant garden and 70ft obelisk, commemorating the royal visit of Frederick, Prince of Wales in 1738, was particularly popular.

Dinner was a much anticipated event at Bath. Even Sarah, Duchess of Marlborough (1660–1744), who disliked Bath because of its 'Stinks and Dirt', conceded that the city provided a 'great Plenty of Meat, and very good', so much so that she deemed it impossible to starve at Bath.[53] There were further opportunities for Murray to sell her goods in the mid-afternoon when the Company reconvened at the Pump Room for a second time in the day, before walking off dinner by strolling in Orange Grove or the exclusive Harrison's Walk. There, a subscription fee enabled those wishing to escape 'from *Crouds* [sic], and *empty Noise*' to walk by the riverside where 'Round the *green Walk* the *River* glides away'.[54] It was then time for the Company to gather once again at the Assembly Rooms, for afternoon tea. It is little wonder that some found the regimented social life at Bath wearisome – Mrs Montagu, writing to Margaret Cavendish Bentinck, Duchess of Portland, on 4 January 1740, remarked that 'the only thing one can do to-day, we did not do the day before is to die'.[55]

Murray's day still might not have been done, and even on the coldest of winter nights, she might have waited outside Harrison's Assembly Rooms on Tuesdays, and Lindsay's on Fridays. Punctually, at six o'clock the Company arrived in all its finery for the weekly public balls, and left just as promptly at eleven, when Murray had her last opportunity of the day to make a sale.[56]

As Murray mingled with the Company, selling her flowers and souvenirs, she witnessed at close quarters the contrast between her own poverty and the beau monde prosperity of her affluent customers. This disparity could have made Murray hungry to escape her penury and ripe for seduction. It certainly gave an edge to her character that would make her appear a steely, impulsive and opportunistic courtesan. It did not, however, give her a good business head, and her fluctuating fortunes within the sex trade have already been noted. Although her childhood deprivations gave her a lifelong fear of poverty, and she followed money intently, even when it belonged to the most disreputable of men, as a courtesan she was unskilled at managing her finances. Living for the moment, she allowed vast sums to run through her fingers, spending rashly and conspicuously as if to compensate for the privations of her youth. In the end, it was a fear of creditors braying at her door that ultimately led her to renounce prostitution and put her house in order.

By the time Murray had reached the age of 13, she might have been selling more than just posies and Bath rings. If so, she would not have been the first flower-seller to accept propositions that offered a step up from street-hawker to the role of mistress. The famous actress Frances Abington (1737–1815) had also been a flower-seller before she began selling sex.

It is also possible that Murray had begun to sell herself with her family's knowledge, for it is well-documented that even middle-class fathers in straitened circumstances acknowledged that their daughters might 'have to turn out whores' to help support the family.[57] Such a step, however, was fraught with danger for those without connections – had it not been for Nash's timely intervention, Murray could have easily ended her days as a miserable streetwalker. As it was, her refashioning, from low-born prostitute into a polished and sophisticated demi-rep was more easily effected in this city of manners. Bath schooled Murray well, giving her such a gloss of sophistication that within a couple of years she was mistress to some of the country's elite men, a gracious companion in public and suitably whorish in private, for those wealthy enough to afford her prices.

There were at least two men who pursued the prepubescent Murray. One was the 23-year-old Edward 'Ned' Harvey (1718–78) whose 'gallantries' with the actress Peg Woffington and the opera singer Signora Giulia Frasi (1720–79), among others, were reputed to have 'resounded throughout the kingdom, and even been extended to the continent'.[58] The other was the Hon. John Spencer, who is probably most noteworthy today for being five times great-grandfather of the late Diana, Princess of Wales, and thereby a direct ancestor of the future kings, Princes William and George.

Harvey was a cornet (a junior commissioned cavalry officer) in the 10th Dragoons in 1741, at the time of Murray's seduction.[59] A portrait now in the Dundee Art Gallery, by the Scottish artist Allan Ramsay, portrays him as a handsome, confident and manly young officer. Painted in 1747, some six years after his purported affair with Murray, he strikes a natural pose in semi-military dress with the lining of his red coat and gorget patches showing the 10th Dragoons' regimental yellow. Little is known of Harvey at the time of their alleged affair, but he went on to have a successful military and political career, becoming adjutant general to the forces (1765–78), governor of Portsmouth (1773–78), and MP for Gatton (1761–68) and Harwich (1768–78). The *Town and Country Magazine*'s gossipy 'tête-à-tête' feature for October 1774, in an exposé of Harvey's *amour* with the courtesan Gertrude Mahon (1752–*c*. 1808), claimed that it was Harvey who had first seduced Murray, but that Spencer took the credit – 'to Gen. H----- is ascribed the introduction of the celebrated Fanny M----- to the world, though the renowned Jack Sp----r plumed himself upon this conquest'.[60] Remarkably, the claim that Harvey was Murray's original seducer has slipped almost completely from all accounts of Murray's early life, and it is Spencer who has always been credited with her first seduction. By a quirk of history, Harvey has been all but erased from Murray's life.

If it is possible to believe the 'tête-à-tête' claim, then Murray might have been sexually experienced before she met Spencer, and sufficiently practised to know how to hoodwink a new lover, eager for a virgin, into believing her chaste. Indeed, the brothel-keeper Charlotte Hayes (1725–1813), who ran the famous King's Place 'nunnery' in Pall Mall, believed that 'a Woman might lose her Maidenhead five hundred times, and be as good a Virgin as ever'.[61] As the fictional Fanny Hill demonstrated, counterfeiting maidenheads was a well-practised art and would-be seducers could be easily duped by the seeming innocence of young girls:[62]

> Six years have past since first I knew a man;
> Then but fifteen, now turn'd of twenty-one,
> To most folks for a virgin still I've gone;
> My coy behaviour, and my looks demure,
> Give me the character – of chaste and pure.[63]

Harris's *List of Covent Garden Ladies*, a directory of prostitutes working in Covent Garden, included in its 1761 edition, Polly Jenkinson, described as 'a little fluttering child'. Said to have been first debauched by a Captain Jones around the age of 13, when she 'could not have been fit, at that time, for any man even of *middling parts*', she was noted for having learnt how to sell her virginity twenty times over in order to secure a better price for herself.[64] The brothel-keeper, Mrs Cole, was able to sell Sally R[o]bi[n]son's maidenhead for 30 guineas, when a prostitute might otherwise only expect to earn a 'whore's curse' of 5s 3d, or, at most, a couple of guineas.[65]

Murray's virginal state at the time she met Spencer is crucial, since her subsequent career hung upon the universal belief that Spencer was her original seducer. If Murray was revirginising herself, then she not only succeeded in deceiving Spencer, but also every biographer and commentator who has since told her story.

Men who consorted with adolescent and premenarche girls were not vilified in the eighteenth century as they are today. Indeed, the 80-year-old rake Field Marshal Ligonier could claim with impunity 'that no woman past fourteen is worth the trouble of pursuing'.[66] It was said of the actress Ann Catley (1745–89) that 'at thirteen many serious overtures of love had been made her, and innumerable schemes were continually laid for her seduction'. She had just turned 14 when she was seduced by a linen merchant.[67]

The courtesan Constantia Phillips stated in her memoirs that she was raped at the age of 13 by the son of an earl, whom she referred to as 'Mr Thomas Grimes' and 'whose peculiar Taste was for Girls of that Age'.[68] Murray was not alone, therefore, in having her first sexual encounter at a young age, yet such early introductions to sex were not the norm for women in the eighteenth century. Although 12 was the legal marriageable age for females, it is well documented that lower-class women usually delayed marriage, and sex, until they were in their mid to late twenties.[69]

Murray's experience, however, was replicated in the lives of prostitutes and courtesans throughout the eighteenth and nineteenth centuries. Apart from men's individual tastes and preferences, there were compelling reasons why prepubescent girls were in demand – young girls were more likely to be virgins and, as such, free from venereal disease. The governors of the Lock Hospital in Hyde Park, London – the first charitable hospital established specifically for the treatment of venereal disease – despaired at the prevalent belief that intercourse with a virgin cured venereal disease, by passing it to the virgin and cleansing the infected person. Although the governors attempted to discredit the old wives' tale, and decried 'the Motives of *wicked People* to so vile an Act', they estimated, in 1751, that of the 1,154 patients admitted to their care since the hospital was founded in January 1747 over fifty were aged between 2 and 12.[70]

Unsurprisingly, there was a well-established market in Bath for young girls. In August 1779, the Reverend James Woodforde noted in his diary how he had met two 'common Prostitutes', one aged about 15, the other 17, as he walked in the fields around Bath.[71] Some years later, in 1829, the Reverend John Skinner, rector of Camerton, noted how the streets of Bath were 'crowded with prostitutes, some of them apparently not above fourteen or fifteen years of age'.[72] *The Bath Miscellany* for 1740, allegedly written by 'the Gentleman and Ladies of that Place', contained a poem 'Upon Capt. L[indse]y' that described the captain's predilection for the child–woman:

> Since Girls of Twelve or Thirteen only Charm,
> And *L[ind]sey's* Bosom, with Love's Fire warm,
> What cruel Torments must those Virgins move,
> Whose riper Years excludes them from his Love.
> Fifteen Despairs! Nay Thirteen, scarce can Boast,
> She ever was, the charming *Lindsey's* Toast.[73]

Prostitutes like Polly Jenkinson and those who ended up in the Lock Hospital were very much victims of the sex trade, trapped into poverty, often abused by hard-nosed brothel-keepers, and exposed to violence and venereal disease by their punters. There were, however, a select few like Murray, who manipulated the sex trade to their advantage and rose to the very top of their profession. Exhibiting feistiness and bravura, vivacity and impertinence, they demonstrated self-determination in choosing to use sex to achieve their ambitions for wealth and/or status.

Even though their lives sometimes ended in penury, at the height of their power these models of female agency prospered by taking control of their bodies and successfully exploiting male desire. Mary Robinson, for example, only agreed to become mistress to the 17-year-old Prince of Wales, the future George IV, once he had made promises to her (which he broke) of £20,000. Their liaison began in December 1779, shortly after the young prince had seen Robinson in a production of

Shakespeare's *A Winter's Tale* – she was known as 'Perdita' ever afterward. As already noted, courtesans such as Constantia Phillips and Harriette Wilson also successfully navigated the sexual marketplace and used their memoirs to create lucrative sources of income for themselves by black-mailing former lovers who were keen to avoid exposure.

Murray's remarkably successful career probably began around 1742 when she was 13 years old and already attracting male attention at Bath. Indeed, the *Memoirs* (1:17) claimed that Nash actually fought a duel with one of her suitors. The notorious adulteress Frances, Lady Vane (*c*. 1715–88), demonstrated vividly how the compactness of Bath made it the perfect hunting ground for predatory males in search of young girls.[74] She recalled her first visit to Bath as a 13-year-old in 1728, when she found herself 'surrounded by a croud of admirers, who courted [her] acquaintance, and fed [her] vanity with praise and adulation'. When she returned a year later 'many proposals of marriage were made to [her] parents; but, as they came from people whom [she] did not like, [she] rejected them all'.[75] This type of male behaviour was so taken for granted that it appeared in fiction. In *Humphry Clinker*, for example, pretty Julia Melford attracted so much attention from 'some coxcombs in the Rooms', that her uncle, Mr Bramble, considered removing her from Bath altogether.[76] It was in this milieu, that 'the Bath goddess', as the *Memoirs* (1:87) dubbed her, first caught the eye of one of the most notorious rakes of his age, the tall and aristocratic John Spencer. He would change Fanny Murray's life forever.

Notes

1 Edward Ward, *A Step to the Bath: with a Character of the Place* (1700), p.16.

2 Mary Chandler, *A Description of Bath: A Poem. Humbly Inscribed to Her Royal Highness the Princess Amelia* (1734), p.9.

3 Elizabeth I visited Bath in 1574, and again in 1591. For comprehensive studies of the development of Bath in the eighteenth century see A. Barbeau, *Life & Letters at Bath in the Eighteenth Century* (Stroud: The History Press, 2009); Peter Borsay, *The English Urban Renaissance: Culture and Society in the Provincial Town 1660–1770* (Oxford: Clarendon Press, 1989); Peter Borsay, *The Image of Georgian Bath, 1700–2000: Towns, Heritage, and History* (Oxford: Oxford University Press, 2000); Graham Davis and Penny Bonsall, *A History of Bath: Image and Reality* (Lancaster: Carnegie Publishing, 2006); R.S. Neale, *Bath, A Social History, 1680–1850, or A Valley of Pleasure, yet a Sink of Iniquity* (Routledge & Kegan Paul, 1981).

4 Neale, *Bath*, p.46.

5 Henry Chapman, *Thermae Redivivae: The City of Bath Described* ... (1673), p.2.

6 Neale suggested that there were 669 houses in Bath in 1700, and used Wood's estimate that there were 1,339 in 1743. See Neale, *Bath*, p.44.

7 Barry Cunliffe, *Roman Bath Discovered* (Routledge & Kegan Paul, 1971), p.6.

8 John Wood, *A Description of Bath...* (1765) (Facsimile edition, Bath: Kingsmead Reprints, 1969), pp.216–17.

9 Chandler, *Description of Bath*, p.12.

10 Daniel Defoe, *A Tour Thro' the whole Island of Great Britain ...*, 3 vols (1724–27), vol. 2 (1725), Letter III, p.51.

11 William Tyte, *Bath in the Eighteenth Century* ... (Bath: 1903), p.2.

12 Wood, *Description of Bath*, p.232.

13 See Philip Carter, 'Beau Nash', in Matthew and Harrison (eds), *Oxford Dictionary of National Biography*, vol. 40, pp.225–32.

14 Quoted in Marjorie Williams, *Lady Luxborough Goes to Bath* (Oxford: Basil Blackwell, 1946), p.6.

15 Philip Carter, *Men and the Emergence of Polite Society, Britain 1660–1800* (Longman, 2001), p.176.

16 Wood, *Description of Bath*, p.338.

17 [John Wilson Croker (ed.)], *Letters to and from Henrietta, Countess of Suffolk, and her second husband, the Hon. George Berkeley, from 1712 to 1767 ...*, 2 vols (John Murray, 1824), vol. 2, pp.116–17.

18 Tobias Smollett, *The Expedition of Humphry Clinker*, edited with an introduction by Angus Ross (Harmondsworth: Penguin, 1967, repr. 1985), p.78.

19 Oliver Goldsmith, *The Life of Richard Nash, of Bath, Esq ...* (1762), p.13.

20 Smollett, *Humphry Clinker*, p.78.

21 Smollett, *Humphry Clinker*, p.80.

22 *T&C* (July 1769 issue), p.360.

23 Neale, *Bath*, p.17.

24 Henry Fielding, *Tom Jones*, edited with an introduction by R.P.C. Mutter (Harmondsworth: Penguin, 1966, repr. 1985), Book 10, Ch. 5, p.440.

25 Lisa Hilton, *Mistress Peachum's Pleasure: The Life of Lavinia, Duchess of Bolton* (Weidenfeld & Nicolson, 2005), p.131. Just weeks after the death of his wife in October 1751, the duke made Fenton a duchess.

26 Wood, *Description of Bath*, preface.

27 See, for example, Horace Bleackley, *Ladies Fair and Frail*, p.3; E.J. Burford, *Wits, Wenchers and Wantons, London's Low Life: Covent Garden in the Eighteenth Century* (Robert Hale, 1990), p.79; Sir Charles Wentworth Dilke (ed.), *The Papers of a Critic. Selected from the Writings of the Late Charles Wentworth Dilke...*, 2 vols (John Murray, 1875), vol. 2, p.275 (footnote); Jones, *Clubs of the Georgian Rakes*, p.86; Linnane, *Madams, Bawds & Brothel-Keepers*, p.126; Donald McCormick, *The Hell-Fire Club: The Story of the Amorous Knights of Wycombe* (Jarrolds, 1958), p.146; Nickie Roberts, *Whores in History: Prostitution in Western Society* (Grafton, 1993), p.176.

28 BL – Add MS 75714.

29 Thomas Hinde, *Tales from the Pump Room. Nine Hundred Years of Bath: the Place, its People, and its Gossip* (Victor Gollancz Ltd, 1988), pp.40–41. Kinsman de Barri claimed Murray spent her childhood in London's Lewknor Lane, a red-light district in the rookeries of St Giles. See de Barri, *Bucks and Bawds*, p.107. See also, John Walters, *Splendour and Scandal: The Reign of Beau Nash* (Jarrolds, 1968), p.73.

30 BCL – Arthur J. Jewers (ed.), *The Registers of the Abbey Church of SS. Peter and Paul, Bath*, 2 vols (The Harleian Society (vols. 27–28), 1900–01), vol. 1 (1900), p.206. (Ref: B.929.3 BAT).

31 BCL – *The Register of St James's Bath*, 4 vols (n/d), vol. 1, p.36a. (Ref: B.929.3 SAI).

32 BCL – *Register 1560–1586*, in 'The Register Book of the Parish of Wolley [sic]', in *Parish Registers: Bathwick, Wooley*, [sic] *Englishcombe*, (n/d), p.2 (Baptisms). (Ref: L.929.3 BAT).

33 BCL – Bath Council Book, vol. 3 (1751–83), no. 7 (21 November 1751–16 March 1761), p.51, entry for 24 October 1755. (Ref: B.352.0422).

34 BCL – City of Bath Rate Books, vol. 1 (1766–73), Section for 1771, p.64. (Ref: B.942.38).

35 BCL – For John Rudman, see 'St James's Register Burialls 1686–1718' in *The Register of St James's Bath*, vol. 1, p.10b. For Rose Rudman, see Jewers (ed.), *Registers of the Abbey Church*, vol. 2 (1901), p.429.

36 BRO – Minute Book of the Blue Coat School 1711–73, p.47. See also, p.46. (Ref: 103/1/2/1).

37 BRO – Minute Book of the Blue Coat School, p.11.

38 Ward, *Step to the Bath*, p.15.

39 Francis Fleming, *The Life and Extraordinary Adventures, the Perils and Critical Escapes, of Timothy Ginnadrake ...*, 3 vols (Bath: 1771), vol. 3, p.27.

40 Burford, *Wits, Wenchers and Wantons*, p.79; See also, Kenneth E. James, 'Concert Life in Eighteenth-Century Bath' (unpublished doctoral thesis: University of London, 1987), pp.139 and 401 (note 2).

41 Fleming, *Timothy Ginnadrake*, vol. 3, pp.23 and 25. For a discussion of music in Bath, see Ian Bradley, *Water Music: Music Making in the Spas of Europe and North America* (Oxford: Oxford University Press, 2010), pp.31–56; Robert and Nicola Hyman, *The Pump Room Orchestra Bath: Three Centuries of Music and Social History* (Salisbury: Hobnob Press, 2011).

42 BCL – Bath Council Book, vol. 2 (1684–1751), no. 5 (1728–38), p.39. (Ref: B.352.0422). In the Minutes for 26 March 1733 it was agreed 'that the City Waits, now established by this Corporation whose business is to attend the Corporation on all occasions shall have 4 guineas per annum for their trouble'.

43 Smollett, *Humphry Clinker*, p.58. See also, Philip Thicknesse, *The New Prose Bath Guide, for the year 1778 ...* [1778], p.91.

44 Ward, *Step to the Bath*, p.16.

45 James, 'Concert Life in Eighteenth-Century Bath', p.55.

46 *N&Q*, 6 Ser. II (18 December 1880), p.486.

47 Williams, *Lady Luxborough goes to Bath*, p.29.

48 Smollett, *Humphry Clinker*, pp.87–88.

49 Smollett, *Humphry Clinker*, p.103. See also, R.A.L. Smith, *Bath*, 2nd rev. ed. (B.T. Batsford Ltd, 1945), pp.56–62; Wood, *Description of Bath*, pp.437–44.

50 Ward, *Step to the Bath*, p.13; Defoe, *Tour Thro'* ... *Great Britain*, vol. 2, Letter III, p.51.

51 Wood, *Description of Bath*, p.438.

52 William Somerville, 'The Fortune-Hunter', in *William Somerville* [sic], *Esq; Occasional Poems, Translations, Fables, Tales, &c.* (1727), p.261.

53 Hon. Charles Spencer Cowper (ed.), *Diary of Mary Countess Cowper, Lady of the Bedchamber to the Princess of Wales, 1714–1720*, 2nd ed. (John Murray, 1865), p.197. Extract of a letter from the Duchess of Marlborough to Lady Cowper dated 3 September 1716.

54 Chandler, *Description of Bath*, p.16.

55 Matthew Montagu (ed.), *The Letters of Mrs Elizabeth Montagu, with some of the Letters of her Correspondents* ..., 4 vols (1809–13), vol. 1 (1809), p.77.

56 Fleming, *Timothy Ginnadrake*, vol. 3, pp.29 and 50–51. See also, Walters, *Splendour and Scandal*, pp.66–67.

57 Rubenhold, *Covent Garden Ladies*, p.124.

58 *T&C* (October 1774 issue), p.513.

59 See Stuart Reid and Paul Chappell, *King George's Army 1740–1793*: (3) (Osprey, 1996), pp.13 and 16.

60 *T&C* (October 1774 issue), p.513.

61 *Nocturnal Revels: or, the History of King's-Place and other Modern Nunneries ... By a Monk of the Order of St. Francis*, 2nd ed., 2 vols (1779) vol. 1, p.164.

62 John Cleland, *Memoirs of a Woman of Pleasure*, 2 vols (1749), vol. 2, pp.119–20. See also, Tassie Gwilliam, 'Female Fraud: Counterfeit Maidenheads in the Eighteenth Century', in *Journal of the History of Sexuality* (April 1996), vol. 6, no. 4, pp.518–48.

63 *An Essay on Woman. The Fourth Epistle. With Explanatory Notes* [1763], p.10.

64 *Harris's List of Covent-Garden Ladies; or New Atalantis for the Year 1761* ... (1761), pp.83–84. Jenkinson's profile also appeared in *Harris's List* for 1773, which suggests careless or hasty editing. See *Harris's List of Covent-Garden Ladies: or Man of Pleasure's Kalendar* ... (1773), pp.83–84.

65 *Harris's List* (1761), pp.91 and 55.

66 *T&C* (April 1770 issue), p.178.

67 Miss [E.] Ambross, *The Life and Memoirs of the Late Miss Ann Catley, the Celebrated Actress* ... [1789], pp.8–9.

68 Phillips, *Apology for the Conduct of Mrs Teresia Constantia Phillips*, vol. 1, p.25; Lynda M. Thompson, *The 'Scandalous Memoirists' Constantia Phillips, Laetitia Pilkington and the Shame of 'Publick Fame'* (Manchester & New York: Manchester University Press, 2000), pp.35–36 and 76 (note 34). See pp.44–53 for a discussion of the identity of 'Mr Grimes'.

69 Lawrence Stone, *The Family, Sex and Marriage in England 1500–1800* (New York: Harper & Row, 1977), especially pp.50–54. See also, Peter Laslett, *The World We*

Have Lost – Further Explored, 3rd ed. (Methuen, 1983), pp.81–90;. W.A. Speck, 'The Harlot's Progress in Eighteenth-Century England', in *British Journal of Eighteenth-Century Studies* (1980), vol. 3, pp.127–39.

70 'An Account of the Proceedings of the Governors of the Lock-Hospital, near Hyde-Park-Corner … By Order of the General Court held Tuesday, March 12, 1750–1' [1751], p.2.

71 John Beresford (ed.), *The Diary of a Country Parson: The Reverend James Woodforde, 1758–1781*, 5 vols (Humphry Milford, Oxford University Press, 1924–31), vol. 1 (1924), p.258.

72 Howard Coombs and the Rev. Arthur N. Bax (eds), *Journal of a Somerset Rector: John Skinner, A.M., Antiquary 1772–1839* (John Murray, 1930), p.231.

73 *The Bath Miscellany. For the Year 1740* … (Bath: 1741), p.33.

74 Born Frances Anne Hawes, her salacious 'Memoirs of a Lady of Quality' appeared as Chapter 88 in Tobias Smollett's *The Adventures of Peregrine Pickle* (1751).

75 Tobias Smollett, *The Adventures of Peregrine Pickle*, edited by James L. Clifford and Paul-Gabriel Boucé (Oxford: Oxford University Press, 1983), pp.433–34.

76 Smollett, *Humphry Clinker*, p.77.

2

Rakes and Royals

The late Mr Spencer, the Duke of Marlboro's brother, had this disease [the love of low company] to such a height, that he for years before his death never was seen in good company.[1]

By the close of 1743, Murray had had at least three lovers. She had been taken up, and as quickly dropped, by both John Spencer and Edward Harvey, and by the time she was 14, she had become mistress to Richard Nash.[2]

With little happening in Bath without Nash, as master of ceremonies, knowing about it, he had taken a personal interest in the plight of the abandoned and newly debauched flower-seller. After her desertion by both Spencer and Harvey, Nash took Murray to live with him and she remained his paramour for about a year.[3] Harvey disappeared completely from Murray's life, and the claim, made in *Town and Country Magazine* that he was her original seducer has been ignored in all subsequent accounts of Murray's affairs, in favour of the *Memoirs'* assertion that Spencer was her first lover. It is universally accepted, therefore, that Spencer's brief dalliance with Murray, before he too passed out of her life forever, paved the way for her career as one of the great *impures* of her day.

When Murray first met Spencer, around 1742, he was 34 years old, and well known for his 'riotous course of life'.[4] Born on 13 May 1708 at the family seat of Althorp in Northamptonshire, he was a member of one of the wealthiest landowning families in England. His maternal grand-parents were the renowned military genius John Churchill, 1st Duke of Marlborough and his redoubtable duchess Sarah Jenyns (or Jennings), whose home was the dramatic Blenheim Palace at Woodstock in Oxfordshire. In 1733, Spencer became head of the Althorp estates when his elder brother Charles succeeded their aunt, Henrietta Godolphin, as 3rd Duke of Marlborough and inherited the Blenheim estates.[5]

Like his grandmother, Spencer was a regular visitor to Bath, where his reputation for unruliness went before him, and he was credited with masterminding one of the most extravagant practical jokes ever played on the city. The prank involved turnspit dogs, a now extinct breed of small dog that were used in the city's kitchens. They were made to run for hours on end inside wheels attached to pulleys, which turned joints of meat basting over an open fire. It was said that Spencer deprived Bath of its roast dinners for a whole day by arranging to have the city's 3,000 turnspit dogs locked away for an afternoon.[6] The story is undoubt-edly apocryphal, and was also credited to Smollett's eponymous hero Peregrine Pickle, but it says something of Spencer's reputation for rogu-ishness that he was associated with the prank.[7]

Spencer was the author of a number of other mischievous stunts including, for example, hosting dinner parties where the guest list was made up entirely of either hunchbacks or stutterers.[8] His love of practical jokes was matched only by his love of public exhibitionism, and on one occasion this landed him before a magistrate after he accepted a bet to drive a coach and horses stark naked along the Strand in London.[9]

Spencer's reputation as 'a man of great humour' was outweighed, how-ever, by his notoriety as a drunk, rake and rabble-rouser.[10] He had been a heavy drinker since his youth, often staying up all night in London's brothels, taverns and bagnios to carouse with friends and prostitutes. By 1744, when Spencer was 36, he was an alcoholic, dependent upon 'drams and small beer in the morning', and was as intemperate with women as he was with drink.[11] The anonymous author of *Satan's Harvest Home* (1749), an exploration of the seamier side of sexual life in England, painted a graphic picture of the extent of Spencer's promiscuity and powers of seduction:

> If you meet with any of our Trading Madams, and ask them *who debauch'd her*, it is ten to one, but her Answer will be *Jack* – I have heard of above

500 unfortunate Women, who have laid their *Virginities* at the Door of this *young Gentleman*.[12]

Spencer's self-destructive dissipations were, in part, the result of his grandmother's emasculating influence. On the death of his mother, Anne Churchill, Countess of Sunderland, in 1716 (his father Charles, 3rd Earl of Sunderland, died in 1722), 8-year-old Spencer and his four older siblings came under Sarah's guardianship. From an early age, therefore, Spencer lived within a matriarchal household, headed by a domineering and fiery-tempered 'old Fury of a Grandmother'.[13]

In the years that followed, Sarah slowly sapped Spencer's will as she controlled nearly every aspect of his life, arranging both a career and marriage for him that reflected her political convictions. An influential supporter of the Whig party, Sarah was behind Spencer's 1732 election as MP for Woodstock – a seat he held until his death in 1746. She was also behind his marriage to the beautiful Georgiana Caroline, Lady Carteret (1716–80), the daughter of John Carteret, 2nd Earl Granville. He shared with Sarah a fierce antipathy to Robert Walpole, credited with being first to hold the office of prime minister.

The story goes that Sarah drew up an alphabetical list of suitable brides from which she invited Spencer to make his choice. Spencer acquiesced, demonstrating a flash of defiance as he did so, by picking a wife quite randomly and plumping for the name that happened to be first on his grandmother's list.[14] The prospect of a wife did not change Spencer's ways and, three weeks before his wedding, he was spotted at the opera with an unnamed mistress.[15]

Lady Carteret and Spencer were married, once Spencer had undergone yet another cure for venereal disease, on Valentine's Day 1734, with the bride radiant in 'white satin embroidered with silver, very fine lace; and the jewels the Duchess of Marlborough gave'.[16] Their only son and heir, John (1734–83), who was born ten months later on 19 December 1734, was destined to play an influential part in Murray's later life.

Sarah's desire to control Spencer and to bend him to her political will was undoubtedly motivated by feelings of deep affection and a desire to do what she thought best for her favourite grandchild while also advancing the Whig cause. Years of Sarah's domestic tyranny, belligerent manner and quarrelsome nature had, however, turned her youngest grandson against her.

There is a story that when his grandmother remarked at an annual family dinner on 'the pleasure she felt on seeing so flourishing and numerous an Assembly around her', Spencer whispered under his breath 'how much better [they] might all flourish if the old stump [they] sprang from was under ground'. Hurt and offended by the remark, Sarah told her grandson to leave and never enter her doors again. The following morning, so the anecdote goes, Spencer was on his knees in her dressing room winsomely begging her forgiveness. To Sarah's admonishment that she had forbidden him ever to enter her doors again, came the disarming reply, 'you did, Madam ... and therefore I came in at the window'.[17] It is not surprising that Mary 'Perdita' Robinson, should describe Spencer as 'the misery at once and the darling of his grandmother'.[18]

As this anecdote demonstrates, Spencer was adept at hiding his true feelings for his formidable grandmother behind a veneer of charm and attentiveness. As in his dealings with women in general, Spencer learnt to be plausible and to manipulate Sarah just as she manipulated him. If he appeared compliant in his grandmother's choice of bride or acquiescent to her demands and caprices; if he were charming, flattering and engaging; if he tempered his behaviour or seemed contrite after displeasing her, it was not from affection but rather, to serve his own ends in protecting his inheritance. Sarah made twenty-six wills in her lifetime and Spencer knew from experience that she was not above vengefully disinheriting him, if provoked.[19]

As Sarah's sole heir, Spencer stood to inherit 'not so much a fortune as an empire – with no less than thirty-nine separate manors in a dozen counties', all her personal wealth – amounting to some £500,000 – and five large residences including Wimbledon House and Marlborough House near St James's Park.[20] Lady Bolingbroke estimated that Spencer could expect a yearly income of £27,000, while Amanda Foreman has calculated that on Spencer's death in 1746, his son John 'had an income of £700 a week in an era when a gentleman could live off £300 a year'.[21] The yearly income of Murray's father in 1733 might have been as little as 4 guineas. Yet, as Spencer waited for his grandmother to die, he was 'under the greatest difficulties' financially and forced to borrow heavily against the expectation of his inheritance. Careful to conceal his financial arrangements from his grandmother 'for fear it should prejudice him in her favour; and hurt him in regard to the hopes he had from her will', Spencer's debts, by 1738, were thought to exceed £20,000, or approximately £2.5 million in today's figures.[22]

Frustrated by years of his grandmother's controlling influence, Spencer developed into a disappointed young man who squandered his abilities and ruined his health in drinking and whoring. Indeed, by the time Murray met Spencer he was a sick man, having wilfully neglected his health for years. His surgeon, Mr Middleton, said that Spencer had once confided to him that 'he did not desire to live longer than his constitution would enable him to live in the manner he liked' – it was as if Spencer was determined to assert an authority that was beyond the reach of his grandmother.[23] As a result, Spencer's addiction to chewing tobacco, his alcoholism and his uncompromising promiscuity took its toll.

Wracked by bouts of rheumatic pain and atrophied by alcoholism and 'frequent venereal disorders', his 'weak and decayed constitution' had continued to deteriorate throughout the 1730s.[24] By November 1739, it was reported that he was 'dangerously ill at Bath'.[25] In November 1741, he was undergoing yet another aggressive mercury, or salivation, cure for venereal disease which placed further stresses upon his health.[26] Mercury was administered by pill, potion or ointment as a treatment for both gonorrhoea and syphilis under the mistaken belief that they were variations of the same disease. An immediate side-effect was salivation, as the body worked to flush out the mercurial poisons. Sufferers produced litres of fetid saliva daily over a four to six week period, and this, in turn, inflamed already swollen and ulcerated gums, loosened teeth and led to mercurial gingivitis and a stinking odour from the mouth. The toxicity of the mercury also caused abdominal, bone and joint pain, skin ulcerations, profuse sweating, incessant diarrhoea, organ failure, aneurysm and disintegrating nose and jaw tissue. It was not for nothing that the cure was often regarded as worse than the disease.[27]

Spencer regularly took the waters at Bath to ease the rheumatic pains that had first afflicted him in 1739, and to relieve 'his complaint of want of appetite, and indigestion [... which] were notoriously the effects of former drinking, and a broken constitution'.[28] He might also have undergone his mercury cures at the spa. It was on one such visit that the raddled Spencer first took notice of Murray as she mingled with the Company selling her nosegays and souvenirs.

Writers on Murray have tended to follow the *Memoirs'* (1:3) ambiguous suggestion that her seduction took place when she was 12 years old.

It is more likely, however, given the chronology of Murray's early life, that the liaison took place around 1742 when she was aged 13.[29] Spencer, as a practised debauchee, might have seduced her with cheap trinkets and false promises, or simply by the purchase of her Bath rings and posies of flowers. Perhaps no such inducements were necessary and, as the *Memoirs* (1:3) suggested, Murray 'might have then been corrupted, with less powers than [Spencer] used to effect his intent'.

Murray had quite possibly decided that, like the Duke of Bolton with his paramour Lavinia Fenton, the aristocratic *roué* represented her best opportunity for escaping impoverishment and securing her rise in the world. If Murray entertained such naïvely grandiose dreams then she was soon disabused of them, for Spencer was far too seasoned a rake to consider her as anything more than a momentary diversion.

Those who have argued that Murray was born in London have suggested that she was debauched by Spencer in the darkness of the steps of Covent Garden Theatre, and that Spencer then took her to live with him as his mistress.[30] Peter Cunningham, the nineteenth-century editor of Horace Walpole's letters, even suggested that Murray lived with Spencer until his death in 1746, before moving to Bath to live with Nash.[31] Similarly, Charles Spencer, in his history of his family, has suggested that Spencer kept Murray as his mistress in the full knowledge of his wife, Georgiana, Lady Spencer.[32] It is, however, more in keeping with the chronology of Murray's eight-year career as a courtesan, that the *Memoirs* (1:5) are correct and Spencer soon tired of her and abandoned her almost immediately without any provision – 'in fine, a vender of nosegays he found her, and such he left her, after a few weeks enjoyment'. News that Murray had been discarded by Spencer and also by Harvey would have spread like wildfire among the gossips of Bath, and a pretty young girl with a lost reputation was fair game to young bloods in search of sexual encounters.

Nash's interest in Murray's plight was not unusual. It was part of the myth that Nash perpetuated about himself, as the benevolent sovereign of Bath, that he protected the naïve and defenceless from the city's iniquities.[33] In theory at least, Nash's successful regulation of Bath rested upon his reputation for generosity toward those in financial need and his willingness to defend the vulnerable. Anecdotes attested to his numerous interventions on behalf of fledgling gamblers, against the legion charlatans, gamesters and sharpers who worked Bath's gaming rooms, and of the protective advice he offered to the lovelorn against the designs of plausible fortune hunters:

> Th'unwary and beautiful Nymph would he guide;
> Oft tell her a Tale, how the credulous Maid
> By Man, by perfidious Man is betray'd.[34]

Even so, Nash did not make a habit of taking in Bath's newly debauched girls to live with him. His reputation in the city, and the sheer numbers of girls involved precluded such a deed. That is not to say that Bath's master of ceremonies had not enjoyed his fair share of mistresses. Oliver Goldsmith, in his 1762 biography of Nash, embellished the legend of Nash as lothario with stories of youthful intrigue. It was generally believed, for example, although without sure foundation, that he had been sent down from Jesus College, Oxford, where he matriculated in 1692, for a liaison with a disreputable woman of the town. A more creditable ill-fated romance with a Miss Verdun, who rejected his marriage proposal in 1696, gave Nash a certain cachet by making him the inspiration for John Vanbrugh's play *Aesop* (1697).

Nash appears to have abandoned thoughts of marriage sometime after this doomed affair, for later anecdotes, apocryphal or otherwise, refer only to liaisons with a succession of mistresses. According to *Court Tales* (1717), for example, Nash once took a lady's necklace in settlement of a gambling debt 'and at the next Assembly his own Dirty Mistress appear'd with it, to the terrible Mortification [of the lady] and the wonderful Delight of the whole Company'.[35]

Nash's reasons for taking Murray to live with him by early 1743 are unrecorded.[36] He might have been motivated by his friendship with Spencer's grandmother and his desire to save her embarrassment from gossip about her grandson's indiscretions. Over the years, a bond had developed between the master of ceremonies and the widowed duchess, to the extent that she trusted Nash's opinion on most things, from land leases to liveries for her footmen.[37] Another possibility is that Nash knew the Rudman family, and had been in contact with Murray's father at various times over the years regarding professional engagements in the city. Rudman, for his part, might have encouraged Murray's liaison with Bath's wealthy celebrity as the best means of support for himself and his family. Alternatively, the 'protection' extended to Murray by Nash might have been no more than an act of benevolence within eighteenth-century terms of gallantry, offering Murray pecuniary advantage and a magnificent roof over her head in exchange for sexual intimacy and companionship, as the ageing Nash rattled around his fine house in St John's Court by himself.

Whatever Nash's motives, once Murray was installed in his sumptuous mansion, disapproving gossip soon began to circulate about the toothless, 67-year-old 'Monarch of Bath' and his 14-year-old flower-seller. Accused by one indignant observer of being a whoremonger, Nash confronted his traducer full-square:

> I acknowledge, says [Nash], I have a Woman lives in my House, and that may have occasioned the Mistakes [that Nash was a whoremonger]; *but if I did keep her, a Man can no more be deemed a Whoremonger, from having one Whore in his House, than a Cheesemonger, for having one Cheese.*[38]

Murray was something of a shadowy figure during the year or so that she lived with Nash. There are no accounts of her accompanying him to the public balls over which he presided, or to other social events at the theatre or in the gaming rooms. While Murray's position as Nash's mistress made public appearances together inappropriate, such niceties had not prevented Nash from parading a previous 'Dirty Mistress' at the Assembly Rooms in a newly acquired necklace.

In truth, Nash preferred to hobnob with distinguished members of the Company, and upper-class ladies in particular, without a mistress to detract attention away from himself. According to his biographer John Walters, Nash 'tolerated no female companion. Her presence would have spoiled his flirtations, his strolls and dances with high-born ladies.'[39] Murray, therefore, inhabited her own domestic sphere, largely excluded from her keeper's public life. Goldsmith's description of the domestic arrangements at St John's Court confirmed the separateness of their lives. According to him, it was Nash's custom to get up at five in the morning and to spend his day socialising with the Company in the Pump Room, coffee houses and Assembly Rooms.[40] As a result, Nash was 'seldom at home but at the time of eating or rest'. When he dined at home, he returned around nine or ten o'clock in the evening, otherwise, it would be nearer midnight. As soon as he had enjoyed his favourite hot supper of boiled chicken or roast mutton, followed by a particular small potato which Nash dubbed the English pineapple, and which he ate 'as others do fruit, after dinner', he would go to bed.[41]

As Nash's mistress, Murray was experiencing luxury for the first time in her life. St John's Court was 'furnished with the Beauties of the Age' and was 'both within and without, a first Sight for Strangers' who came to gaze on its grandeur.[42] As a budding courtesan, Murray's domestic arrangements taught her invaluable lessons on how to inhabit refined spaces and how elegant households were run. To this extent, luxury, as Mary Peace suggested, was a refining rather than corrupting influence upon her. In addition, Murray was developing an eye for fashion, as she observed the most stylish women in England who were in Bath for the season. According to the *Memoirs* (1:7–8), 'she dressed equal to any woman at B[at]h' and, certainly, within a few short years Murray had emerged as *the* fashion leader of the *bon ton*.

Nash, who had once famously quipped that 'wit, flattery, and fine cloaths … were enough to debauch a nunnery', was now meeting all her expenses.[43] As a result, where once she had stared enviously in Bath's shop windows, she could now afford the 'Tippets and Trimmings; Artificial Flowers; Bath Lamb Gloves; Muslins, Cambricks and Lawns' that she saw for sale in millinery shops such as Rebecca Griffith's at the lower end of Orange Grove.[44] She could also join the general excitement when, for the Bath season only, the weavers and mercers P & J Ferry from the Strand opened their shop at the second door in Pierrepont Street to display the 'newest and genteelest Taste London can produce' and sell 'a great Variety of the richest and most fashionable Brocaded, Flower'd, Figur'd, Strip'd and Plain SILKS'.[45]

More valuable than such outward trappings of her status as mistress, Murray's time with Nash began a transformation in her manners, conversation and bearing that enabled her to hold an unassailable position for almost a decade within the rarefied and elegant world of the demi-rep. The *Memoirs* (1:44) described how 'all the rusticity of a nosegay girl, or a B[at]h-ring seller, was softened into that easy deportment, which is peculiar to those who move in the most elevated sphere' and attributed her metamorphosis to a refined young woman called Mrs Stevens. Described as the daughter of a Welsh baronet, Mrs Stevens was a fictional creation whose autobiographical account of conspiracy, adultery and betrayal added spice to the early chapters of the *Memoirs* (1:21–36).

It was, of course, Nash, the acknowledged arbiter of good conduct and correct manners, who was really instrumental in polishing and refining Murray into a suitable companion and mistress. Nash had, after all, successfully transformed himself from the son of a glass manufacturer into the friend of royalty and the aristocracy. She would have been an attentive pupil, keen to improve herself and shrewd in observing Nash at his own table and in emulating the fine manners of the ladies she saw in Bath.

Nash might have arranged lessons to improve on the 'indifferent' education (1:3) she had received from her parents. These could have included singing and music lessons to capitalise on any natural ability she had inherited from her father (1:150). What was most lacking in Murray, however, were the superior refinements that could only be acquired at the hands of a dancing master such as 'the eminent John Stagg who kept a profitable boarding school in Kingsmead' in the city.[46] Trevor Fawcett, in his study of dance in eighteenth-century Bath, has described how 'the fundamental importance of a dancing master' lay not only in teaching the intricacies of dance technique, but also 'in the coaching he provided in etiquette, in deportment, and in the cultivation of that air of relaxed assurance so much admired by contemporaries'.[47] In Murray's case, however, when the taught qualities of propriety and graciousness of manner were combined with her own natural allure, the resultant refinements proved a remarkably heady mix of sex and sophistication. It was these attributes that enabled Murray to pass elegantly and seamlessly within the demi-monde and the social circles of elite gentlemen: in time, her captivated admirers would respond by making her 'the greatest *purchaseable* beauty of her day'.[48]

Murray's affair with Nash probably ended in early 1744. Nash might have grown bored with his young mistress, or perhaps he was jealous of her growing popularity. As a beautiful and sexually awakened young woman, Murray would have undoubtedly attracted a train of youthful admirers. It could have been Murray, of course, who ended the affair, having wearied of her elderly protector's inattentiveness and his rude, testy manner which grew worse with age.[49] With the mindset of a courtesan already established, she might have suspected that Nash was not going to be a good financial prospect for much longer. Indeed, laws for the suppression of gaming bankrupted Nash during the 1740s, much of whose wealth had been derived from the cuts he took at the gaming tables of Bath and Tunbridge Wells, where he was also master of ceremonies.

Nash does not appear to have been especially wounded by his estrangement from Murray, and he soon found himself a replacement.[50] It was one of his *bons mots* that 'women were as plentiful as mushrooms, and always to be had for the asking'.[51] His new mistress was the eccentric Juliana Papjoy (or Popjoy or Pobjoy) (1710–77), the daughter of an innkeeper from Bishopstrow, near Warminster, some 19 miles from Bath. Known as 'Lady Betty Besom' because of her distinctive multi-thonged horsewhip, she regularly rode around Bath on a grey horse given to her by Nash.[52] It is said that Nash abandoned her when penury forced him to give up his mansion, and that he did not wish her to suffer his degradations. Papjoy, however, chose degradations of her own and, vowing never again to sleep in a bed, she slept in the hollow of a tree until her death in 1777. There are romantic stories that she returned to Nash in his old age and cared for him until his death in 1761.[53] However, Nash's executor George Scott suggested that for the last twenty years of his life, Nash lived with another woman who was of such a 'fierce Disposition' that 'poor Nash had no small Degree of Punishment in living with this termagant Woman, Solomon could not describe a worse'.[54]

By the age of 15, Murray was about to become Bath's most valuable export to London's sex trade. The former flower-seller was on the brink of early womanhood and possessed of an alluring beauty that would enthral the capital and beyond. Nash had smoothed Murray's roughened edges to reveal a nascent sophistication and elegance in her person and character. Imbued with the sexually charged atmosphere of Bath, Murray had also begun honing her lascivious arts. Her ability to offer blissfully erotic experiences wrapped in an outer casing of refinement and urbanity would prove an intoxicating and irresistible combination. She would soon be the unrivalled choice of elite men in search of exquisite pleasure.

It was time for Fanny Murray to spread her wings and London was calling.

Notes

1 The Earl of Ilchester and Mrs Langford-Brooke, *The Life of Sir Charles Hanbury-Williams, Poet, Wit Diplomatist* (Thornton Butterworth Ltd, 1928), p.235. Letter from Hanbury-Williams to his son-in-law William Anne Capell, 4th Earl of Essex dated January 1751.

2 *Memoirs*, vol. 1, p.7. See also, Dilke (ed.), *Papers of a Critic*, vol. 2, p.275 (footnote).

3 A.H. Batten Pooll, *A West Country Potpourri* (Bath: published privately, 1969), p.168, suggested that Nash tired of Murray after two years. David Gadd, *Georgian Summer: Bath in the Eighteenth Century* (Bath: Adams & Dart, 1971), p.76, stated that Murray lived with Nash 'for many years' before he replaced her with Papjoy.

4 John Tracy Atkyns (ed.), *Reports of Cases Argued and Determined in the High Court of Chancery, in the Time of Lord Chancellor Hardwicke* ... (1765), vol. 1, p.303.

5 Henrietta, Sarah's only surviving daughter, was 2nd Duchess of Marlborough from 1722 until her death in 1733. A special dispensation from the Crown, first granted during the reign of Queen Anne, allowed the Marlborough family the rare privilege of having its title pass down the female as well as the male line.

6 Thicknesse, *New Prose Bath Guide*, p.88. See also, John Eglin, *The Imaginary Autocrat: Beau Nash and the Invention of Bath* (Profile Books, 2005), p.67.

7 Smollett, *Peregrine Pickle*, Ch. 76, pp.376–78.

8 Taylor, *Records of My Life*, vol. 1, pp.213–14. The anecdote of a dinner party of stutterers was also attributed to the Duke of Montagu at Bath. See Frank Laurence Lucas, *The Art of Living: Four Eighteenth Century Minds* ... (Cassell, 1959), p.98.

9 *The Sporting Magazine: or, Monthly Calendar* ... (August 1799 issue), vol. 14, p.275. See also, Basil Cozens-Hardy (ed.), *The Diary of Sylas Neville, 1767–1788* (& New York & Toronto: Geoffrey Cumberlege, Oxford University Press, 1950), pp.99–100. Much to the mortification of his grandmother, Spencer had several brushes with the law. See, for example, *Satan's Harvest Home...* (1749), pp.2–3; *Walpole Correspondence*, vol. 1, pp.191–92. See also, Tim Hitchcock, '"You bitches [...] die and be damned": Gender, Authority and the Mob in St Martin's Roundhouse Disaster of 1742', in Tim Hitchcock and Heather Shore (eds), *The Streets of London from the Great Fire to the Great Stink* (& Sydney & Chicago: Rivers Oram Press, 2003), pp.69–81.

10 Thicknesse, *New Prose Bath Guide*, p.88. See also, *The Lady's Magazine: or, Entertaining Companion for the Fair Sex* ... (August 1778 issue), p.399.

11 Atkyns, *Reports of Cases Argued and Determined*, vol. 1, p.329.

12 *Satan's Harvest Home*, p.30. This quotation also appeared on p.39 of an earlier version of *Satan's Harvest Home* by Father Poussin entitled *Pretty Doings in a Protestant Nation* ... (1734). See Cruickshank, *Secret History of Georgian London*, pp.25–26.

13 Charles Spencer, *The Spencer Family* (Harmondsworth: Penguin Books, 2000), p.96. Sarah's temper tantrums and quarrelsome nature had led, in 1710, to a very public and irrevocable rift with Queen Anne to whom Sarah had been close confidante and advisor.

14 Ophelia Field, *The Favourite: Sarah, Duchess of Marlborough* (Hodder & Stoughton, 2002), p.420.

15 Ilchester and Langford-Brooke, *Life of Sir Charles Hanbury-Williams*, p.37 (footnote 1). Letter from Charles Wyndham to Hanbury-Williams dated 22 January 1734.

16 Lady Llanover (ed.), *The Autobiography and Correspondence of Mary Granville, Mrs Delaney ...*, 3 vols (Richard Bentley, 1861), vol. 1, p.427. See also, John Pearson, *Blood Royal: The Story of the Spencers and the Royals* (HarperCollins, 1999), p.86.

17 John Croft, *Scrapeana: Fugitive Miscellany* ([York]: San Souci, 1792), pp.287–88.

18 Mary Robinson, *Beaux & Belles of England*, (The Grolier Society, n/d), p.296.

19 Iris Butler, *Rule of Three: Sarah, Duchess of Marlborough, and her Companions in Power* (Hodder & Stoughton, 1967), pp.337–38; Field, *Sarah, Duchess of Marlborough*, p.414. See also, Frances Harris, *A Passion for Government: The Life of Sarah, Duchess of Marlborough* (Oxford: Clarendon Press, 1991), pp.306 and 327.

20 Pearson, *Blood Royal*, p.93.

21 Lady Bolingbroke's estimate is quoted in David Green, *Sarah Duchess of Marlborough* (Collins, 1967), p.308; See also, Amanda Foreman, *Georgiana, Duchess of Devonshire* (HarperCollins, 1998), p.4. When Spencer died in May 1746, Walpole wrote to Sir Horace Mann on 20 June 1746 saying that Spencer had had an income of £30,000 per year. See *Walpole Correspondence*, vol. 2, p.30.

22 Atkyns, *Reports of Cases Argued and Determined*, vol. 1, p.306. See also, pp.303 and 315–16.

23 Atkyns, *Reports of Cases Argued and Determined*, vol. 1, p.328.

24 Middleton's view of Spencer's health in the 1730s was contested in a Chancery suit in 1750. The executors of Spencer's will had refused to settle his debts with Sir Abraham Janssen of Wimbledon, claiming that the contract had been 'unreasonable and usurious'. Acting as an expert witness for Janssen, the surgeon James Napier who had attended Spencer before 1738, claimed Spencer had been in robust health from 1736 until shortly before his death. Other witnesses confirmed Napier's evidence. See Atkyns, *Reports of the Cases Argued and Determined*, vol. 1, pp.304 and 329.

25 *Read's Weekly Journal: or, British Gazetteer*, 3 November 1739.

26 Atkyns, *Reports of Cases Argued and Determined*, vol.1, p.328. Spencer had undergone mercury cures since at least 1732, when he had one in May and one in November. See Harris, *Passion for Government*, pp.285 and 290.

27 David Innes Williams, *The London Lock: A Charitable Hospital for Venereal Disease 1746–1952* (& New York: Royal Society of Medicine Press Ltd, 1995), pp.6–8.

28 Atkyns, *Reports of Cases Argued and Determined*, vol. 1, p.328.

29 E.J. Burford, *Royal St James's: Being a Story of Kings, Clubmen and Courtesans* (Robert Hale, 1988), p.163, suggests Murray was seduced by Spencer at the age of 14.

30 Hinde, *Tales from the Pump Room*, p.40; Walters, *Splendour and Scandal*, p.73. Molloy, *The Queen's Comrade*, vol. 2, p.618, claimed that Spencer lived with Murray 'on intimate terms', while Lewis Melville, *Bath Under Beau Nash* (Eveleigh Nash, 1907), p.266, suggested that Murray lived with Spencer as his mistress for an unspecified period of time. See also, de Barri, *Bucks and Bawds*,

p.108; Willard Connely, *Beau Nash: Monarch of Bath and Tunbridge Wells* (Werner Laurie, 1955), p.59.

31 *Walpole Correspondence*, vol. 4, p.133 (footnote 1).

32 Spencer, *Spencer Family*, p.104.

33 Carter, 'Beau Nash' in Matthew and Harrison (eds), *Oxford Dictionary of National Biography*, vol. 40, p.228.

34 Christopher Anstey, *The New Bath Guide*, with introduction and notes by Gavin Turner, (Bristol: Broadcast Books, 1994), p.84. See also, Barbeau, *Life & Letters at Bath*, p.49 (footnote 43).

35 [John Oldmixon], *Court Tales: or, a History of the Amours of the Present Nobility ...* (1717), pp.95–96. Nash is referred to as 'Nessus' in the anecdote, and his name given in the key at the end of the book as 'N-s-h'.

36 Keith B. Poole, *The Two Beaux* (East Ardsley: E.P. Publishing, 1976), p.31 and Connely, *Beau Nash*, p.60, both suggested that Nash lived with Murray from about the time his mansion was built *c.* 1720. This was nine years before Murray was born.

37 William and Robert Chambers (eds), *Chambers's Journal of Popular Literature, Science and Arts* (Edinburgh: W. & R. Chambers, 1860), vol. 12, p.252.

38 *The Jests of Beau Nash, Late Master of the Ceremonies at Bath ...* (1763), p.48.

39 Walters, *Splendour and Scandal*, p.75.

40 Goldsmith, *Life of Richard Nash*, pp.232–33.

41 Goldsmith, *Life of Richard Nash*, pp.231–32; *Jests of Beau Nash*, p.68.

42 Thicknesse, *New Prose Bath Guide*, p.81.

43 Goldsmith, *Life of Richard Nash*, p.74.

44 *The Bath Journal*, 17 September 1744.

45 *Bath Journal*, 24 September 1744.

46 Trevor Fawcett, 'Dance and Teachers of Dance in Eighteenth-Century Bath', in *Bath History* (Gloucester: Alan Sutton, 1988), vol. 2, pp.33–34.

47 Fawcett, 'Dance and Teachers of Dance', p.27.

48 Taylor, *Records of My Life*, vol. 1, pp.362–63.

49 Poole, *Two Beaux*, p.38, suggested Murray left Nash for an unnamed man.

50 Eglin, *Imaginary Autocrat*, p.99.

51 Richard Bentley, *Bentley's Miscellany* (Richard Bentley, 1837), vol. 2, p.423.

52 The whip was reminiscent of a 'besom' or broom made of twigs.

53 Poole, *Two Beaux*, p.57.

54 BL – Egerton MS 3736, f. 139. Letter from George Scott to Dr Thomas Wilson, dated 11 June 1761. If Nash did live with such a woman, it was for between ten and fifteen years.

3

London and the 'Sisters of Carnality'

While Fair F---- whom each Fop admires,
The Talk of Courtiers, and the Toast of Squires,
Tho' once in B[ath] the Lowest of her Kind,
In T[own], did a Panegyrist find.[1]

Murray set off on the 107-mile cramped and bone-jostling journey from Bath to London in the April of 1744.[2] She probably reserved her seat through Mr Brewer, the booking agent for the London Flying Stage-coach, who operated out of the Sadlers Arms in Stall Street. According to its advertisements in the earliest editions of the *Bath Journal*, the first coaches of the year set out 'from *Bath* on *Monday* the First of April, and Inns at the *One-Bell*, in the *Strand, London*'.[3]

If Murray travelled alone, as suggested by the *Memoirs* (1:48), then the journey was a particularly brave undertaking, since coach travel was notoriously perilous; so much so that passengers commonly made their wills before embarking on journeys of the shortest distance.[4] Roads were in a constant state of disrepair, coaches overturned and at certain times of the year thick fogs descended suddenly to disorientate drivers. To make matters worse, heavy rains turned roads into quagmires and snowdrifts caused whiteouts.[5] Then there were the highwaymen to contend with, who lay in wait along the length of the lonely and exposed

Bath road. It was not for nothing that travellers called coaches 'god per-mits' and credited their safe arrival at their destination to 'god willing'.[6]

The *Memoirs* provide the only narrative of Murray's first months in London and, in the absence of corroborating evidence; writers on Murray have accepted their account of her rapid descent into street prostitution at the hands of mercenary brothel-keepers, and her sub-sequent emergence as a triumphant new toast of the town. It makes for a good story, and is retold here, but is without sure foundation. The *Memoirs'* description of Murray's early experiences in London's brothels, for example, was formulaic and owed much to set-piece narratives in which innocent young women were tricked into prostitution. In these, ingénues were hoodwinked into believing that they were being offered honest employment, only to discover too late that their employers were bawds and that the food, lodging and clothes they had accepted came at a heavy price. A fictional account which appeared in 1755 in the weekly periodical *The World* described succinctly how this entrapment worked:

> I desired to understand her, and was informed (though not in plain words) that my benefactress was a bawd, and that she had taken me into her family for the most infamous of purposes. I trembled with amazement, and insisted on leaving the house that instant. She told me, I was at full liberty to do so; but that first I must pay her for my lodging and clothes.[7]

William Hogarth gave pictorial expression to such narratives in *The Harlot's Progress* (1732), one of his series on 'Modern Moral Subjects'. In the first plate, Moll Hackabout was depicted as she arrived in London, fresh-faced from the country, at the moment she was befriended by the famous real-life brothel-keeper Elizabeth Needham (d. 1731). As Hackabout responded to Needham's seeming benevolence, she took her first steps toward ruination, and in Needham's patched face was written the inno-cent Hackabout's future demise, at the age of 23, as a diseased prostitute.

The story of Murray's arrival in London differed markedly in two respects from such narratives, in that she was already sexually experi-enced when she arrived in the capital and, if the *Memoirs* (1:67) are to be believed, she entered her first brothel of her own volition – 'neces-sity obliged her to have recourse to Mrs Softing'.[8] Although the author of the *Memoirs* claimed that Murray had chosen to turn prostitute, he was characteristically benign in his treatment of her. He insisted that she had retained her charming innocence, and that she was still sufficiently honest to hope for marriage or 'something [that] might be obtained in an honourable way'. Thus, Murray, as presented in the *Memoirs*, conformed to the stereotype of the hoodwinked maiden in so far as she was innocent of the world of brothels and was hastened into the profession by the stratagems of a practised brothel-keeper.

In this, there were certain parallels between Murray's story and that of Fanny Hill, the heroine of John Cleland's novel, *Memoirs of a Woman of Pleasure* (1749). These similarities, and a shared Christian name, led the Austrian historian, Lujo Bassermann, to suggest that Cleland had based his novel on episodes from Murray's life. 'Even if it need not be assumed that Fanny Murray was the original of the celebrated Fanny Hill,' Bassermann argued, 'certain aspects of her career were certainly embodied in Cleland's novel.'[9] While this is indeed true of Murray's first experiences in London, little in the novel was so specific to Murray's life to differentiate her from countless other women who came to London from the provinces and ended up in the sex trade. It is more likely that the parallels Bassermann noted resulted from the anonymous author of the *Memoirs* borrowing scenes from Cleland's novel to recreate Murray's early life as a prostitute.

In both narratives, the two women were befriended by bawds who quickly drew them into a state of financial indebtedness and dependence. Both were given food and lodging and, in Fanny Hill's case, 'a white lute-string [dress], flower'd with silver … a *Brussel*-lace cap, [and] braided shoes'.[10] Mrs Softing set Murray up with one of her houses near the Haymarket, a 'waiting-job chariot' (1:67) and a clothing account with some mercers. Both bawds encouraged the young women in their mounting debts, before offering them a predictable solution to their financial difficulties. Murray (1:81) was introduced to one of Mrs Softing's clients, the elderly Mr F, complete with gouty leg and such severe halitosis that it drove Murray to her smelling bottle. Similarly, Fanny Hill's bawd, Mrs Brown, presented her to the equally foul-breathed Mr Crofts, who was 'past threescore, short and ill-made, with a yellow cadaverous hue, [and] great goggling eyes'.[11]

Fanny Hill managed to escape Brown's establishment *virgo intacta*, to become mistress to a handsome young man of her own choosing. Murray, on the other hand, went through with her assignation. The author of the *Memoirs*, in his account of Murray's introduction to brothel life, claimed that her previous sexual experiences meant that she 'was not much shocked at the proposal' (1:80). Consequently, when Mr F presented her with a snuffbox containing two £20 notes (equivalent to £5,000 today), Murray was easily persuaded to go ahead with the transaction. According to the *Memoirs* (1:82), Murray's night with Mr F was a defining one, for she was said to have emerged the following morning as a fully fledged prostitute having 'played her part so well behind the scenes'. Thus, without further explanation, Murray's momentous step from Richard Nash's mistress to London prostitute was colourfully imagined and brightly passed over for the amusement of readers.

Murray having been deserted by both Mrs Softing and her elderly lover following a quarrel, the *Memoirs* (1:88–9) went on to describe her rapid descent into 'nocturnal incontinence and repeated debauch' with the 'beastly drunkard, [and] the nauseating rake'.[12] Venereal disease, reasoned the author of the *Memoirs* (1:89), was the inevitable consequence. *The Humours of Fleet-Street* also asserted that Murray contracted the disease, but there is no corroborating evidence to support the claims of either biography beyond the high probability that as a prostitute Murray would have fallen victim to the clap (gonorrhoea) or the pox (syphilis) at some point in her career.

As already noted, both diseases were to be feared. Syphilis, which can be deadly if untreated, begins innocuously enough with a painless chancre (ulceration), while gonorrhoea often has silent symptoms in women.[13] Left untreated, gonorrhoea can cause pelvic inflammatory disease and infertility. Perversely, this was a blessing in disguise to prostitutes whose livelihoods were forfeit by pregnancy and unwanted children.[14] Although her biographer in *The Humours of Fleet-Street* claimed that Murray gave birth, other sources suggest that Murray never fell pregnant. For example, in *An Essay on Woman* (printed 1763) by John Wilkes and Thomas Potter, which is discussed in chapter nine, a scurrilous comparison was made between Murray and the Virgin Mary when it was claimed that Murray '*never had a Child*, nor I truly believe did she ever conceive'.[15]

The possibility of infection, reinfection and repeated curative treatments, to say nothing of frequent abortions, helps explain why so many courtesans, including Elizabeth Armistead (1750–1842), Nancy Parsons (c. 1735–c. 1814), Harriet Powell (d. 1779) and Murray, remained childless even after marriage. Barrenness, which had been such a boon to their working lives, was perhaps the cause of wistful regret in marriage.

Murray might have made 'use of all the precaution possible', as the prostitute Mrs L[e]w[i]s of Market Row on Portland Street had done; however, as the author of *Harris's List* remarked in pseudo-philosophic terms, 'who can withstand the power of numbers?'[16] Cures, which took anything from ten weeks to four months depending on the severity of the infection, were expensive. The writer and diarist James Boswell, who had as many as nineteen bouts of gonorrhoea in his lifetime, paid 5 guineas (about £600 today), for a cure following his intimacy with the actress Mrs Louisa Lewis.[17] Thus, when Murray first became aware of her condition, she might have been tempted, for economy's sake, to cure herself with anti-venereal pills bearing such names as 'Grand Anti Siphylicon' which were regularly advertised in the newspapers.[18] According to the *Memoirs* (1:89), however, Murray, like Boswell, sought the safer but more expensive option and trusted her treatment to a surgeon who cured her but made her destitute into the bargain: 'Her small stock [was] exhausted in chirurgical fees; her cloaths were pledged upon the same account; her surgeon took his last fee, produced by her last gown.'[19]

At her lowest ebb, and with the threat of debtors' prison looming, the *Memoirs* (1:90) claimed, rather melodramatically, that Murray was on the brink of suicide but that she chose instead to earn her keep as a streetwalker operating from a seedy brothel near the Old Bailey. The brothel, as described in the *Memoirs*, was a far cry from the fashionable bordellos of Covent Garden, being on the east side of the city beyond St Paul's – the haunt of the lowliest prostitutes.

According to the ten-point 'Gradations of Whores' described by the 'Reformed Rake' in his *Congratulatory Epistle*, streetwalkers were just above the most wretched categories of pickpocketing prostitutes, known as bunters and bulk-mongers, who drifted in and out of Bridewell correctional institutions.[20] If the *Memoirs* (1:92 and 95–7) were correct, then Murray was living on these criminal fringes among rough-trade prostitutes and bound to a blackmailing bawd who threatened to inform against her and have her sent to Bridewell should she try to escape.[21]

In these miserable circumstances, Murray would have been sent out berouged and 'dressed up in dabs for the patrole of Fleet-street and the Strand' (1:92). The Strand, in particular, was synonymous with desperate streetwalkers like Miss Kitty E[mer]son, who was noted in *Harris's List* as having sunk so low that 'she can now toss off a glass of gin as well as the commonest bunter in the Strand, and, like them, stoop to every meanness'.[22]

Boswell knew the type well, and remarked in 1763 on 'the civil nymph with white-thread stockings who tramps along the Strand and will resign her engaging person to your honour for a pint of wine and a shilling'.[23] Twenty years earlier, in the mid-1740s, when Murray walked the same streets, her weekly earnings were recorded in the *Memoirs* (1:92) as £5 10s 6d, so that she might have been turning tricks for as little as sixpence. If so, she could have serviced 100–200 men a week, which possibly accounts for the uncorroborated anecdote from Murray's later career that she was well able to satisfy 100 men a day. According to the anecdote, she 'boasted of once earning a hundred guineas in one day simply by asking one hundred gentlemen, "What is your pleasure sir?"'[24]

The *Memoirs* (1:92) claimed that Murray was only allowed to keep sixpence from her weekly earnings after her Old Bailey bawd had deducted charges for her clothes and her board and lodgings in a garret above a chandler's shop. The brothel-keeper's list of Murray's weekly requirements, and the extortionate rates the bawd charged for them were reproduced in the *Memoirs* (1:93–4). The document is undoubtedly an invention, for it is unlikely that one of Murray's old bills would have survived thirteen years before finding its way to her biographer as he worked on the *Memoirs* during 1758. The published reckoning is nonetheless valuable as a creative response to the financial exploitation of those 'sisters of carnality' who, like Murray, found themselves caught up in the sex trade:[25]

	£	s	d
To board and lodging (in a garret, upon small beer and sprats)	1	15	0
To washing (two smocks, two handkerchiefs, and two pair of stockings)	0	7	0
To the use of a brocade gown (of the intrinsic value of a crown)	0	8	0
To the use of a pair of stays (not worth a shilling)	0	3	0
To the use of a pair of silk shoes (ditto)	0	2	6
To the use of smocks (coarse, old, and patched)	0	7	0
To the use of ruffles (darned, of the original value of half a crown)	0	2	0
To the use of petticoats (all of the lower sort, except one water-tabby petticoat, piss-burnt)	0	4	0

To seeing the constable of the night, for preventing her going to Bridewell (peace-officers fee'd – in buckram)	0	10	6
[Blank]			
To the use of a hat (worthless)	0	2	0
To the use of ribbands (unused)	0	3	6
Pins (a few)	0	0	6
To the use of a capuchin (a cloak for imposition)	0	8	0
To the use of a gauze apron (of Rag-fair genealogy)	0	5	0
To the use of a gauze handkerchief (ditto)	0	2	6
To the use of a pair of silk stockings (yellow, and pieced)	0	2	6
To the use of a pair of stone buckles (most of the stones out. No price)	0	4	6
Carmine, tooth-powder, and brushes (carmine, alias brick-dust. Tooth-powder ditto. Brushes, unseen)	0	3	0
	5	10	6

Murray's experiences as a street prostitute might have been created by the *Memoirs* for dramatic effect or reader titillation but they were nevertheless accurate reflections of the abuses prostitutes sometimes suffered at the hands of autocratic and mercenary brothel-keepers. Indictments taken from the Old Bailey *Session Papers* suggest that working girls were often little more than sex slaves until age or the final stages of disease released them from the clutches of their bawds. While Murray might have felt aggrieved by her sixpenny wages, Margaret Cassady, who ran her operation from Eagle Court in the Strand, took every last penny from her prostitutes in payment for their clothes, board and lodgings. They were not allowed to keep any part of their earnings.

A sympathetic customer gave one of Cassady's girls, Mary Caton, an 18*s* piece and half a guinea specifically for her to buy her own clothes and escape the brothel. Possessing one's own clothes was critical to any getaway, since runaway prostitutes could be charged with theft and imprisoned or hanged if taken in clothes that brothel-keepers alleged belonged to them. Cassady doggedly tracked Caton down to Tothill

Fields Bridewell in Westminster, where she had been taken on a charge of disorderly conduct. Caton was probably too browbeaten a creature to make any bid for freedom. Instead, and still dressed in clothes belonging to Cassady, she had gone on a drinking binge with her customer's generosity. Cassady assaulted Caton there and then, and retrieved the 18*s* piece and the 2*s* remaining from the half guinea.[26]

Murray appears to have shown greater resolve than Caton. According to the *Memoirs*, she escaped from her brothel-keeper, and set herself up in her own lodgings in fashionable St James's with 7 guineas that she had concealed from her bawd. In reality, without a generous client like Caton's to help with an extra guinea or two, it would have taken Murray two or three years to save a sufficient stash of extra sixpences and shillings from her apprentice-boy punters to afford the lodgings, furnishings and smart clothes she required for her upmarket address.

Murray's success once she escaped the brothel was portrayed as immediate and spectacular – according to the *Memoirs* (1:99–100) she was soon employing a double called 'Miss G' who assisted by servicing surplus customers. The historian Julie Peakman has tentatively identified her as 'bouncing Miss *Gif[for]d*' who, by the time she had reached her mid to late thirties, had 'lai[n] with more men, than she has hairs upon her head'.[27] Even if Miss G were no more than a spurious invention designed for reader entertainment, there were real-life prostitutes who did good business from their resemblances to toasts of the town. In her youth, the prostitute Mrs Pritchard of Wardour Street in Soho was said to have borne a handsome resemblance to the notorious adulteress Lady Sarah Bunbury, the daughter of Charles Lennox, 2nd Duke of Richmond. Similarly, Polly Davies traded on her likeness to the celebrated Kitty Fisher and took particular pride in the fact that she had a better nose than Fisher's.[28]

Around 1745, Murray's fortunes actually changed spectacularly when she came to the attention of John Montagu, 4th Earl of Sandwich, 'the most profligate character in the kingdom' and grandson of the famous libertine John Wilmot, Earl of Rochester.[29] Interestingly, the *Memoirs* made no mention of this significant liaison. In December 1744, Sandwich had been appointed a lord commissioner of the Admiralty and he would spend most of his political career at the Admiralty Office, serving as First Lord of the Admiralty on three occasions between 1748 and 1782.[30] The writer Donald McCormick suggested that Sandwich found Murray, then 16 years of age, in a brothel run by a Mrs Stanhope, who had 'decked her out as a parson's daughter to such good effect that she soon became Sandwich's mistress'.[31]

Tall and athletic-looking, Sandwich captivated women. This was despite an awkward gait that made him look, some said, as if he were walking down both sides of the street at once and an ungainliness on the dance floor which led his Parisian dancing master to beg him 'never [to] tell anyone of whom [he] learned to dance'.[32] Indeed, the *Town and Country Magazine* for 1770 remarked how he was 'still *a buck of the first water*, and love[d] his bottle and his lass, though now in his 52nd year'.[33]

His long-term mistress was the beautiful Martha Ray (1745–79), the daughter of a stay-maker in Holywell Street, whom Sandwich had met around 1762 when she was a 17-year-old milliner's apprentice. The couple lived together in relative harmony for over sixteen years until Ray's murder, just before midnight on 7 April 1779, at the age of 34. She was shot dead as she left Covent Garden Opera House by the infatuated Reverend James Hackman, whom Ray had first met in the winter of 1775.[34] Her lifeless body was then carried to the Shakespear's Head Tavern, one of Murray's youthful haunts. Sandwich was devastated by Ray's loss; and yet, within a year, he had taken up with another mistress, Nelly Gordon, with whom he lived until his death in 1792.

Murray might not have been one of Sandwich's long-term mistresses, but when he was involved in an exposé in November 1769, it was his liaison with Murray, and also Lucy Cooper, that was recalled. The revelations appeared in a 'tête-à-tête' when Sandwich and Ray were the featured lovers of the month. Never a stickler for accuracy, the exposé gave the impression that Murray and Cooper were concurrent mistresses with Ray, when in fact, Murray had been married for six years when Sandwich and Ray first met, and Cooper had already entered her 'fair but faded' years.[35] The 'tête-à-tête' piece described how Sandwich had once been a rival to 'Sir Richard Atk[i]ns, in the embraces of Fanny M----y, whilst he supported Lucy Cow--r [Cooper] for her wit and sprightliness. He was, nevertheless, united to an agreeable and accomplished lady, [Martha Ray] who bore him several *pledges* of *her* constancy and affection.'[36]

The refinements that Murray had acquired at Bath appear to have stood her in good stead as she sought to distinguish herself to Sandwich as a high-quality prostitute and budding courtesan. Like Nash before him, Sandwich might have smoothed some of Murray's roughened edges. The *Memoirs* (1:145–6) hinted that during this period Murray continued to perfect her arts, so that she probably learnt to make the best of her natural beauty, to dress tastefully in the latest fashions and in particular, to offer elegant companionship at the theatre or pleasure garden and pleasing conversation at the dinner table.

No matter how fleeting the intrigue, Murray's conquest of Sandwich was a great coup, and instrumental in establishing her as a peerless, purchasable beauty. With Sandwich's reputation well established as 'a professed admirer of every reigning toast', his liaison with Murray was a public acknowledgement of her superior qualities as a 'votary of Venus'.[37] Her position as the latest toast of the town was assured and reflected in the increasing number of admirers who began to mob her. 'Whenever she walked abroad a troop of gallants crowded around her [...]. Such a favourite did she become that the wits declared "it was a vice not to be acquainted with Fanny; it was a crime not to toast her at every meal".'[38]

Among their number were two lovers, both on the cusp of highly successful careers, who were proof of the elite clientele that Murray was beginning to command. One was Henry Gould (1710–94) of Sharpham Park in Somerset, a first cousin of the novelist Henry Fielding. The other was Joseph Yorke (1724–92), who was created 1st Baron Dover in 1788.[39] Gould was a barrister at the time he consorted with Murray, having been called to the Bar in June 1734, and by 1763, he had risen to become a judge of the Court of Common Pleas.[40] Yorke, on the other hand, pursued a military career and was a lieutenant at the time of his liaison with Murray. He advanced quickly to attain the rank of general before pursuing a diplomatic career at the Hague, first as British minister from 1751 to 1761 and then as ambassador between 1761 and 1780.

Career-minded and ambitious, both men were careful to avoid reckless intrigues that could damage their prospects or ruin their reputations, so that they were fairly abstemious by the sexual standards of the day. It was said that Gould 'never lost sight of prudence, or sacrificed those hours to amusement, which should be devoted to more useful application'.[41] Similarly, Yorke turned his back on gallantry after he took up his diplomatic posting at the Hague in 1751, and severed all connections with the *impures* in England with whom he had enjoyed his youth.

Yorke and Gould's pasts caught up with them, however, when gossipy retrospectives on their youthful indiscretions appeared in the 'tête-à-tête' series. Yorke's exposé as 'the experienced ambassador' was published in September 1779, when he was 55, and Gould's as 'the humane judge' in November 1781, when he was 71. Both men were portrayed as having been connoisseurs of the female form in their youth and as having consorted exclusively with the select beauties of their day, such as the courtesan Constantia Phillips and the actress Peg Woffington. As a result, they had shared several women in common, including the opera singer Signora Campioni and Murray, whom Gould was noted to have placed on the 'list of his favourite Thaïs's'.[42]

It was during this period of her life, and possibly with the assistance of Sandwich, that Murray sat for two of her earliest portraits, both of which have been the subject of controversy and debate. The earlier of the two portraits was first mentioned in Richard Cooksey's 1791 biography of Yorke's father, Philip, 1st Earl of Hardwicke, who was Lord Chancellor of England from 1737 to 1756.[43] The story goes that around 1740, shortly after he had bought Wimpole Hall in the Cambridgeshire village of Arrington, Hardwicke made an impromptu visit to one of his new neighbours. This happened to be Sandwich's volatile and slightly unhinged younger brother, the naval captain William Montagu, known as 'Mad Montagu'.[44] According to Cooksey, Montagu did not recognise his unexpected visitor when he invited him in and offered him a tour of his house. As they walked through the elegant rooms, Montagu stopped before a portrait of Murray and Kitty Fisher 'beautifully painted in all their native naked charms'. Even though the portrait captured perfectly their 'most striking likenesses', Hardwicke did not recognise the two women. Appalled by his ignorance, Montagu immediately upbraided his visitor:

> Why, where the devil have you led your life, or what company have you kept, says the Captain, not to know Fanny Murray and Kitty Fisher, with whose persons I thought no fashionable man like you could be unacquainted?[45]

The anecdote was dismissed by George Harris, another of Hardwicke's biographers, as an attempt by Cooksey to tarnish Hardwicke's reputation by linking him, albeit tangentially, with prostitutes.[46] By the mid-1840s, however, the story of Hardwicke's encounter with the naked courtesans had been made flesh when John Campbell, in his *Lives of the Lord Chancellors of England*, refuted claims that Hardwicke had had affairs with both Murray and Fisher. Defending Hardwicke from accusations of alleged liaisons with a Lady B and a Mrs Wells, Campbell insisted that such charges had 'as little foundation as for his conjectured intimacy with Fanny Murray and Kitty Fisher'.[47]

The literary critic Charles Wentworth Dilke was also sceptical about the Cooksey anecdote. According to his reckoning, if Hardwicke had bought Wimpole Hall in 1740 then he must have seen the portrait no later than 1741, since Montagu would not have delayed in showing 'so distinguished a man the neighbourly respect of a visit'.[48] While this demolished the effect of the anecdote, which relied for its humour on Montagu being unaware that he was remonstrating with the Lord Chancellor of England, it also meant that Murray was no older than 12 when the nude portrait was painted, and Fisher aged 2.[49] Whether or not the anecdote was genuine, the important point is that it might once have had a basis in truth and that Fisher was only added to embellish the tale. It seems to be more than coincidental that Montagu should be credited with owning a portrait of a woman once intimately connected with his brother, and it is possible that Sandwich commissioned the portrait for him or, at the very least, arranged for his beautiful young mistress to be the model.

If this portrait ever existed it is now lost, as indeed is a later portrait of Murray by Henry Robert Morland which was widely copied for the print-shop market. As a result, another early portrait of Murray, in which Sandwich might have also played a small part, is of particular importance as it is now the only known oil painting thought to be of Murray still in existence. The painting is also significant in confirming that by the age of 16 Murray had left the stews of the Old Bailey and Covent Garden behind her and was operating as a high-class prostitute.

Her portrait is one of four oriental studies of female sitters that now hang either side of *Il Faquir Dashwood Pasha* (*c.* 1745) in the Palmyra dining room at West Wycombe Park in Buckinghamshire, the sumptuous home of the Dashwood family. Aside from Murray, the sitters were all members of Sir Francis Dashwood's close family – his wife Sarah Gould, the widow of Sir Richard Ellys, whom Dashwood had married in 1745; his sister Rachel, Lady Austen; and his half-sister Mary Walcot (or Walcott).[50] Taken together, the visual effect of these oriental paintings, with Dashwood's portrait as the centrepiece, is stunning. All four women are richly dressed in the height of 'turquerie' fashion in 'gold dresses with ermine wraps' and their portraits mounted within heavy gilt frames, topped with centrally placed carved turbans and crescents.

Painted around 1745 by the artist Adriaen Carpentiers (fl. 1739–78), Murray looks older than her 16 years and exudes a dazzling coquettishness as she stares from the canvas. Susan Griffin, in her study of courtesans, has remarked on 'the frank quality' of the subjects' gaze in courtesan portraiture, and the way courtesan eyes 'do not flinch or shrink or apologise but instead meet you with unremitting candour'.[51] Murray's portrait is no exception; she draws the gazer into her deep, shining almond-shaped eyes. She is luxuriously costumed in a gold brocade dress over which she wears a pale blue, ermine-trimmed cloak. A belt with a bejewelled clasp encircles her waist and her right hand rests on an opulently jewelled turban. She wears two strands of pearls on her left arm and a pair of large pearl drop earrings, while her thick, dark hair is ornamented with a pearl braid, set off by a pretty feather-like pearl and ruby ornament. Her left breast and nipple are fully exposed and a long string of pearls hangs seductively across the expanse of her translucent neck and décolletage. Her naked breast might be 'a pun on the word "sultana"', as the 11th Baronet Dashwood suggested in his history of his family, but it is also likely, given the long tradition of bare-breasted whores and mistresses in art, that Murray's nakedness worked as a visual code to denote her status as a high-class prostitute.[52]

The provenance of Murray's exotic portrait is connected to the short-lived Divan Club, which was founded by Sandwich in 1744.[53] At its first meeting on 8 January, Sandwich, Dashwood and eight other inaugural members resolved to 'form themselves forthwith into a Turkish Club'.[54] Sandwich's interest in the East had been sparked during a three-year sailing trip around the Mediterranean, which began in 1737 and included two journeys into Asia Minor. Dashwood also travelled to the Levant in the late 1730s.[55]

Divan Club membership was restricted to those who had travelled, or were about to travel, in the Ottoman Empire and, since Europe rather than Asia was the usual well-trodden route for the Grand Tourist, the Divan Club remained small and exclusive, with no more than twenty-two members.[56] It disbanded after twenty-eight months, holding its last meeting, with only three members present, on 25 May 1746.

Claims that Murray's portrait was commissioned by the Divan Club in January 1744 (when she was actually still in Bath) and formally recorded in *Al Koran*, the club's irreverently named minute book, have proved unfounded.[57] It is more likely that Sandwich recommended his mistress of the moment to Dashwood, and that Dashwood engaged Carpentiers to paint Murray's portrait as a companion piece to *Il Faquir Dashwood Pasha*, commissioned to celebrate Dashwood's membership of the Divan Club. This would account for the particular visual unity in the two portraits, especially the dark blue ermine-trimmed cloaks, which is less apparent in the three other oriental studies. In *Il Faquir Dashwood Pasha*, named after one of his Divan Club titles, Dashwood is dressed for a club meeting in 'a gold brocade shirt, richly encrusted with jewels', his ermine-trimmed cloak and a jewelled turban. Captured in jovial mood, Dashwood holds a full glass of wine in his raised hand as if about to give the Divan Club's standing toast to 'the Harem'.[58]

This provocative toast and Murray's bare-breasted portrait, which was undoubtedly enjoyed by club members, has given rise to speculation that the Divan Club was open to women, and that it functioned as a form of seraglio. It has been suggested, for example, that club members 'cavorted with their harem' and that, 'dressed up as Sultans (and Sultanas) [they] revelled in the worship of Bacchus'.[59] Indeed, Murray's semi-naked portrait led the 11th Baronet Dashwood to propose that 'it is unlikely that the activities [of the club] were wholly intellectual'.[60]

As the portrait of Dashwood shows, there was a strong element of fantasy to the Divan Club, in that members attended the fortnightly meetings in full oriental costume, complete with robes, daggers and turbans. In addition, they adopted Turkish names for the officers of the club so that, for example, the chairman of each dinner was designated the '*vizier*' and the Divan Club secretary, the '*reis effendi*'.[61] Even so, the Divan Club was not a 'private bordello'; rather, it was a gentlemen's club where respected scholars like Sir Richard Pococke, and those interested in Ottoman civilisation and culture, could talk about their travels and enjoy intellectual discussion on convivial evenings when 'the Master of the Tavern provide[d] a Dinner at a Crown a head'.[62] This is not to say, however, that on occasion, and given 'the erotic undercurrent of masculine Orientalist discourse', conversations did not range over less scholarly subjects such as the exoticism of Turkish women or ruminate on life in the seraglio.[63] Neither does it disregard the possibility that, at the close of the evening, club members made their way 'to some nearby house of carnal recreation'.[64]

Rachel Finnegan, in her study of the Divan Club, has suggested that, rather than an invitation to promiscuous nights with paid prostitutes like Murray, the club's standing toast to 'the Harem' was to honour Lady Mary Wortley Montagu (1689–1762) for her contribution to the study of the Ottoman Empire. Finnegan also claimed that Lady Mary was 'indirectly one of the major influences on the establishment of the all-male Turkish Club' while the historian Eric Towers has suggested that she might have been made an honorary member.[65] Lady Mary had penned a series of fifty-two 'Turkish Embassy Letters' to her friends during a fifteen-month residence in Constantinople, from August 1716 while her husband Edward Wortley Montagu was ambassador. These letters, which were published posthumously in 1763, were highly influential as they unveiled to male audiences for the first time the private and forbidden world of Turkish women and especially the harem.

The 11th Baronet Dashwood has also argued for female involvement in the Divan Club, which he dated to the time of his half-sister Mary Walcot's death in 1741. The four oriental portraits at West Wycombe, and especially the unity in the style of the costumes and their similarity to that worn by Dashwood in *Il Faquir Dashwood Pasha*, suggested to the 11th Baronet that an informal precursor to the Divan Club might have existed which permitted the inclusion of women who had travelled to Turkey.[66] He also suggested that Walcot and Murray might have accompanied Dashwood on his trip to the Levant in the late 1730s. There is, however, no evidence that Murray ever visited Turkey, and she would have been about 9 years old at the time of Dashwood's voyage.

Murray's portrait is important not only as the earliest surviving rendition of her youthful beauty but also for demonstrating how quickly she appears to have moved from low prostitution and into the elite circles she would dominate for almost a decade. Her liaison with Sandwich had introduced her to Dashwood, and Sandwich might have also introduced her to Joseph Yorke, since the two men moved in similar diplomatic circles.[67] Dashwood, in his turn, introduced her to his friends, such as the politician George Bubb Dodington, and it would not be long before Dashwood would re-enter her life and make her famous as one of the 'Nuns of Medmenham'.

Carpentiers had immortalised Murray's beauty in paint for the private enjoyment of Divan Club members, but the politician Richard Rigby, who had described her spat with the diplomat and politician Thomas

Robinson, was about to ensure that she was eternalised in poetry, so that the nation as a whole should know the name of Fanny Murray.

Notes

1 *The Modern Courtezan, an Heroic Poem. Inscrib'd to Miss F---y M----y ...* [1750], pp.3–4.
2 *Memoirs*, vol. 1, p.48. Roberts, *Whores in History*, p.176, suggested Murray moved to London in 1743.
3 *Bath Journal*, 25 March 1745.
4 See, for example *The Miscellaneous Works of William Hazlitt ...*, 5 vols (New York: Derby and Jackson, 1857), vol. 5, p.92; Tyte, *Bath in the Eighteenth Century*, p.78.
5 *Bath Journal*, 23 February 1747.
6 *Bath Journal* for 28 April 1746 carried an advertisement for the 'Frome Flying-Waggon' which travelled between Frome, near Bath, and London. This claimed that the journey was to be 'perform'd (if GOD permit) by Joseph Clavey'. See also, *Bath Journal*, 1 October 1744.
7 Edward Moore [pseud. Adam Fitz-Adam], *The World ...*, 6 vols (1755–57), vol. 3 (1755) no. 97, pp.243–44 (entry for 7 November 1754).
8 The name 'Mrs Softing' might be a play on words since a Mrs Harding was a well-known bawd in London. See John Brewer, *Sentimental Murder: Love and Madness in the Eighteenth Century* (HarperCollins, 2004), p.129.
9 Bassermann, *Oldest Profession*, p.148. The *Memoirs* are described as an 'imitation of Fanny Hill; less indecent' in George Watson et al. (eds), *The New Cambridge Bibliography of English Literature*, 5 vols (Cambridge: Cambridge University Press, 1969–77), vol. 2, (1971), p.999.
10 Cleland, *Memoirs of a Woman of Pleasure*, vol. 1, p.36.
11 Cleland, *Memoirs of a Woman of Pleasure*, vol.1, p.41.
12 See also, Ch. 4, below, p.98.
13 Williams, *London Lock*, especially pp.5–7. Margaret Leeson (1727–97), a Dublin-born prostitute, contracted venereal disease after being gang-raped in the autumn of 1796. She died within six months on 22 March 1797.
14 I.M. Davis, *The Harlot and the Statesman: The Story of Elizabeth Armistead & Charles James Fox* (Bourne End: Kensal Press, 1986), p.91.
15 Quoted in Arthur H. Cash, *An Essay on Woman by John Wilkes and Thomas Potter: A Reconstruction of a Lost Book with a Historical Essay on the Writing, Printing, and Suppressing of this 'Blasphemous and Obscene' Work* (New York: AMS Press Inc., 2000), p.99 (verse 8).
16 *Harris's List* (1773), p.24.
17 Boswell arrived in London from Scotland in 1762 at the age of 22. See Frederick A. Pottle (ed.), *Boswell's London Journal 1762–1763* (& New Haven: Yale University Press, 1992), p.175; Stone, *Family, Sex and Marriage*, pp.572–602.

18 *Whitehall Evening Post*, 29–31 May 1760.

19 Pottle (ed.), *Boswell's London Journal*, p.156.

20 *Congratulatory Epistle of a Reformed Rake*, p.8.

21 Peakman has suggested that the bawd might have been Mrs Maddox. See Peakman, *Whore Biographies*, vol. 3, p.2.

22 *Harris's List* (1773), p.76.

23 Pottle (ed.), *Boswell's London Journal*, pp.83–84.

24 De Barri, *Bucks and Bawds*, p.101.

25 *Harris's List*, (1761), p.25.

26 http://www.oldbaileyonline.org – 2 July 1766 – trial of Margaret, wife of Michael Cassady. (Ref: t17660702-12).

27 See Peakman (ed.), *Whore Biographies*, vol. 3, p.2, and vol. 4, pp.13 and 451 (note to p.13); *Kitty's Attalantis* (1766) p.11.

28 Mrs Pritchard in *Harris's List* (1773), pp.32–33; Polly Davies in *Harris's List* (1761), p.36.

29 Quoted in Michael J. Franklin, *Orientalist Jones: Sir William Jones, Poet, Lawyer, and Linguist, 1746–1794* (Oxford: Oxford University Press, 2011), p.126.

30 The most comprehensive study of Sandwich is N.A.M. Rodger, *The Insatiable Earl: A Life of John Montagu, 4th Earl of Sandwich 1718–1792* (& New York: W.W. Norton & Co., 1994).

31 McCormick, *Hell-Fire Club*, p.153. Cruickshank, in *Secret History of Georgian London*, p.407 suggested that Murray might have been introduced to Sandwich and Dashwood by the pimp Jack Harris. See also, Evelyn Lord, *The Hell-Fire Clubs: Sex, Satanism and Secret Societies* (& New Haven: Yale University Press, 2008), pp.91–92.

32 Joseph Cradock, *Literary and Miscellaneous Memoirs* …, 4 vols (J.B. Nichols, 1828), vol. 4, p.166.

33 *T&C* (January 1770 issue), p.40. The anecdote refers to Sandwich by his nickname 'Jemmy Twitcher', the character who betrayed Captain Macheath in *The Beggar's Opera*. It was a name that stuck with Sandwich after his prosecution in 1763 of his former friend John Wilkes for obscene libel.

34 For a comprehensive discussion of the murder of Martha Ray, see Brewer, *Sentimental Murder*.

35 Taylor, *Records of My Life*, vol. 1, p.51.

36 *T&C* (November 1769 issue), p.561.

37 *T&C* (November 1769 issue), p.561.

38 Bleackley, *Ladies Fair and Frail*, pp.16–17. This quotation was attributed to Richard Rigby in Burford, *Wits, Wenchers and Wantons*, p.82 and Linnane, *Madams, Bawds & Brothel-keepers*, pp.129–30. Part of the quotation, however, originated with the *Memoirs*, vol. 1, p.149.

39 For a life of Yorke, see Daniel A. Miller, *Sir Joseph Yorke and Anglo-Dutch Relations, 1774–1780* (The Hague & Paris: Mouton, 1970).

40 Edward Foss, *The Judges of England; with Sketches of their Lives* …, 9 vols (John Murray, 1848–64), vol. 8 (1864), pp.294–95; *The Gentleman's Magazine and Historical Chronicle* … (March 1794 issue), p.283.

41 *T&C* (November 1781 issue), p.569.

42 *T&C* (November 1781 issue), p.569. See also, *N&Q*, 11 Ser.V (11 May 1912), pp.361–62. The *Memoirs* (2:93–94) imagined a wager whereby a gentleman bet £100 that for every man who had lain with Campioni, he could produce fifty, if not a hundred that had lain with Murray.

43 Richard Cooksey, *Essay … [and] Sketches of an Essay on the Life and Character of Philip Earl of Hardwicke …* (Worcester: 1791).

44 G.H. Wilson, *The Eccentric Mirror …*, 4 vols (1807), vol. 4, pp.28–31.

45 Cooksey, *Philip Earl of Hardwicke*, pp.102–03.

46 George Harris, *The Life of Lord Chancellor Hardwicke …* 3 vols (Edward Moxon, 1847), vol. 3, pp.158–60.

47 John, Lord Campbell, *The Lives of the Lord Chancellors of England and Keepers of the Great Seal of England …*, 2nd series, 8 vols (John Murray, 1846–69), vol. 5 (1846), p.170.

48 Dilke, *Papers of a Critic*, vol. 2, p.275.

49 Bleackley, *Ladies Fair and Frail*, p.313; *N&Q*, 2 Ser. 81 (18 July 1857), pp.41–42 (taken from Dilke, *Papers of a Critic*, vol. 2, pp.272–79). See also, *N&Q*, 10 Ser. XI (19 June 1909), pp.493–94.

50 See also, Lord, *Hell-Fire Clubs*, p.91. Walcot's portrait is entitled *Sultana Walcotonia*, and *Lady Dashwood of West Wycombe* was painted shortly after her marriage in 1745. Until its recent identification as Lady Austen, the portrait of Dashwood's sister, Rachel, was thought by the 11th Baronet to have been that of Lady Mary Wortley Montagu.

51 Susan Griffin, *The Book of the Courtesans: A Catalogue of their Virtues* (Macmillan, 2002), p.51.

52 Sir Francis Dashwood, *The Dashwoods of West Wycombe* (Aurem Press, 1987), p.24; Gill Perry with Joseph Roach and Shearer West, *The First Actresses: Nell Gwyn to Sarah Siddons* (National Portrait Gallery, 2011), p.64.

53 For a comprehensive discussion of the Divan Club, see Rachel Finnegan, 'The Divan Club, 1744–46', in *Electronic Journal of Oriental Studies*, IX (2006), no. 9, pp.1–86. It has also been suggested that the club was founded by Dashwood, or jointly by Dashwood and Sandwich. See, for example, Eric Towers, *Dashwood the Man and the Myth: The Life and Times of the Hell Fire Club's Founder* (Crucible, 1986), p.63; Lord, *Hell-Fire Clubs*, p.90.

54 NMM – *Al Koran*, entry for 8 January 1744. (Ref: (microfilm) SAN/V/113).

55 Dashwood, *The Dashwoods*, p.22. See also, Towers, *Dashwood*, p.58.

56 A full list of members is given in Dashwood, *The Dashwoods*, p.24. See also, Finnegan, 'Divan Club', in *Electronic Journal of Oriental Studies*, pp.24–67.

57 Franklin, *Orientalist Jones*, p.126. See also, John Sainsbury, *John Wilkes: The Lives of a Libertine* (Aldershot & Burlington, Vermont: Ashgate Publishing, 2006), p.104 (and footnote 95).

58 Dashwood, *The Dashwoods*, pp.22–23; NMM – *Al Koran*, entry for 20 January 1744.

59 Franklin, *Orientalist Jones*, p.126; Toby Musgrave with Mike Calnan, *Seven Deadly Sins of Gardening and the Vices and Virtues of Gardeners* (National Trust Books, 2006), p.74.

60 Dashwood, *The Dashwoods*, p.24. See also, Rodger, *Insatiable Earl*, p.7; Sainsbury, *John Wilkes*, p.104.

61 Finnegan, 'Divan Club', in *Electronic Journal of Oriental Studies*, p.19.

62 Finnegan, 'Divan Club', in *Electronic Journal of Oriental Studies*, p.21. Richard Pococke (1704–65) was the author of *A Description of the East and of some other Countries* (1743–45).

63 Patricia Plummer, '"The free treatment of topics usually taboo'd": Glimpses of the Harem in Eighteenth- and Nineteenth-Century Literature and the Fine Arts', in Michael Meyer (ed.), *Word & Image in Colonial and Postcolonial Literatures and Cultures* (Amsterdam & New York: Rodopi, 2009), p.63.

64 Towers, *Dashwood*, p.63.

65 Finnegan, 'Divan Club', in *Electronic Journal of Oriental Studies*, p.1; Towers, *Dashwood*, p.63.

66 Dashwood, *The Dashwoods*, p.23; Finnegan, 'Divan Club' in *Electronic Journal of Oriental Studies*, pp.3 and 23; Towers, *Dashwood*, pp.58 and 63.

67 Albinia Lucy Cust, *Chronicles of Erthig on the Dyke*, 2 vols (John Lane, The Bodley Head, 1914), vol. 1, p.357.

Poetic Lists and Whores' Directories

How pretty Flora, wanton Maid,
By Zephyr woo'd in Noon-tide Shade,
With rosy Hand coquetly throwing
Pansies, beneath her sweet Touch blowing;
How blithe she look'd, let FANNY tell,
Let Zephyr own if half so well.[1]

One lazy afternoon in July 1746, Horace Walpole found himself at a loose end while staying as the house guest of his good friend Richard Rigby at Mistley Hall near Manningtree, in Essex. To pass the time while Rigby was at a cricket match, Walpole decided to put his deliberations on the most beautiful women in Britain into poetic form. In 'less than three hours' he had dashed off 140 lines of rhyming couplets and had managed to whittle down his long-list of the great beauties of the age to a score of names.[2] Entitled, unimaginatively, *The Beauties*, Walpole intended the poem for the amusement of Lady Caroline Fox *née* Lennox (1723–74) who had eloped, in May 1744, with Walpole's friend, the politician Henry Fox. Ironically, Walpole did not feature Lady Caroline in his poem, although he did include her sister, Lady Emily Fitzgerald (1731–1814), later Duchess of Leinster. In a letter dated 19 July 1746, Walpole explained to his cousin and lifelong correspondent, Henry Seymour Conway, that he had felt able to exclude

Lady Caroline because she was magnanimous enough to acknowledge herself less beautiful than her sister.[3]

Walpole also excluded Murray from his constellation of beauties, and it was her omission that led to a light-hearted contretemps between the two friends. Rigby championed Murray's charms with such determination that he forced a witty compromise, which restored harmony between the two men and won for Murray a special place within Walpole's encomium on beauty. Rigby, who was just starting out on his political career when he and Walpole had their good-humoured falling out, had entered Parliament in 1745 as MP for Castle Rising in Norfolk and was a career sinecurist. By 1768, at the age of 46, he held 'the most lucrative office in the gift of the crown' as paymaster of the forces, a post he held until 1782.[4]

In his youth, before fine dining made him corpulent and heavy drinking gave his face a purplish hue, he was 'an advantageous and manly person' and reputed to have been 'a constant votary to the Cyprean queen'.[5] There is no evidence, however, that Murray was ever his mistress, even though it was said that 'there was scarce a *demirep* in Dublin or London, who judged herself a reigning toast, without being ambitious of having Mr R---- amongst the number of her admirers'.[6] Instead, his eye wandered to the handsomest 'wives of men provided for by the liberality or the gratitude of the paymaster of the forces'. Rigby never married and attributed his 'countenance of festive conviviality, and a heart at ease' to this fact.[7]

The Beauties was written in imitation of Joseph Addison's epistle to the painter Sir Godfrey Kneller (1646–1723). In Walpole's poem the addressee was John Giles Eckhardt (d. 1779), a German artist whom Walpole had commissioned to paint portraits of his friends for his gothic home Strawberry Hill House in Twickenham. Walpole exhorted Eckhardt, in his quest for beautiful models, to abandon the Ancients in favour of the women to be found in Britain:

> In *Britain's* Isle observe the Fair,
> And curious chuse your Models there.[8]

By providing Eckhardt with a score of recommendations, drawn mostly from his own acquaintance, Walpole used *The Beauties* to pay tribute to his circle of female friends, which probably explains Murray's initial omission from the poem. *The Beauties* listed friends such as Penelope, Lady Atkins (*c.* 1725–95), regarded as 'the handsomest woman of her day'; Juliana, Lady Fermor (1729–1801) whom Lady Mary Wortley Montagu once described as having 'few equals in beauty, or graces'; and Conway's fiancée, the 'dimpled beauty' Lady Caroline Campbell (1721–1803).[9] The poem also paid tribute to friends such as Lucy Fortescue (*c.* 1717–46) who had married George, Lord Lyttleton in 1742; Sophia, Lady Fermor (*c.* 1720–45), sister to Juliana; and Mary Evelyn (d. 1744), who had all died tragically young. Evelyn's surviving sisters, Anne (d. 1781) and Elizabeth, who became the wives of Daniel Boone, MP for Ludgarshall, and Peter Bathurst of Clarendon Park respectively, were also admired within the poem 'in all the melting Pow'r of Tears'.[10]

Murray's presence in *The Beauties* was all the more remarkable, therefore, given the personal nature of most of Walpole's choices. It also speaks of Rigby's strength of purpose in winning a place for her among such intimate company, and of Murray's great beauty by the age of 17. Rigby might have argued that not all the women on Walpole's shortlist were close friends, since two of his beauties, Barbara Palmer, Duchess of Cleveland (1640–1709), mistress to Charles II, and Isabella Fitzroy (1667–1723), the wife of Henry, 1st Duke of Grafton, were from a previous age. Nor was Murray's notoriety an impediment to her inclusion, since some of the beauties in the poem were of questionable reputation. The licentious Elizabeth Chudleigh (*c.* 1720–88), who had secretly married Augustus Hervey, afterward 3rd Earl of Bristol, in August 1744, would scandalise society when, in 1749, she appeared bare-breasted as Iphigenia at a masquerade ball.[11] Of greater notoriety was the 'resplendent Fair' Lady Caroline Fitzroy (1722–84), whose reputation for promiscuity invited much ribald comment.[12] Walpole once gossiped that when the acid-tongued George Selwyn observed her one day in conversation with her sister-in-law Lady Euston, Selwyn had remarked, 'there's my Lady Euston, and my Lady *us'd to't*'.[13]

Walpole enclosed *The Beauties* in a letter to Conway dated 19 July 1746, in which he explained that 'Rigby makes me send you these verses'. Walpole was understandably defensive about his attempt to distil the most beautiful women in Britain into a score of names, especially since, Walpole explained, Rigby had 'contended a great while for a set of beauties of his own, who he swears by God are handsomer than any one (except Lady Emily) that I have mentioned'. Walpole stood firm and only agreed to send his poem to Conway on condition that the names stood as he had intended them. Rigby acquiesced, but was still determined to win a special dispensation for Murray, and eventually succeeded in wearing down his house guest. 'I have fought them all off,' conceded Walpole, 'but Fanny Murray.'[14]

The compromise that the two friends reached was only possible because one of the women on Walpole's original list shared the same initials as Murray. This was the Irish poetess Frances Macartney (or MacCartney) (*c.* 1724–89), the 'Flora' and 'Fanny' described in the extract from *The Beauties* at the head of this chapter. She eloped with the diplomat, gambler and dandy Fulke Greville in 1748 but is better remembered today as the godmother of the novelist Fanny Burney (1752–1840). Exceptionally beautiful in her youth, it was only the passage of time that gave her the appearance of 'a penetrating, puissant, and sarcastic fairy queen'.[15] Bowing to Rigby's intransigence over Fanny Murray, Walpole agreed that 'the description of Flora shall at least be left doubtful by the letters F. M. in the margin, and may be wrote at length in the Covent Garden editions'.[16] With the initials FM meant for Frances Macartney, but passing for Fanny Murray, Rigby was satisfied and so Murray found her unorthodox entry into Walpole's poem.[17]

Although Murray now had a place of sorts within *The Beauties*, her exposure to a wider audience was far from assured, as Walpole affected reluctance to have the poem published, preferring for it to remain private and 'just to divert anybody one loves for half an hour'. He pleaded the haste with which it had been written, and quipped that he did not wish to make enemies of all the women in England. More poignantly, he objected that 'the conclusion of the poem is more particular than [he] would choose publicly to subscribe to'.[18] It was there that he had chosen Elizabeth Evelyn, the future Mrs Bathurst, as the fairest of the fair. There was speculation that Walpole was in love with Elizabeth and it was said that when Walpole's niece, Maria, Duchess of Gloucester, read of the death of a Mrs Bathurst in the newspapers in 1777, she wrote to ask her uncle 'Is it your old love?'[19]

Despite Walpole's hesitations, the poem was 'handed about till it got into print, very incorrectly' in September 1746 and, to Walpole's evident surprise, it was well received.[20] Insisting, with a touch of false modesty, that he 'never wrote anything that [he] esteemed less, or that was seen so incorrect', Walpole claimed, in a letter to Horace Mann, that he could not 'at all account for their [the lines] having been so much liked, especially as the thoughts were so old and so common'.[21] The poem was soon re-published in *Dodsley's Collection of Miscellaneous Poems* (1748), and again in 1758, when it appeared in *Fugitive Pieces in Verse and Prose*, published by Walpole himself from his printing press at Strawberry Hill.[22]

In the end, the 1746 edition of the poem identified Flora in the foot-notes, not as FM but as 'F-nny M-cc-rtn-y', and by 1758, when the poem appeared in *Fugitive Pieces*, Frances Macartney's name was given in full alongside a note of her marriage to Greville. Even so, the good-humoured debate over the rival charms of the two FMs undoubtedly rumbled on between Rigby and Walpole and possibly spilled over into their circle of friends, to become the subject of animated discussion in elegant drawing rooms and gentlemen's clubs. These discussions might have filtered down to coffee houses and taverns in the winter of 1747 after the poet Mr Thomson, probably James Thomson (1700–48), tried to put the matter beyond doubt in a fulsome, nineteen-stanza poetic tribute to Murray, entitled 'An Ode on Miss Fanny Murray'. The poem featured in *The New-Year's Miscellany*, a collection of ephemera that was widely advertised in newspapers throughout January 1747.[23] Thomson referenced Walpole's poem, and 'Ye Beauties of the *British* Isle' but was unequivocal in his praise of Murray, insisting that:

Of *Fanny's* Charms none can refuse
To sing, whilst they have Breath.[24]

The Beauties placed Murray on a poetic par with members of Walpole's inner circle of female friends and acquaintances, who, apart from the odd *scandaleuse*, were mostly titled and respectable women of high social standing. This poetic parity, due solely to Rigby's playful and mischievous meddling, guaranteed Murray an association in the public imagina-tion with women from a superior social class and by connotation, with wealth, taste and status. *The Beauties* was also an early acknowledgement of Murray as a great beauty of the age. The success of the poem, and the unusual circumstances of her inclusion in it, were instrumental in bring-ing Murray to the attention of a wider audience. In no time at all *The Beauties*, and also Thomson's 'Ode', set in train a curiosity about Murray that would grow into an almost universal adulation among both male and female admirers, who, unfazed by the shamefulness of her profession, saw only her beauty, cachet and éclat.

As 1746 turned into 1747, and away from the poetic worlds created by Walpole and Rigby, business was booming, and a new side to Murray's character began to emerge. With clients willing to lavish extravagant amounts of money on her, all vestiges of the reluctant prostitute seemed to disappear and she was, by turns, avaricious, profligate and wildly dissipated. Her intemperance might have been intentional, since her success as a courtesan depended upon her ability to trade successfully on male fantasies of female abandon.

The *Memoirs* (1:95), in keeping with their view of Murray as naturally virtuous, excused the changes in her as superficial and as a consequence of her profession that 'obliged her to throw off her real character, humanity, and a charitable disposition for her fellow-creatures'. Her profligacy, therefore, might have been an occupational expense, designed to attract the high-spenders by becoming one herself. Successful courtesans had to be seen to afford expensive addresses and the writer EJ Burford claimed that by 1750, Murray was living in 'an elegant lodging' at 22 St James's Place.[25] Then there were the extravagant, ever-changing fashions to pay for, as well as the jewels, the box at the theatre, and of course, the expense of a private carriage. Murray's reputation as grasping and greedy probably originated from this time, when she appeared to worship money above all other considerations. Commanding high prices, Murray could afford to take the pick of her lovers, yet she went for the highest bidder, regardless of background or disposition. As a result, she made no distinction between refined, elite men like Henry Gould and Joseph Yorke, and rougher sorts who had neither reputation nor character to commend them, but who could fund her excesses.

Captain Jasper, a young naval officer, who was said to have ruined himself bankrolling Murray's profligate lifestyle, was a case in point. He was probably the ne'er-do-well Richard Jasper, ill-famed for his 'irritable irascible temper', who spent much of his naval career overseas, serving in Africa, Jamaica and the West Indies until he was court martialled in 1753 for misconduct. He was in England intermittently, however, between taking command of the *Phoenix* frigate in 1745 and the *Prince Henry* man-of-war in 1747, at the time Murray was coming to public notice.[26]

His ruinous involvement with Murray was brought to light by an elderly, anti-duelling campaigner who wrote into the *Town and Country*

Magazine in 1784 to protest against 'the barbarous custom'. To illustrate his point, and from a distance of almost forty years, the writer recalled one of Jasper's duels, which he claimed Jasper had initiated as part of a desperate ploy to avoid arrest for debt. The elderly campaigner laid the cause of Jasper's financial ruin squarely at Murray's door, claiming that Jasper had 'squandered many thousands' upon her and that she was one 'of the most extravagant Thaïs's then upon the *ton*'.

Jasper had deliberately provoked a duel by insulting a gentleman from Exeter at Munday's coffee house in Round Court near Covent Garden. In the words of the elderly campaigner, 'the captain fell a victim to his temerity, which was what he proposed, as he was then compelled to confine himself within the verge of the court, to avoid arrests'.[27] Jasper's chequered career came to an end some fifteen years later, on 11 May 1761, when he was killed in a duel at the Cardigan Head Tavern in Charing Cross, in an argument over a game. His fellow duellist, Joseph Brice, was acquitted of murder, and found guilty of the lesser charge of manslaughter, since it was accepted that Jasper had been 'intirely the aggressor'.[28]

It was also in 1747, if the claims of the *Memoirs* (1:100) are to be accepted, that Murray's growing fame as a Cyprian beauty brought her to the attention of Jack Harris, 'the celebrated negociator in women' – the Harris of *Harris's List*.[29] Murray and Harris would have undoubtedly noticed each other in the busy taverns around Covent Garden – in Bob Derry's Cyder Cellar, Weatherby's or the Castle, Rose or Shakespear's Head taverns, where prostitutes in search of custom would congregate.[30] However, there is no evidence beyond the claims made in the *Memoirs* that Murray ever used Harris's pimping services. In 1747, Harris was plain John Harrison, whose father George ran the Bedford Head Tavern in Maiden Lane, on the edge of Covent Garden. By the time the *Memoirs* were published in 1758, Jack Harris, as he was then known, was beginning a three-year sentence in Newgate Prison, following a government clampdown on brothels.

Between Maiden Lane and Newgate Prison lay a remarkable story of reinvention, as John Harrison transformed himself into Jack Harris, head waiter of the Shakespear's Head Tavern and 'pimp-general of all England'. The *Memoirs* (1:126–37) perpetuated the Harris myth by including, within its pages, one of the earliest accounts of his formative years. Presented as a self-contained autobiography, this version of

Harris's life made no mention of his father, George, or of the Bedford Head Tavern. Rather, Harris was portrayed as the eldest son from 'a good family in Somersetshire' (1:126) whose father had died impecuniously in King's Bench Prison. Heeding his late father's advice to 'let no scruple of conscience preponderate with [him]', so the *Memoirs* (1:133–5) asserted, Harris had soon realised that 'nature designed [him] for a pimp'.

This fictitious and largely generous account of Harris's early life was counterbalanced in the *Memoirs* (1:115–25) by another first-person narrative presented by a character named Charlotte S---. Her history, which was probably an amalgam of many women's experiences, sought to expose Harris as the venal debaucher of countless virgins.[31] Charlotte described how she had been the respectable daughter of a Newcastle coal merchant until Harris prostituted her. Conniving at her downfall, so the narrative related, Harris was employed by an unnamed lord whom Charlotte had previously rejected, to obtain her hand in marriage and to take her to London, where a sham marriage ceremony was to be performed. After the ceremony, Harris was to take her to the wedding chamber where, in the darkness, the spurned lord would possess Charlotte in Harris's stead. Once ruined, Charlotte had little option but to become mistress to her seducer, who arranged for her to be placed on *Harris's List* after he had tired of her. This mercenary aspect of Harris's character was given full vent in John Hill's *The Remonstrance of Harris* (1759), where Harris was painted in altogether darker hues as wholly cold, scheming and evil-minded.[32]

In 1747, Harris was probably working as a waiter in his father's tavern in Maiden Lane, where he would have observed from an early age the money to be made by tavern waiters who procured prostitutes for inebriated customers. The profitability of the trade was remarked upon in the *Town and Country Magazine*, where it was reported that 'many an imprudent young man has been starving in a jail, whilst a tavern-pimp, whom he has lavishly rewarded, has been riding in his carriage'.[33] As a result, pimp waiters gained a dubious reputation as swindlers, and were even rumoured to spy on copulating couples through peepholes in walls.[34]

James Boswell was especially suspicious of them, having witnessed at first hand, in April 1762, 'the rascality of the waiters in these infamous sort of taverns. They connive with the whores, and do what they can to fleece the gentlemen. I was on my guard, and got off pretty well.'[35] In the long run, however, Boswell did not get off 'pretty well' at all.

Pimp waiters were an insurance of sorts against venereal disease, since their reputations depended upon providing clean girls. Boswell, by contrast, was at constant risk of infection from his casual encounters with streetwalkers like Elizabeth Parker and Alice Gibbs, whom he picked up when desire overtook him.[36]

Central to the pimp waiters' trade were their personally compiled, handwritten lists of prostitutes whom they could send for when customer need arose. These tavern waiters' lists, which were highly organised, regularly updated and encyclopaedic in length, were most probably arranged into pocket-sized volumes, with each girl allocated a parchment sheet to herself. According to the narrator of *A Congratulatory Epistle from a Reformed Rake*, he was in a tavern one evening with drunken friends who asked 'the *Gentleman-porter*' to procure some girls. 'To my great Surprize', related the 'Reformed Rake', 'he pulled out a *List*, containing the Names of near *four Hundred*, alphabetically ranged, with an exact Account of their Persons, Age, Qualifications, and Places of Abode'.[37] These qualifications might have included the girl's performance in bed and any special skills she possessed. Every taste could be catered for, from the shoe fetishist to the sadomasochist. Scotty Hamilton, for example, who was first introduced to prostitution by a waiter from the Shakespear's Head Tavern, entertained her customers by alternately singing bawdy songs and repeating scripture.[38]

All that remains of Harris's ephemeral parchment list is a reproduction in the *Memoirs* (1:101–2) of a single sheet, dating from 1747 which featured Murray. If genuine, it would be of immense interest as a unique example of the layout and format of Harris's original list. It would be of greater value to this study, however, as proof that Harris was Murray's pimp and as the only extant description of Murray as she approached her 19th birthday.

Unfortunately, Murray's profile is probably a fabrication as it is highly unlikely that this single sheet from Harris's parchment list, said to have been 'ingrossed upon a whole skin of parchment', would have found its way into the hands of Murray's biographer a decade after Harris had written it. It is always possible, of course, that Murray's biographer reconstructed, from memory, the sheet that he might have once seen in Harris's possession. The profile is nonetheless valuable as an imaginative recreation of Murray, three years after she had posed for her Divan Club portrait. It presented Murray as a high-class prostitute and 'a good side-box piece' who would be a gracious companion at the theatre and, it is assumed, other fashionable venues.

Like Moll Hackabout in the second plate of *A Harlot's Progress*, Murray was judged an ideal mistress for a Jew, the inference being that only wealthy Jews could afford the carriages, fine lodgings and jewels that a top-ranking prostitute like Murray could command. Despite having worked London's brothels for four years, the profile described Murray as a new face on the town who had only been in the West End for the previous six months, and who could still pass for a virgin. Thus, both the profile and the *Memoirs* were agreed that Murray's success as a prostitute had not cost her her charming innocence:

Name	Condition	Description	Place of Abode
FANNY M----	Perfectly sound wind and limb.	A fine brown girl, rising nineteen years next season. A good side-box piece – will shew well in the flesh-market– wear well– may be put off for a vir-gin any time these twelve months – ne-ver common this side Tem-ple-Bar, but for six months. Fit for high keeping with a Jew mer-chant. – N.B. A good prae	The first floor at Mrs. –'s, milli-ner at Cha-ring Cross.

-mium from
ditto. – Then
the run of the
house – and if
she keeps out
of the Lock,
may make her
fortune, and
ruin half the
men in town.

According to the *Memoirs*, before Murray could join Harris's 100-strong herd of harlots and her name be added to Harris's parchment list, she had to undergo an enrolment process. Even if this was a fiction, created by the *Memoirs* for the amusement of its readers, the account provided an intriguing glimpse into how pimping enterprises like Harris's might have been organised.

The enrolment process (1:100) required Murray to submit to a thorough medical examination by an attending physician. Once pronounced infection-free, she was then expected to sign a legally binding document, agreeing to forfeit £20 if statements about her health proved false. She was also expected to agree to hand over a quarter of her earnings ('five shillings in the pound') to Harris for his pimping services. The *Memoirs* (1:109) claimed that Harris collected his dues at regular Sunday night meetings of the so-called Whores' Club which he was credited with establishing, and to which Murray would have had automatic membership, as one of Harris's girls.

Aside from settling their accounts, these Sunday evenings would have afforded members an opportunity to talk over 'their various successes, compare notes, and canvas the most probable means of improving them the week following' (1.109). Club membership, so the *Memoirs* (1:111–2) claimed, entailed a weekly subscription of half a crown, sixpence of which went straight into Harris's pocket to cover his management charges. Of the remaining 2s, 1s was put aside for the support of club members infected with venereal disease but denied free treatment at the Lock Hospital, and the other paid for the alcohol for the evening. It is not surprising, then, that the *Memoirs* described these Sunday night assemblies as wildly drunken affairs.

There was a precedent for Harris's Whores' Club in that the notorious bawd Elizabeth Wisebourne (1653–1720) had reputedly run a 'Society of Ladies' for the mutual support of its members and as an arbiter in their disputes.[39] Even so, Harris's Whores' Club, where 100 women regularly congregated together in drunken abandon, was most likely another of the *Memoirs'* inventions for purposes of entertainment. In particular, the club's set of rules which were reproduced in the *Memoirs* (1:110–4) – and especially Harris's privilege, stated in rule ten, of choosing one of his girls as his bedfellow for the night – smacks of male fantasy and a desire to titillate:

1. Every member of this society must have been debauched before she was fifteen.
2. Every member of this society must be upon the negociator H----s's list; and never have incurred the penalty of being erased therefrom; either on account of not paying poundage, making proper returns of her health, or any other cause whatever.
3. No modest woman whatever to be admitted a member of this society.
4. No member of this society must have been in Bridewel above once.
5. Any member of this society, that may have been tried at the Old-Baily, for any crime except picking of pockets, shall not be objected re-instating, if acquitted, upon condition she did not plead her belly.
6. Any member of this society who may become with child, shall be struck off the list, no longer coming under the denomination of a whore.
7. Each member to pay half a crown; one shilling whereof to be applied to the support of such members as may be under a course of physic, and not fit for business, or cannot get into the Lock; another sixpence thereof to the use of our negociator, for his great care and assiduity in the proper conducting this worthy society; and the remaining shilling to be spent in liquor, at the option of the members – Gin not excluded.
8. [Rule 8 is missing from the text].
9. Any member, who may become a modest woman by going into keeping, shall, upon quitting the society, make a donation thereto, in proportion to her settlement or allowance.
10. No man whatever to be admitted into this society, except our nego-ciator; who has the privilege of chusing what member he pleases for his bedfellow that night, she not being pre-engaged.

11. No conversation is prohibited but religion and politics; as the first always indicates a drunken assembly, and the latter generally terminates in party feuds.

12. Any member who shall get so intoxicated as not to be able to walk, shall be immediately sent home in a coach or chair, at the expence of the society, to be refunded by her at the ensuing meeting.

13. Any member who shall break any glasses, bottles, etc. or behave in a riotous manner, shall be immediately expelled, and the damages made good before she be re-admitted.

14. If any member by any overcharge of liquor, should, in clearing her stomach, spoil any other member's cloaths, she shall be obliged to take the same off her hands, and furnish her with new ones, or in some other manner compensate the damages.

N.B. Every member, before she be admitted of this society, must engage, under the penalty of one guinea and a dram round, to conform herself to the foregoing rules, for the proper decorum thereof.

If Harris had highly popular prostitutes like Murray in his stable, then his parchment list was worth its weight in gold and, by the mid-1750s, after Murray had retired from prostitution, Harris's list had made his name, if not his fortune. Harris appears to have come to an arrangement with the Irishman Samuel Derrick (1724–69) whereby, for a one-off payment, he agreed to lend his name to *Harris's List of Covent Garden Ladies*.[40] This purported to be Harris's own parchment list of prostitutes, in printed form, and, as part of the agreement, Harris might have handed over his handwritten list to Derrick. Beyond this, however, Harris had no further involvement in the publication that bore his name. The first *Harris's List*, which appeared in 1757, was the spur to a sex-trade phenomenon. Selling as many as 8,000 copies a year, *Harris's List* enjoyed an unbroken annual run for thirty-eight years until 1795, the year after Harris's death, and outlived Derrick, who remained its ghostwriter until his death in 1769.[41]

Harris, no doubt irked by having missed out on the runaway success of *Harris's List*, published his own rival directory entitled *Kitty's Attalantis* in 1766, but the venture failed, if only because Harris lacked Derrick's witty and immediate writing style, the humour, double entendres and 'astonishing variety of his descriptions' that made *Harris's List* the essential accessory of every gentleman in search of a whore, or of pleasure in the privacy of his own home.[42]

A close reader would have noted, however, that Derrick was often slapdash in his writing and paid scant attention to accuracy. He would flesh out his annual directory by repeating the same entry several years running, or spice it up by plundering other sources for added colour. Thus, he plagiarised the *Memoirs* while he was preparing *Harris's List* for 1761, and repurposed Murray's profile to suit a Miss Evans of Castle Court in the Strand. Closely following Murray's description, Miss Evans appeared as 'a Black-eyed, neat girl, rather tall, rising twenty-one next season; shews well in the flesh-market; never common on the other side Temple-bar. If she keeps out of the Lock, may make her fortune.'[43] Similarly, an impassioned diatribe against prostitution, spoken by the 20-year-old reluctant prostitute Kitty A[-]chison in which she complained of 'nocturnal incontinence and debauch', was also lifted almost verbatim from the *Memoirs* (1:88–9).[44]

An appearance in *Harris's List*, whether on an earlier parchment list or in the later published editions, was a guarantee to most prostitutes of greater kudos and increased business. The careers of several celebrity courtesans and brothel-keepers including Kitty Fisher, Lucy Cooper and Charlotte Hayes can be traced back to an early appearance in *Harris's List*.[45] By the same token, a damning description could destroy a prostitute's livelihood. It is hard to imagine any prostitute recovering from descriptions such as that lodged for Mrs Fowler who was said to have been uglier than all the other prostitutes in *Harris's List* for 1761 – 'she possesses everything, in our opinion, that is disgustful; drinks, takes snuff, and swears like a trooper'.[46]

After Murray featured on Harris's parchment list, the *Memoirs* (1:102) claimed that she 'never went under two guineas', a sum which would have taken one of Nash's top musicians in Bath a week to earn. Even so, and as Fergus Linnane has remarked, 2 guineas was a rather modest sum for a prostitute of Murray's calibre.[47] By 1773, 2 guineas was considered the mark for middling prostitutes, like Miss Ver[no]n of Frith Street in Soho, who were pleasing company, performed well but with few distinguishing qualities.[48] The going rate for classier prostitutes, like the 'extraordinary piece' Betsy C[o]k[e]r[y]n with her hair 'of a beautiful flaxen colour; eyes blue, and shape elegant' was at least 5 guineas.[49]

As Murray turned 19, her star was very much in the ascendant. She had wealthy, well-connected patrons and a lavish lifestyle that gave her control over the men she chose as her clients. She did not forget, however, those streetwalkers who had no such control and who were threatened with venereal infection by their every indiscriminate sexual encounter. Having undoubtedly seen at first hand the devastating effects wrought by the disease when left untreated, she became one of the earliest supporters of the Lock Hospital near Hyde Park Corner, which first opened its doors on 31 January 1747.

Established by William Bromfeild (1712–92), a governor of St George's Hospital from 1742 and surgeon to Frederick, Prince of Wales from 1745, the Lock was the first charitable hospital in London, established specifically for the treatment of venereal disease.[50] Financed entirely by voluntary subscription, the Board of Trustees resolved 'that every Person who subscribes £5 a Year; shall be a Governor of this Hospital; and whoever gives a Benefaction of £50 at one time a Governor for Life'.[51]

Appealing to potential donors in sufficient numbers was a perennial problem for the Lock, and it regularly attracted 'significantly fewer annual and lifetime governors than other charity hospitals'.[52] A charity devoted to the cure of venereal disease was both unfashionable and controversial since it was objected that the Lock was an encouragement to vice and, as such, an affront to morality. Only sixty-seven subscriptions were minuted in the Lock's court records for the six-month period between the inaugural First General Board on 4 July 1746 and the opening of the hospital in January 1747. Murray was one of at least twenty-three new subscribers whose names were recorded during the hospital's first year of operation.[53] By 1749 when 'An Account of the Proceedings of the Governors of the Lock Hospital' was published, the number of subscribers had only risen to 168, and to 178 by 1751. This tally can be adjusted upward slightly as the names of all women subscribers were omitted from the published lists for the sake of propriety as there were 'several Ladies, who subscribe annually, but don't chuse to have their Names inserted in the List'.[54]

In the unpublished court records which are lodged in the library of the Royal College of Surgeons of England, only four other women were registered as subscribers by the time Murray's name was entered in the minutes of the Quarterly General Court held on Tuesday 23 November 1747. They were Mrs and Miss Guerin, probably the wife and daughter of Maynard Guerin, named as a trustee at the second meeting of the board on 24 July 1746, Mrs Hamilton and Mrs Sarah Pauls.[55] Murray is not recorded as renewing her subscription, but that is not to say that she abandoned her interest in the Lock. It is more than likely that she persuaded Sir Richard Atkins (1728–56), who became her principal keeper around 1746, to support the hospital and his 5-guinea subscription is noted in 'An Account of the Proceedings of the Governors of the Lock Hospital' for both 1749 and 1751. Atkins was still involved with the Lock at the time of his death in 1756 and was mentioned in the newspapers as one of the stewards of the governors' anniversary dinner, which was held at Ranelagh Gardens on 15 June 1756, five days after his death.[56]

Murray's support of the Lock at the time of its establishment – and she was possibly the only high-ranking courtesan to do so – was an act of altruism that placed her, and her fellow subscribers, ahead of their time in their concern to improve public health. Her involvement with the Lock is also noteworthy because of her willingness to associate herself, as the most fashionable of women, with the most unfashionable of charities. It might have been her identification with the work of the hospital that led the author of *The Gentleman and Lady's Palladium* (1751) to choose her as the proposer of a facetious question regarding the licensing of brothels as a means of preventing, among other distresses, the spread of venereal disease:

> Would not the licensing of publick *Brothel-Houses* in *Britain*, as well as in other *Christian* Countries, be of Advantage to the Publick, and prevent *Diseases, Rapes, Robberies, Murders*, and the *Ruin* of many Families? And whether it would hurt the *Protestant* Religion more than the *Catholick*?[57]

The record of Murray's 5-guinea subscription, written with a bold flourish in black ink in the court records, is almost symbolic of the immense transformations she had undergone since she had left Bath at the age of 14. In the space of four years she had experienced and overcome poverty, disease and low prostitution. She had also risen beyond the stews of Covent Garden to become the subject of refined teatime conversation over her relative merits as one of Walpole's beauties of the age. The poem had placed her on a poetic par with elite women of her day and she was rubbing shoulders, on the page at least, with some of the country's most powerful men such as Robert Walpole, 2nd Earl of Orford (1701–51), and John Russell, 4th Duke of Bedford, whose subscriptions for the Lock were recorded alongside her own.

Her willingness to be named in the court records, and to align herself with a controversial charity associated in the public imagination with immorality and licentiousness, revealed steeliness in her youthful character as well as a benevolent compassion for victims of the sex trade. Her support for the Lock also signalled a laudable degree of self-knowledge and awareness. Here was no soundless, anonymous and shame-faced submission to her prostituted fate, but rather, a clear declaration in front of the most respectable of company, of herself as prostitute for whom the most shameful of diseases was an occupational and quotidian hazard. She embraced prostitution with her sense of self-worth and self-esteem intact and in doing so, made the profession her own.

Notes

1 Horace Walpole, *The Beauties: An Epistle to Mr Eckhardt, the Painter* (1746), p.7.
2 *Walpole Correspondence*, vol. 2, p.37. Letter to Henry Seymour Conway dated 24 July 1746.
3 *Walpole Correspondence*, vol. 2, pp.35–36. Letter to Conway dated 19 July 1746.
4 *Sporting Magazine* (January 1793 issue), vol. 1, p.206. See also, *Authentic Memoirs, and a Sketch of the Real Character, of the late Right Honorable Richard Rigby* (1788).
5 Horace Walpole, *Memoirs of King George II* ..., edited by John Brooke, 3 vols (& New Haven: Yale University Press, 1985), vol. 2, p.285. This description of Rigby dates from 1757 when Rigby was 35. See also, *T&C* (June 1774 issue), p.290.
6 *T&C* (June 1774 issue), p.290.
7 Oliver Oldschool (ed.), *The Port Folio. New Series* (Philadelphia: John Watts, 1806), vol. 2, p.308 (issue no. 46, dated 22 November 1806).
8 Walpole, *The Beauties*, p.4.
9 [Louis Dutens], *Memoirs of a Traveller. Now in Retirement* ..., 5 vols (1806), vol. 2, p.56; Lord Wharncliffe, *The Letters and Works of Lady Mary Wortley Montagu* ..., 2nd rev. ed., 3 vols (Richard Bentley, 1837), p.376. Letter to Mr Wortley Montagu dated 8 May 1744.
10 Walpole, *The Beauties*, p.8.
11 Cindy McCreery, *The Satirical Gaze: Prints of Women in Late Eighteenth-Century England* (Oxford: Clarendon Press, 2004), p.161. Chudleigh was found guilty of bigamy in 1776 for her marriage to Evelyn Pierrepont, 2nd Duke of Kingston-upon-Hull.
12 Walpole, *The Beauties*, p.4.
13 *Walpole Correspondence*, vol. 2, p.436. Letter to George Montagu dated 4 May 1755.

14 *Walpole Correspondence*, vol. 2, pp.35–36. Letter to Conway dated 19 July 1746.

15 Madame D'Arblay, *Memoirs of Doctor Burney arranged from his Own Manuscripts* ..., 3 vols (Edward Moxon, 1832), vol. 2, p.103.

16 *Walpole Correspondence*, vol. 2, p.36. Letter to Conway dated 19 July 1746. It has been suggested that 'Covent Garden editions' was a topical reference to the area's dual connection with printing and prostitutes. See E. Beresford Chancellor, *The Annals of Covent Garden and its Neighbourhood* (Hutchinson & Co. Ltd, 1930), p.60 (footnote 2).

17 See *N&Q*, 2 Ser. 81 (18 July 1857), p.42; 7 Ser. V (30 June 1888), pp.511–12; 8 Ser. I (23 January 1892), pp.73–74.

18 *Walpole Correspondence*, vol. 2, p.37. Letter to Conway dated 24 July 1746.

19 R.W. Ketton-Cremer, *Horace Walpole: A Biography*, 3rd ed. (Methuen & Co. Ltd, 1964), p.107.

20 Horace Walpole, 'Short Notes of My Life (1717–1779)', in *Walpole Correspondence*, vol. 1, p.lxv.

21 *Walpole Correspondence*, vol. 2, p.67. Letter dated 12 November 1746.

22 See Harry M. Solomon, *The Rise of Robert Dodsley: Creating the New Age of Print* (Carbondale: Southern Illinois University Press, 1996), p.148; Horace Walpole, *Fugitive Pieces in Verse and Prose* (1758), pp.28–35.

23 See, for example, *London Evening Post*, 20 January 1747.

24 [James] Thomson, 'Ode on Miss Fanny Murray', in *A New-Years Miscellany* ... (1747), p.29.

25 Burford, *Royal St James's*, p.163. Burford stated erroneously that Murray lived in St James's Place from 1750 to her marriage in 1758. At the time of her marriage, which was in May 1756, Murray was living in New Palace Yard.

26 John Charnock, *Biographia Navalis: or, Impartial Memoirs of the Lives and Characters of Officers of the Navy of Great Britain* ..., 6 vols (1794–98), vol. 5 (1797), pp.394–96.

27 *T&C* (October 1784 issue), p.531.

28 *The Universal Magazine of Knowledge and Pleasure* ... (June 1761 issue), vol. 28, p.333. See also, Robert B. Shoemaker, 'Public Spaces, Private Disputes? Fights and Insults on London's Streets, 1660–1800', in Hitchcock and Shore (eds), *Streets of London*, p.64.

29 This discussion of Harris draws particularly on Rubenhold's comprehensive study of *Harris's Lists*. See Rubenhold, *Covent Garden Ladies*.

30 For a discussion of the 'prominent role for inns and alehouses as sites for prostitution', see John Black, 'Illegitimacy, Sexual Relations and Location in Metropolitan London, 1735–85', in Hitchcock and Shore (eds), *Streets of London*, pp.106–08.

31 Rubenhold identified Charlotte as 'The Honourable' Charlotte Spencer, and her seducer as Lord Robert Spencer. Spencer (1747–1831), who was the youngest son of Charles, 3rd Duke of Marlborough and nephew of Hon. John Spencer, was 11 years old when the *Memoirs* were published. Charlotte Spencer, a former milliner, and unrelated to the Spencer family, belongs

to a later generation of courtesans. She was mistress to William Cavendish, 5th Duke of Devonshire and bore him a daughter named Charlotte Williams about the time of his marriage to Lady Georgiana Spencer in 1774. See *T&C* (March 1777 issue), pp.120–24; Foreman, *Georgiana*, p.21; Rubenhold, *Covent Garden Ladies*, pp.61–62.

32 Rubenhold, *Covent Garden Ladies*, pp.183–86; *Monthly Review* (1758), vol. 19, pp.202–03.

33 *T&C* (April 1776 issue), p.201.

34 *Harris's List* (1761), p.143.

35 Pottle (ed.), *Boswell's London Journal*, pp.240–41.

36 Pottle (ed.), *Boswell's London Journal*, pp.227 and 262.

37 *Congratulatory Epistle from a Reformed Rake*, p.16.

38 *Harris's List* (1761), p.63.

39 Anodyne Tanner [pseud.], *The Life of the late Celebrated Mrs Elizabeth Wisebourn* ... [1721], p.15. See also, Linnane, *Madams, Bawds & Brothel-keepers*, p.115.

40 Derrick had been a linen draper in Dublin before pursuing unsuccessful careers as an actor, poet and playwright. He became master of ceremonies at Bath following the death of Murray's former lover, Richard Nash, in 1761.

41 Johann Wilhelm von Archenholz, *A Picture of England: Containing a Description of the Laws, Customs, and Manners of England* ..., 2 vols (1789), vol. 2, pp.101–02. See Rubenhold, *Covent Garden Ladies*, p.285.

42 *Characters of the Present Most Celebrated Courtezans* ... (1780), p.8. See also, Sophie Carter, *Purchasing Power: Representing Prostitution in Eighteenth-Century English Popular Print Culture* (Aldershot: Ashgate Publishing, 2004), p.55.

43 *Harris's List* (1761), p.117.

44 *Harris's List* (1761), p.105. See Ch. 3, above, p.69.

45 For Kitty Fisher, see *Harris's List* (1761), p.49; Lucy Cooper (1761), p.28; and Charlotte Hayes (1761), p.55.

46 *Harris's List* (1761), p.75. Fowler was still being featured in *Harris's List* in 1773, pp.75–76: another example, perhaps, of Derrick's careless editing.

47 Linnane, *London: Wicked City*, p.132.

48 *Harris's List* (1773), p.98. See also, Miss Hart, *Harris's List* (1761), p.101.

49 *Harris's List* (1761), p.132.

50 See Donna Andrew, 'Two Medical Charities in Eighteenth-Century London: The Lock Hospital and the Lying-in Charity for Married Women', in Jonathan Barry and Colin Jones (eds), *Medicine and Charity before the Welfare State* (& New York: Routledge, 1991), pp.82–97; Kevin P. Siena, *Venereal Disease, Hospitals and the Urban Poor: London's 'Foul Wards', 1600–1800* (Rochester: University of Rochester Press, 2004), pp.181–97.

51 RCS – Minutes of 'A Special General Court' held on 29 January 1747, p.17. See also, minutes of 'First General Board' convened on 4 July 1746, p.1, in *Lock Hospital General Court Book* (July 1746–May 1762). (Ref: MS0022/1/3 Series no. 1).

52 Linda E. Merians, 'The London Lock Hospital and the Lock Asylum for Women', in Linda E. Merians (ed.), *The Secret Malady: Venereal Disease in Eighteenth-Century Britain and France* (Kentucky: University Press of Kentucky, 1996), p.129.

53 Merians, 'London Lock Hospital', p.129.

54 'An Account of the Proceedings of the Governors of the Lock Hospital' [1751], p.3.

55 Mrs Hamilton might be the same woman who accompanied Murray to the masquerade ball hosted by Gertrude, Duchess of Bedford in February 1748. See Ch. 5, below, pp.111–12.

56 *Public Advertiser*, 3 June 1756.

57 Robert Heath, *The Gentleman and Lady's Palladium* ... [1751], p.16.

5

Lovers and Keepers

Fanny's genteel, none can deny,
Fanny is handsome, all reply
Fanny is fair and young:
Of every Glass let her be Toast,
Of every Muse the Pride and Boast,
The Theme of every Song.[1]

The high point of any courtesan's career was to be taken into keeping by a wealthy protector. Men of privilege and position spent extravagantly on their kept mistresses as an outward mark of their own status and wealth, so that their lovers could expect generous allowances, elegant homes, carriages, fine clothes and finer jewels. The rivalry among elite men to possess the most sought-after courtesans of the day was captured in the *Memoirs* (1:68), when one of Murray's young admirers was said to be 'ravished with the expectation of out-rivalling so many fine fellows as daily and nightly attended her in public'. In their turn, courtesans vied with each other in ostentatious displays of extravagance, to attract to themselves the richest and most prestigious lovers. Mary 'Perdita' Robinson, for example, was one of a select group that included Mary Anne Clarke and Grace Dalrymple Eliot (*c.* 1754/58–1823) who achieved, albeit fleetingly, the ultimate prize for any courtesan – the status of royal mistress.

An equally rarefied number, including Nelly O'Brien (d. 1768) and Sophia Baddeley (1745–86), enjoyed immense wealth as courtesans to the aristocracy. The more successful among them even managed to secure their upwardly mobile futures by marrying their titled protectors. This had been the case with the actress Lavinia Fenton and Harriette Wilson's sister, Sophia Dubochet (1794–1875), who married Thomas Noel Hill, 2nd Baron Berwick of Attingham. It was also true of Harriet Powell and Nancy Parsons (c. 1735–1814/15), who married Kenneth Mackenzie, 1st Earl of Seaforth and Charles Maynard, 2nd Viscount Maynard, respectively. Some even found love. Such was the happy outcome for Elizabeth Armistead, who married the politician Charles James Fox. Few courtesans, however, had the integrity of Lucy Cooper, who reputedly refused Sir Orlando Bridgeman's proposal of marriage so that 'she might not bring a scandal upon his family'.[2]

Courtesans lived in an uncertain world, therefore, where they might be abandoned at any moment in favour of a more desirable toast of the town. Mary Robinson, for example, only knew she had been dropped by her royal lover, George, Prince of Wales, when she saw her rival 'the Armistead' returning from an assignation with him.[3] Such a fate was not, of course, the lone preserve of the courtesan. The prostitute Rebecca Smith of Cumberland Court, who appeared in *Harris's List* for 1773, had been taken into keeping and then abandoned several times by the age of 25.[4]

Since protectors often proved mercurial lovers, and few liaisons ended in the security of marriage, women in keeping often made discreet provision for themselves by setting up potential protectors in reserve against the day their present keepers wearied of them. It was a dangerous and invariably furtive game that could cost the courtesan dear if she was caught. Some women, however, were quite open about conducting business as usual while in keeping. *Harris's List* for 1773 described 'a tall, black woman' called Mrs Edmonds, of Church Street in Soho, as 'seldom idle, tho' in keeping; her dress is always elegant, and yet she may be found most nights in the gallery at Covent Garden'.[5] Murray proved no less skilled at this game of double-dealing while she was in the keeping of Sir Richard Atkins, 6th Baronet of Clapham, who became her protector around 1746, when he was 18 years of age. She was more flagrant than most, however, in flaunting her numerous lovers, so that Atkins was soon regarded as 'a very great dupe to her' for allowing Murray to take advantage of him as she did.[6]

Atkins was the youngest child of Sir Henry (*c.* 1707–28), 4th Baronet of Clapham, and Penelope Stonhouse (*c.* 1708–34), the daughter of John Stonhouse, 7th Baronet of Radley in Berkshire. According to the *Memoirs* (1:138), Murray first met Atkins when she was visiting one of his tenants at Clapham, then a small village in Surrey.[7] It is more likely, however, that Murray and the young baronet chanced upon each other in a favourite tavern such as the Shakespear's Head, which they both frequented. Like every other young man in her orbit, Atkins was immediately love-struck. It was already common knowledge that Murray's allure was irresistible. William Horsely, writing in 'The Fool', a periodic letter that appeared in the *Daily Gazetteer* between July 1746 and February 1747, paid tribute to her sexual power. He imagined a gentleman who, '*in Imitation of* Horace, *professes himself past the Love of Woman, and yet keeps the Taint, is, tho' without Abilities, in love with one* Fanny Murray'.[8] What hope then for an impressionable young baronet impassioned with the impetuosity of youth?

Atkins appears to have taken Murray into high-keeping shortly after meeting her and, according to the *Memoirs* (2:1–2 and 1:146–7), set her up with all the accoutrements of a fine courtesan, including 'a splendid equipage, a numerous retinue, an elegant furnished house, and a handsome allowance'. He remained her keeper for about eight years, until approximately 1754. Life with the beautiful but impetuous Murray was undoubtedly a bittersweet experience for Atkins, and she quickly emerged as an ungovernable and dominant force within their relationship. Yet, despite her numerous infidelities and her petulant nature, Atkins was a doting protector whose every thought, according to the *Memoirs* (2:1–2), 'centred in pleasing and diverting her'.

Atkins was quite a catch for Murray. In 1742, aged 14, he had inherited 'a very considerable Estate' on the death of his older brother Henry and, at his coming of age, was said to be worth a substantial £6,000 per annum (about £740,000 today).[9] Apart from being wealthy, Atkins was also handsome, having inherited his family's good looks. Atkins's mother was remembered as 'a fine creature', while his older sister Penelope was described by her friend Horace Walpole, who included her in *The Beauties*, as 'all loveliness within and without'.[10] Atkins was tall and willowy and, in an effort to disguise his height, walked with a noticeable stoop. This led his actor friend Samuel Foote (*c.* 1721–77) who was, by contrast, of 'middle size, [and] rather clumsily made', to nickname him 'the Waggoner's Whip'.[11] Atkins took such ribbing in good part – an indication perhaps that, as well as the family's good looks, he had inherited his mother's good character and the sweet temper which was so apparent in his sister Penelope.[12] A portrait of him, painted by Joshua Reynolds, might still exist. According to the *Morning Herald*, his portrait lay in the artist's studio for at least forty years, until Reynolds's death in 1796. It was not destroyed but, reported the *Herald*, 'to the eternal disgrace' of Atkins's surviving relatives who failed to claim it, the portrait went under the auctioneer's hammer.[13]

As a member of the landed gentry, Atkins could trace his family connections with Clapham back to *c.* 1616, when Dr Henry Atkins (d. 1635), physician in ordinary to both James I and Charles I, had purchased Clapham Manor for £6,000. In contrast to the family's long ancestry, Atkins's own family life was short-lived and traumatic, and he was orphaned by the age of 6. His father died of consumption in France in March 1728, at the age of 21, just weeks after Atkins's birth. His mother died in August 1734, two months after giving birth to a second daughter, also christened Penelope, following her marriage in 1733 to John Leveson-Gower, 1st Earl Gower. She was 26.

Death continued to stalk Atkins's family – in February 1742, his half-sister, Penelope, died at the age of 7 and, seven months later on 1 September, his brother Henry, the 5th Baronet, and 'a very fine Youth', died at Clapham at the age of 16.[14] Only Atkins's older sister Penelope survived into old age.

Since consumption had claimed both his father and brother, the inevitability of premature death left its mark on the young baronet and, in the event, Atkins was himself dead by the age of 28. He discharged his responsibilities as the head of the family conscientiously, and was active in protecting the family's name and interests. He was High Sheriff of Buckinghamshire between 1750 and 1751, just as his great-great-grandfather Sir Richard had been in 1649–50, and by 1752, he was considering politics after having been approached by 'some of the Inhabitants of Westminster to offer himself Candidate for that City and Liberty'.[15]

Away from family matters, however, Atkins was fervent in his pursuit of pleasure. He had Murray, the most desired woman of her day, in his keeping and counted among his friends some of the wittiest, most talented and dissolute men in town. These included the tall, and remarkably handsome, Sir Francis Blake Delaval (1727–71) of Seaton Delaval Hall in Northumberland, and Foote, who amused everyone with his caustic wit and gift for mimicry. Atkins entertained on a lavish scale and at his coming of age party in spring 1749:

> He gave a most elegant Entertainment to a great Number of Persons of Distinction, at his House at Clapham; at Night there was a very magnificent Firework play'd off, plenty of Liquors given to the Populace, and the whole concluded with the utmost Joy and Harmony.[16]

With a devoted and wealthy protector, the future boded well for Murray. There was even talk of a wedding, and in the summer of 1748 Murray was certainly showing signs of homemaking. An entry in the account book of the painter, engraver and art dealer Arthur Pond shows that Murray bought 'three frames & glasses' of Roman antiquities from him on 15 July 1748, at the modest price of £1 4s 0d.[17]

By autumn 1748, rumours were circulating that the couple planned a 'fleet marriage', the speed and clandestine nature of which would have sidestepped neatly any obstructions or censure from Atkins's extended family.[18] Rumours about Murray's marriage were repeated by Elizabeth, Lady Sherard (*c.* 1723–56) in a letter to her 'dear Papa' Ralph Verney, 1st Earl Verney, dated 17 September 1748. Lady Sherard had married Bennet Sherard, the future 3rd Earl of Harborough, just three months before and so, with weddings very much on her mind, she repeated the latest gossip that Murray's marriage to Atkins had already taken place. 'Mr & Mrs Lester was hear [sic]', she wrote, '& said they heard Sir Richard Atkins of Clapham was married to the famous Fanney [sic] Murray'.[19]

Walpole had also heard rumours of Murray's marriage but poured cold water on the idea in a letter to his friend George Montagu, written on 20 October 1748 – 'it is the year for contraband marriages', wrote Walpole, 'though I do not find Fanny Murray's is certain'.[20] The rumours persisted, nevertheless. Writing to her friend Mrs Eyre on 6 December 1748, Jane, Lady Coke (1706–61) of Longford Hall in Derbyshire, remarked on the 'abundance of weddings talked of but the most extraordinary one', she continued, 'is Sir R. Atkins to the famous beauty, Fanny Murray, which I am told either is, or will be soon'.[21]

Walpole's doubts about Murray's marriage proved well-founded, for a wedding and a new life for Murray as Lady Atkins, never materialised.

The relationship, however, did not falter and Atkins remained a faithful and generous lover. According to the *Memoirs* (1:200), he presented her with the lease on 'an elegant country house near Richmond' which Atkins furnished for her at considerable expense.

There is some truth in this claim, as a newspaper report for December 1749 stated that Atkins had bought a house near Epsom (9 miles from Richmond) from William Belchier, MP for Southwark.[22] The report added that the house had once been the country retreat of Frederick, Prince of Wales which enables its identification as Durdans – a substantial residence that had been rebuilt in the classical style during the 1680s. The traveller Celia Fiennes described it in 1712 as looking 'nobly in a fine park' and with a particularly 'noble lofty hall'.[23] A painting of 'an end front or secondary entrance' to the house by Jacob Scmits (or Smits), completed in 1689, gives an indication of the lavish surroundings in which Murray might have then found herself. The house was even larger than the portrait suggested. As the architectural historian, John Harris, has noted, 'what apparently appears to be a small red-brick domestic-type Williamite house is, in fact, just one end of a long twelve-bay side elevation'.[24]

Atkins did not actually buy the Durdans' estate, as stated in the newspaper, but probably rented it from Belchier on a short-term lease. Belchier, who had bought the house in 1747, demolished it sometime later and built a new house on the site, which burnt down in 1755 before completion.

The amount of gossip about Murray's forthcoming marriage suggests some basis in truth. It seems likely, for example, that Atkins, as the last of the male line and coming from such a short-lived family, would have wished to marry sooner rather than later, and to have fathered an heir. What could have possibly gone wrong with their rumoured wedding plans? Atkins, who took his family responsibilities seriously, might have discovered that Murray was unlikely to bear children, or perhaps he came to the conclusion that a woman of Murray's notoriety and reckless indiscretion was ill-suited to bearing the Atkins name. There were skeletons in the family cupboard to remind Atkins how troublesome unfaithful wives could be. His own great-grandfather, Sir Richard Atkins (c. 1654–96), the 2nd Baronet, believed his wife Elizabeth Byde, whom he married sometime before 1684, to be so promiscuous that he eventually banished her to a parson's house near Newport Pagnell, but not before he had fought several duels in defence of her honour. According to the 2nd Baronet's mother, her son's marital problems had 'hastened his end'.[25]

For her part, Murray, at the height of her success, might have been unwilling to exchange the heady excitement of a courtesan's life for the dull respectability and daunting responsibilities of the lady of the manor at Clapham. Moreover, she had the measure of Atkins, and was pragmatic enough to know that she could keep her compliant lover as her generous provider while at the same time enjoying her Cyprian pleasures. Indeed, her numerous affairs, including those with Captain Jasper, Henry Gould, Joseph Yorke, and probably Lord Sandwich, were all conducted while she was under Atkins's protection.

It is also possible that she had taken a royal lover and, if so, she might have been ambitious of becoming a royal mistress or of marrying into the aristocracy, rather than becoming Atkins's wife. Describing a later stage of Fanny's career, the author of the *Memoirs* (2:90) suggested that she 'imagined she had charms to captivate and retain the first peer in the land, whom she had resolved within herself should not enjoy her, but upon honourable terms'.

It has been claimed that Murray was 'chased by Princes and the greatest noblemen', yet evidence of any royal liaison is both rare and circumstantial.[26] In February 1748, the noted bluestocking and gossip, Frances Evelyn Boscawen, the wife of the naval officer and politician, Admiral Edward Boscawen, spotted Murray in the company of George II's younger son, Prince William Augustus (1721–65), the Duke of Cumberland, at a ball hosted by Gertrude, Duchess of Bedford.[27] The duchess was the daughter of Atkins's stepfather, John Leveson-Gower and the wife of John Russell, 4th Duke of Bedford.

According to Mrs Boscawen, Prince William invited himself to the ball and brought thirty ladies along with him, all of whom, including the prince, were masked. Mrs Boscawen was able to recall eleven by name, including the Duchess of Dorset, Lady Pembroke and Lady Caroline Petersham (*née* Fitzroy). Within the prince's party, Mrs Boscawen also noted that 'three masks appeared who stayed together and did not go to the top of the room with the rest'. She described these three women as 'fine but dirty', suggesting they were richly dressed but disreputable. They were 'soon discovered to be Miss Fanny Murray, Mrs Kitty Hamilton and another lady'.

Their intrusion must have been especially awkward for the duchess who unexpectedly found herself playing host to her stepbrother's notorious mistress. Her husband, the duke, though clearly disconcerted by their presence, was careful not to offend these particular members of the royal party. According to Mrs Boscawen, he offered them cold civility and, in polite tones, 'assured them he would be glad to see them there any other night, but just then must desire they would excuse him, but took care they should be safely escorted to their chairs without any insult'.

Murray's evening at the home of the Duke and Duchess of Bedford is immensely significant as proof of her meteoric rise, within three years, from the brothels of London to the city's most elegant ballrooms. It is also proof that the beautiful Murray radiated enough charm, sophistication, and downright sexiness, to captivate a prince. Despite Murray's royal connection and the *Memoirs'* claim that she aimed at peers of the realm, in reality, Murray does not appear to have harboured such social-climbing aspirations. As previously noted, when Murray was left to her own devices, she was drawn to men who were neither refined nor elite. John Hill hinted at her preferences in *The Inspector* (1753):

> Venus, a semi-demi-rep of Paphos, a fine gay girl, a blooming, laughing, dimpled beauty, such another, for all the world, as our Fanny Murray, was long under the protection of a boisterous, blustering ruffian, who terrified people with his very name.[28]

Indeed, even though she had Atkins as her protector, Fanny continued to consort with rough-edged adventurer types who shared in common her impetuous desire to live in the moment and, crucially, an enthusiasm for squandering their fortunes upon her. In accepting such men as her lovers, Murray was arguably demonstrating the skills of a good business woman who put moral considerations aside in pursuit of profit. Yet, Murray's preference for dissolute ne'er-do-wells, especially when she had the wealthy Atkins to provide for her, and her inability to manage her money suggests dissipation and recklessness rather than business acumen. The men Murray chose for herself were, at best, rash adventurers like Captain Jasper, and at worst, thieves and violent thugs.

Murray's name was linked, for example, with the former officer and petty criminal, Captain Plaistow, whom she had probably known from the early 1750s. According to a retrospective on his life that appeared in the gossipy, and avowedly unreliable, *Town and Country Magazine*, Plaistow had been 'a great noise in the world, as a man of gallantry as well as a professed swindler' whose extravagant lifestyle was financed by fraudulently obtained credit. On one occasion, it was said that Murray had acted as his accomplice as he attempted to escape arrest by debt-collecting catchpoles. They had bundled him into a carriage at the entrance to Marylebone Gardens but, it was claimed, 'Fanny Murray, who was in the secret, placed her carriage in the outer rank, and he slipped from one coach into the other, before the catchpoles were aware of the scheme'.[29] Murray then sped him away to safety.

Other accounts made no mention of his career as a fraudster, por-traying him, rather, as a ruthless polygamist.[30] From his breezy account of himself which featured in the *Memoirs* (1:187), Plaistow emerged as charming and plausible, but deadly in the 'wife trade'. As a predatory fortune hunter, he was said to have casually married 'six different wives in three months' without conscience or scruple.

Murray's name was also linked with the notorious gentleman high-wayman and heart-throb, James MacLaine (or Maclean) (1724–50). Courtesans and highwaymen had often made cosy bedfellows. For example, Richard Ferguson (d. 1800), better known as 'Galloping Dick', was involved with a courtesan named Nancy, while Hogarth linked Moll Hackabout, in the third print of *A Harlot's Progress*, with the highway-man James Dalton (d. 1730) whose wig-box could be seen protruding above her bed. Most famously, the spirited and notorious Laetitia Lade (*c.* 1750–1825) was mistress to the highwayman and dandy Jack Rann (1750–74). After his execution, she successfully transformed herself from highwayman's doxy to royal concubine by becoming mistress to Frederick, Duke of York (1763–1827) and possibly his brother, Mary Robinson's former lover, the future George IV.

The *Memoirs* (2:78–83) claimed that Murray and MacLaine had first met at an assembly in York, where the highwayman had introduced him-self as 'Mr Davis'.[31] The affair was short-lived, however, for according to the *Memoirs*, MacLaine was hanged for a robbery on Hampstead Heath which he committed while accompanying Murray back to London. In reality, MacLaine, who operated mainly around Hounslow Heath, was executed on 3 October 1750 for robbing, with his accomplice William Plunkett, the Salisbury coach between Turnham Green and Brentford, and the Earl of Eglinton on Hounslow Heath.

MacLaine's civility and minimum use of violence earned him a reputation as 'The Ladies' Hero', and it was said that he was popular with both 'Women of Fortune and Reputation' and 'the most noted Ladies of the Town', which might have included Murray.[32]

Other evidence linking Murray to MacLaine is equally circumstantial. John Barrows, in his study of highwaymen, claimed that during MacLaine's ill-fated attack on the Salisbury coach, a passenger named Josiah Higden begged MacLaine to allow him to keep a parcel of ribbons that were a gift for his daughter. MacLaine apparently refused, saying he intended the ribbons for 'a young lady whose favours he was enjoying at that time'.[33] This goes some way to supporting the assertion made by Walpole, who was himself held up by MacLaine in November 1749 that, after MacLaine's arrest when his rooms in fashionable St James's were searched, 'there was a wardrobe of clothes, three-and-twenty purses, and the celebrated blunderbuss, [taken during his robbery of the Earl of Eglinton] found at his lodgings, besides a famous kept mistress'.[34] The mistress was not named but, being at the very height of her fame and well-known to be in the keeping of Atkins, it becomes possible that the *Memoirs* are correct and that Murray had added the infamous MacLaine to her list of conquests.

At the same time as her supposed liaison with MacLaine, Murray was also consorting with the dissolute Robert Tracy (or Tracey) (d. 1756).[35] Regarded as 'one of the handsomest fellows in England', 'Beau Tracy' or 'Handsome Tracy', as he was also known, was the grandson and heir of Robert Tracy (1655–1735), a judge of the Court of Common Pleas. Despite the advantages of wealth, a good classical education and a career in law, Tracy was said to have 'destroyed himself by his vices, before he had attained his thirtieth year', having squandered his fortune, and his health, on prostitutes and mistresses.[36]

Indeed, such was his reputation for philandering that he was the inspiration for the heartless rake Beau Leicart who debauched Lucy Sanson in the Reverend Dr William Dodd's moral tale *The Sisters, or, The History of Lucy and Caroline Sanson, Entrusted to a False Friend* (1754).[37] Contemporary accounts of some of Tracy's better-known liaisons depicted him as a hapless lover and, in a famous story which is all the more remarkable for being true, Tracy, in a drunken stupor, married Susannah Owens, a seller of eggs and butter, the daughter of a washerwoman in Orchard Street, Westminster.[38]

His relationship with his great love, Charlotte Hayes, who became a successful procuress, running a lucrative brothel from King's Place in Pall Mall, was as ill-fated as his other affairs. Like Murray with Atkins, Hayes was said to have had the infatuated Tracy so much at her command that 'she could fleece him at will'.[39] It was reported that she paraded her various lovers before him, and even charged their bills to Tracy's account. Her greatest betrayal, however, was with Tracy's good friend Samuel Derrick, he of *Harris's List* fame, with whom she conducted a public affair, once more financed by Tracy.

The irony implicit in Tracy being so attractive to women, yet emasculated in their company, was fully exploited in the *Memoirs* where he was portrayed, to comic effect, as impotent. A first-person narrative of his life, which took up almost a quarter of the second volume of the *Memoirs* (2:23–77) included a scene in which Tracy was granted a night with Murray after she had taken all his money at her gaming table – the joke in the *Memoirs* (2:21–2) was that he was then unable to enjoy his expensive and hard-won prize:

> He endeavoured to be the happiest man upon earth. His ill-success in love was as great as at play – in the first, it's true, she took all advantages, but in the latter she gave him all imaginable opportunities, and yet he failed.

In fact, Tracy probably enjoyed several months with Murray, and Hallie Rubenhold has described how, 'for most of 1750 he had been seen dangling Covent Garden's current reigning lovely, Fanny Murray, off his arm'.[40]

By spring 1751, however, Tracy had thrown Murray over in favour of Hayes, who, since 1750, had been entertaining an Edward Strode at her home in King's Place. Having lost Hayes to Tracy, Strode wasted little time in replacing her, and by May 1751, he had taken up with Murray.[41] Strode was a deeply unsavoury and violent character who, in August 1745, when he was a clerk at Gray's Inn, had tricked a young heiress named Lucy Naomi Gough (or Goff), into a clandestine marriage at St George's Chapel in Mayfair. He had then viciously abused her and run through her fortune in gaming houses, brothels and presumably in maintaining Hayes, Murray, and other courtesans of the day.[42]

Lucy Strode was granted a divorce in 1755, on the grounds of her husband's cruelty and adultery. Among the divorce papers, held at the

London Metropolitan Archives, is a written statement in which Lucy described Strode as 'a Person of a very wicked, profligate and debauched Life and Conversation and of a very vicious cruel and inhuman Temper and Disposition'.[43] Her statement also disclosed how Strode had committed adultery with 'divers lewd and incontinent Women', although only Hayes and Murray were actually cited. According to Lucy Strode's statement, her husband had lived with Hayes during 1750 and part of 1751, and from May 1751 until 1754, he was living with Murray, spending 'night after night' with her at her house in New Palace Yard and afterward, at her lodgings near Vauxhall Gardens.[44]

Lucy Strode's divorce was not the end of her tragic story. Her uncle and guardian, Ferdinando John Paris (d.1759), in an effort to outwit her ex-husband, left his fortune which he intended for his niece, in trust to her mother. When Mrs Gough's death was announced in *Lloyd's Evening Post* in January 1763, Edward got wind of Lucy's inheritance and, in December of that year, armed men broke into her late uncle's house in Surrey Street in the Strand and forcibly abducted her.[45] Within a fortnight, Edward Strode's remarriage to Lucy at the parish church of St Martin-in-the-Fields was announced in the *London Evening Post*.[46]

Murray does not emerge in a good light from this catalogue of purported liaisons. Her connection with Plaistow, her alleged affairs with Tracy and MacLaine, and her three-year liaison with the violent Strode, suggest that rogues and felons held a particular attraction for her. Despite having access to Atkins's deep pockets, Murray chose to associate with fraudsters, violent bullies and possibly highwaymen, presumably because of the reckless excitement they represented and their largesse with their ill-gotten gains.

Lucy Strode's allegations also raise the question of the exact nature of Murray's relationship with Atkins during the three years she was said to have been involved with Edward Strode. If the *Town and Country Magazine*'s retrospective on Murray's lover Joseph Yorke is to be believed, she made a virtue of humiliating her young baronet by trumpeting her high-profile affairs in front of him:

> At this time Fanny Murray, Peg Woffington, and Campioni, were the three reigning princesses amongst the *grizettes* of the *haut ton*. It was not necessary to be very secret in *amours* with these beautiful females, who considered a variety of admirers as so many conquests; and they

exhibited their trophies in assignations stuck behind their looking glasses. The cards of Sir Richard Atkins, captain W---, count H[aslan]g, and even Beau Tracey, were displayed with triumph. Those of our hero (Yorke) were made still more conspicuous, being considered as a man of superior merit and consequence to any of them.[47]

A poem, which appeared in the 1750s, played on Murray's reputation for infidelity. Reminiscent of the repeated duels fought by Atkins's great-grandfather in defence of his promiscuous wife's honour, the poem imagined a scene where Atkins, the 'angry knight', forcibly removed a young fop from Murray's lodgings whom she intended to seduce. A version of this scene was played out in the *Memoirs* (2:2–4), where Atkins was called upon to defend Murray from an overzealous admirer. Murray's promiscuity was made clear in the poem by the suggestion that, had the young gallant been successful in his attempt upon her, he would have contracted venereal disease and been liable for a sizeable medical bill from his surgeon for a cure:

> Tir'd to the last I seize the cringing Spark
> And drag him nolens volens from the Park
> When Fanny Murray seeing something odd
> Pass by her window gave the Fop a nod
> An added smile set all his soul on fire
> And thro strong vanity and some desire
> Like liquid dew exhald away he hies
> Crosses the street & to her Lodgings flies
> Bounces up stairs and opes her chamber door
> When (sad to tell!) Sr Dick was there before
> Kickd Boxd and Cudgelld by the angry Knight
> Home and to bed he steals in piteous plight
> And had he gaind the Fair and lov'd his fill
> He'd scarce have earnd a longer Surgeons Bill.[48]

Atkins was actually incapable of any degree of violence toward Murray or her lovers; rather, he indulged her petulant tantrums and tolerated her infidelities. His friends, Delaval and Foote in particular, teased him for allowing his mercurial mistress to ride roughshod over him:

Frank Delaval and Foote being over a bottle, the subject turned upon Sir Richard's weakness in being such a dupe to a woman … 'Oh,' said Foote, 'there is nothing surprizing in it; he is not indeed a supple-jack, but you know he is a very *supple Dick*'.[49]

Atkins's patient forbearance toward his mistress gave rise to a celebrated incident which alone assured his otherwise mediocre life a place in anecdotal history, and ensured Murray a lasting notoriety. The story centred on a £20 banknote (about £2,400 today). Writing from Strawberry Hill, Walpole tittle-tattled about it in a letter to George Montagu dated 20 October 1748, mistaking Atkins's name as he did so:

> [Fanny Murray] was complaining of want of money. Sir Robert Atkins immediately gave her a twenty pound note; she said, 'D[am]n your twenty pound! what does it signify?' clapped it between two pieces of bread and butter, and ate it.

Walpole's account was cut short by the arrival of his gardener, and since working with his gardener was 'to be preferred to all the world', even to Fanny Murray, Walpole wrote no more of the incident.[50]

The story of Murray and her £20 sandwich spread like wildfire – rakes with demanding mistresses took note. When Kitty Fredericks, the mistress of William Douglas, 4th Duke of Queensbury, better known as 'Old Q', asked him for more money, it was said that 'he threw another Banknote of a hundred pounds into her lap, saying, he hoped she would not, like FANNY MURRAY, pretend she could not make a breakfast of it'.[51]

Murray's exquisite moment was still being repeated to great comic effect five years after her death. For example, the 1783 poetic satire on the future George IV and his lover Mary Robinson, entitled *The Vis-à-Vis of Berkley-Square*, asked:

> Or what could FANNY MURRAY do,
> Tho' she the Venus of the Stew;
> Profusion all her thoughts!
> To make a Country Booby stare,
> She swore she had no other fare
> To breakfast, than *Bank-notes*.[52]

Murray's £20 sandwich represented the kind of breathtaking bravado that every courtesan wished she had thought of first, and her extravagant gesture was soon credited to other courtesans. The Reverend Dodd added a footnote to his novel, *The Sisters*, that he could 'now produce four, at least, who have excelled and gloried in the very same notable feast'.[53] The beautiful Sophia Baddeley, for example, was said to have made a sandwich of a banknote that had been presented to her by a near relation of George III.[54]

It was Kitty Fisher, however, who had the last word on this epicurean rivalry with Murray for, according to Casanova's memoirs, she ate a £100 banknote between two slices of bread and butter.[55] Fisher further trumped Murray when, in 1759, she sat for a portrait by Joshua Reynolds entitled *Kitty Fisher as Cleopatra dissolving the Pearl*. This recreated Pliny's story of how the Queen of Egypt dissolved one of the largest pearls of all time in a glass of vinegar, and then drank it down to impress Mark Antony with the true meaning of epicurean luxury and excess.

This example of Murray's impetuosity explains, in part, the stormy nature of her relationship with Atkins and why quarrels between them were 'usually the case once a-week'.[56] According to the anonymous author of *Nocturnal Revels* (1779), on one occasion Atkins was so exasperated by yet another spat with Murray that he abandoned her in the Shakespear's Head Tavern, and went home instead with the beautiful one-eyed prostitute Betsy Wemyss (*c.* 1725–65). Known as 'the Little Squinting Venus' or 'the Wall Ey'd Beauty', Wemyss was a familiar face in Covent Garden taverns. She was said to enjoy nothing more than 'to swallow down a Gallon of Wine at least' and was also known for her love of practical jokes.[57] It was one of her ruses to create a commotion by pretending to have lost her artificial eye and to compel 'her *inamorato* to go on hands and knees scrabbling in the sand or sawdust on the floor' for it.[58]

On this particular evening, as the author of *Nocturnal Revels* reported it, Wemyss had genuinely lost her false eye and the oculist Dr Taylor had come to her rescue having a selection of glass eyes on hand for her to choose from. Taylor was well known for his lechery, and it was said that he once tried his luck with Murray. Telling her that 'he knew her thoughts by her eyes', Murray had quickly retorted, 'Do you, by G–d, then I am sure you will keep them secret, for they are not to your advantage'.[59] Wemyss had then made her way to the Shakespear's Head

Tavern, just as Atkins, still seething from yet another row with Murray, was settling their bill. In a fit of pique, the author of *Nocturnal Revels* continued, Atkins abandoned Murray for the night and left the tavern with Wemyss – 'Bet's sparkling eyes prevailed, and proved that TAYLOR was no *Botcher*'.[60]

Atkins's night with Wemyss demonstrated that even the patient and long-suffering Atkins had his breaking point. If the *Memoirs* (2:5–10) are correct, on at least one occasion Atkins actually broke with Murray, replacing her with Charlotte E-----, whom he took into keeping. Indeed much of volume two of the *Memoirs* is concerned with Murray's adventures during their period of estrangement. The *Memoirs* (2:152) eventually engineered a sentimental reconciliation with Atkins, following a chance meeting in Wales where 'tears mingled with their kisses, and caresses interrupted sighs'.

Murray's escapades during their separation, as recounted by the *Memoirs*, were prompted by Murray's fluctuating fortunes and her attempts to escape her creditors or find new clients to support her. The *Memoirs* created mildly titillating adventures out of her penury and, on one occasion (2:131–7), flirted with male fantasies of lesbianism. In that particular escapade, Murray had fled to Holland to avoid imprisonment for £600 of debt. Wishing to return to England, but fearing imprisonment, she had disguised herself as a male opera singer but made such a handsome youth, so the *Memoirs* reported, that she was soon the focus of lustful female attention.

Murray emerged from the late 1740s as a somewhat contradictory figure. She was beautiful and beguiling and, when she chose it, refined and agreeable company. She was also compassionate, as evidenced by her supporting the Lock Hospital. The *Memoirs* (1:146 and 2:17), promoted her qualities of natural goodness, describing her as 'she did the honours of [Atkins's] table with that ease and composure, that could not be surpassed by a woman of the first fashion'. According to the eponymous narrator of 'The Episode of a Petticoat', she was visited by fine company and 'Great Personages'. As to be expected, however, her visitors 'were generally of one Sex; for the Ladies of Figure, except such as were of Miss M----'s own Stamp, never approached her'.[61]

She was also immensely successful, and if Atkins had indeed leased Durdans for her, then this was demonstrable proof of the luxurious trappings prostitution had brought her. Moreover, she commanded wealthy, reputable lovers, such as the barrister Henry Gould and the diplomat Joseph Yorke. She had also captivated a wealthy and well-connected young baronet as her protector and even, perhaps, a royal prince as her lover.

There was, however, another less refined side to Murray, for she was recklessly drawn toward profligate, rough-edged and dissipated lovers at the expense of her long-term best interests. As a consequence, she was described in *The Juvenile Adventures of Miss Kitty F----r* as 'handsome without being genteel'.[62] Careless and neglectful of Atkins, she seemed to live for the moment with men who were as disreputable and uproarious as herself. She also appeared to be grasping and unprincipled in choosing clients on the strength of their disposable wealth no matter how reprehensible their character. As Atkins learnt to his cost with his £20 banknote, she was capable of explosive outbursts of temper if her extravagant needs were not met.

Although Murray liked easy money and did not scruple about its source, she seemed indifferent to her long-term security, and her callous and unfeeling treatment of Atkins probably cost her the chance of marrying into the Atkins family and their substantial estates. This rougher and less attractive side of Murray was well hidden beneath breathtaking shows of magnificence, and her beauty shone forth as she dazzled in shimmering jewels and sumptuous gowns. As the 1740s gave way to the 1750s, the public's unbounded obsession with Murray reached its apotheosis. There was a compulsive and overwhelming outpouring of adulation for her that, in the coming months and years, would find expression in every creative form, from poetry to fashion, from prose to mezzotint; so that Murray's name was on everyone's lips and her image stared out from every print-shop window.

Notes

1 Thomson, 'Ode on Miss Fanny Murray', in *A New-Years Miscellany*, p.30.

2 *Nocturnal Revels*, vol. 1, p.18.

3 Byrne, *Perdita*, p.141.

4 *Harris's List* (1773), pp.35–36.

5 *Harris's List* (1773), p.19.

6 *Yorick's Jests: or, Wit's Common-Place Book …* [1790], p.11.

7 The *Memoirs*, vol. 1, p.146, suggested erroneously that Fanny met Atkins just as he was coming of age, which would date their first meeting as March 1749. Rumours of Murray's marriage to Atkins were circulating by September 1748.

8 *The Fool: Being a Collection of Essays and Epistles* ..., 2 vols (1748), vol. 1, p.285 (issue no. 40, dated 4 October 1746).

9 *London Evening Post*, 31 August–2 September 1742; *The General Advertiser*, 2 March 1749.

10 Philip Bliss (ed.), *Reliquiae Hearnianae: The Remains of Thomas Hearne* ..., 2nd ed., 3 vols (John Russell Smith, 1869), vol. 2, p.319. *Walpole Correspondence*, vol. 3, p.460. Letter to Horace Mann dated 14 November 1761.

11 William Cooke, *Memoirs of Samuel Foote, Esq* ..., 2 vols (1806), vol. 1, p.139; *Yorick's Jests*, p.11.

12 See Emily Symonds [George Paston pseud.], *Lady Mary Wortley Montagu and her Times* (Methuen & Co., 1907), p.356.

13 *The Morning Herald*, 14 April 1796.

14 *London Evening Post*, 31 August–2 September 1742.

15 *Read's Weekly Journal or British Gazetteer*, 22 August 1752.

16 *General Advertiser*, 2 March 1749.

17 BL – Add MS 23724. *An Account of the Receipts & Disbursements of Arthur Pond, the Painter and Engraver, from 1734 to 1750* ..., f.140. See also, Sheila O' Connell, *London 1753* (The British Museum Press, 2003), p.142.

18 Kitty Fisher's marriage in 1766 to John Norris, MP for Rye, took place in Scotland, probably to avoid parental objections. See Marcia Pointon, 'The Lives of Kitty Fisher', in *British Journal for Eighteenth-Century Studies* (2004), vol. 27, p.77.

19 Margaret Maria, Lady Verney (ed.), *Verney Letters of the Eighteenth Century from the MSS at Claydon House*, 2 vols (Ernest Benn Ltd, 1930), vol. 2, p.242.

20 *Walpole Correspondence*, vol. 2, p.133.

21 Mrs Ambrose Rathborne (ed.), *Letters from Lady Jane Coke to her friend Mrs Eyre at Derby, 1747–1758* (Swan Sonnenschein & Co. Ltd, 1899), p.14.

22 *General Advertiser*, 13 December 1749. The name is given erroneously as Belcher.

23 Quoted in Christopher Morris (ed.), *The Illustrated Journeys of Celia Fiennes, c. 1682–c. 1712* (Webb & Bower, 1988), pp.233–34.

24 John Harris, *The Artist and the Country House: A History of Country House and Garden View Painting in Britain, 1540–1870* (Philip Wilson Publishers Ltd, 1979), pp.61–62.

25 Eveline Cruickshanks, Stuart Handley and D.W. Hayton (eds), *The History of Parliament: The House of Commons 1690–1715*, 5 vols (Cambridge: Cambridge University Press, 2002), vol. 3, p.85. Narcissus Luttrell, *A Brief Historical Relation of State Affairs from September 1678 to April 1714*, 6 vols (Oxford: Oxford University Press, 1857), vol. 3, pp.494 and 506.

26 E.J. Burford and Joy Wotton, *Private Vices–Public Virtues: Bawdry in London from Elizabethan Times to the Regency* (Robert Hale, 1995), p.134.

27 Cecil Aspinall-Oglander, *Admiral's Wife: Being the Life and Letters of The Hon. Mrs Edward Boscawen from 1719 to 1761* (& New York & Toronto: Longmans, Green & Co., 1940), pp.79–80.

28 [John Hill], *The Inspector*, 2 vols (1753), vol. 2, p.300.

29 *T&C* (April 1786 issue), pp.208–09.

30 See 'Memoirs of Captain Plaistow' in *T&C* (August 1771 issue), pp.407–08.

31 This section of the *Memoirs* is mispaginated. See *Memoirs*, Ch. 7.

32 *Select Trials for Murder ...*, 4 vols (1764), vol. 2, p.49.

33 John Barrows, *Knights of the High Toby: The Story of the Highwaymen* (Peter Davies, 1962), p.169.

34 *Walpole Correspondence*, vol. 2, p.219.

35 *T&C* (October 1770 issue), p.515.

36 *Nocturnal Revels*, vol. 1, p.21. See also, *T&C* (October 1770 issue), pp.515–16.

37 *Gentleman's Magazine and Historical Chronicle* (July 1777 issue), vol. 47, p.339.

38 In a similar situation, Lady Mary Wortley Montagu's son, Edward, married 'an industrious washerwoman' named Sally in 1730. See, for example, *The Annual Register ... for the Year 1776* (1777), section entitled 'Characters' in the appendix, pp.34–35.

39 *Nocturnal Revels*, vol. 1, p.36.

40 Rubenhold, *Covent Garden Ladies*, p.88.

41 Rubenhold, *Covent Garden Ladies*, p.89.

42 Randolph Trumbach, *Sex and the Gender Revolution: Volume One. Heterosexuality and the Third Gender in Enlightenment London* (Chicago: University of Chicago Press, 1998), pp.206 and 380–81.

43 LMA – Allegations, Libels and Sentence Book, July 1754–June 1759, f. 183. (Ref: DL/C/0173 (microfilm X079/091)).

44 LMA (Ref: DL/C/0173, fols. 183–89. See also, DL/C/0553/149–51). Murray does not appear to have taken up lodgings in Vauxhall Gardens – see Ch. 8, below, pp.174–5.

45 *Lloyd's Evening Post*, 28–31 January 1763 and 14–16 December 1763.

46 *London Evening Post*, 27–29 December 1763.

47 *T&C* (September 1779 issue), p.457.

48 William Mason, 'First Satire of Dr Donne Versified' (*c.* 1750), quoted in Donald A. Low, 'An Eighteenth-Century Imitation of Donne's First Satire', in *The Review of English Studies* (August 1965), vol. 16, no. 63, p.297.

49 *Yorick's Jests*, pp.11–12.

50 *Walpole Correspondence*, vol. 2, p.133; *N&Q*, 7 Ser. XII (12 December 1891), p.470; 10 Ser. XI (5 June 1909), p.447; 10 Ser. XI (26 June 1909), pp.514–15; 6 Ser. II (18 December 1880), p.486. See also, *The Hibernian Magazine: or, Compendium of Entertaining Knowledge ...* (Dublin: April 1784 issue), p.190.

51 *Nocturnal Revels*, vol. 2, Ch. 35, p.214. (Mispaginated).

52 *Vis-à-Vis of Berkley-Square*, p.11.

53 William Dodd, *The Sisters: or, the History of Lucy and Caroline Sanson, Entrusted to a False Friend*, 2 vols (1754), vol. 1, p.36 (footnote).

54 Grantley F. Berkeley, *My Life and Recollections*, 4 vols (Hurst & Blackett, 1865–66), vol. 2 (1865), pp.26–27.

55 Giacomo Casanova, Chevalier de Seingalt, *History of My Life*, translated by William R. Trask, abridged by Peter Washington and introduction by John

Julius Norwich (& New York & Toronto: Alfred A. Knopf, 2006), p.933. Casanova states wrongly that the banknote had been given to Fisher by Atkins.

56 *Nocturnal Revels*, vol. 1, p.37.

57 *Great News from Hell, or the Devil Foil'd by Bess Weatherby* (1760), p.7.

58 Burford, *Wits, Wenchers and Wantons*, p.120.

59 *The English Roscius: Garrick's Jests* ... [1785], pp.84–85. The anecdote is also attributed to an unnamed lady in *Nancy Dawson's Jests* ... (1761), p.24.

60 *Nocturnal Revels*, vol. 1, p.39.

61 'The Episode of a Petticoat', in *Memoirs and Interesting Adventures of an Embroidered Waistcoat*, pp.20–21.

62 *Juvenile Adventures*, vol. 1, p.109.

6

The Height of Fashion

My Name, Sir, is Witwood Borlace, a Name, I believe, once as well known in the gay Life of London, as Fanny Murray's.[1]

By the late 1740s, the public curiosity and adulation that Murray inspired was on an unprecedented scale, outstripping that of any courtesan who had gone before, even the celebrated Sally Salisbury (*c.* 1690/92–1724). Fascination with every aspect of Murray's life, from her lovers to her wealth and beauty, was no longer the lone preserve of male admirers, and extended well beyond the world of gallantry. As already noted, reputable women, who might not have wished to receive Murray in their homes, were nonetheless keen to follow her as a fashion icon and to copy her style. According to the *Memoirs* (1:148), she was 'servilely followed, not only by women in a middling station, but by those in the most elevated'. Thus, in 1754, when the *Connoisseur* asked 'whether Fanny Murray or Lady ---- were the properest to lead the fashion', the question was undoubtedly rhetorical.[2]

Although Murray was thinking about withdrawing from prostitution at this time, and eight years had elapsed since she had first been acclaimed a toast of the town, she was still at the top of her profession, the very personification of style and an unparalleled arbiter of taste. Even after Murray had settled into marital respectability, magazines like the *Centinel* still presented her as a leading trendsetter and influential woman of fashion:

If *Fanny Murray* chuses to vary the fashion of her apparel, immediately
every *Lucretia* in town takes notice of the change, and *modestly* copies the
chaste original. If *Fanny* shews the coral centre of her snowy orbs – *miss* to
outstrip her, orders her stays to be cut an inch or two lower; and kindly
displays the whole lovely circumference.[3]

It was not unusual for society ladies to turn to celebrated courtesans
and actresses for instruction on the latest fashions and, according to
the German traveller Johann Wilhelm von Archenholz, who visited England in the 1780s, the comedic actress Frances Abington was
'constantly employed in driving about the capital to give her advice
concerning the modes and fashions of the day'.[4] By the time the
Connoisseur posed its question, Murray was 25, an advanced age for
a courtesan, and no longer a fresh face, yet the public's fascination
with her and the exclusive world within which she moved burned as
brightly as it had always done.

Murray's success in igniting and, more importantly, sustaining public
interest was in part achieved by what one nineteenth-century writer
described as the 'Cyprian Puff' whereby high-class prostitutes metic-
ulously stage-managed their own extravagant lives in order to attract
maximum publicity, perpetuate their celebrity and, hopefully, attract
wealthy protectors. As a result, the more astute courtesans ensured that
their images dominated every print-shop window and that every glamorous detail of their existence, from fashionable appearances at the opera
to promenades with wealthy new lovers, received the utmost newspaper
or pamphlet coverage. By such means, argued the writer:

A public prostitute, shall, in a few months, by means of newspaper puffs,
raise herself from the rank of a starving strumpet, to be mistress of a lord,
a duke, or even a prince, and after that set up her carriage, keep an elegant
table, and even pretend to give the fashions.[5]

Puffing was in its infancy when Murray was at her height. Compared
to her nearest rival Kitty Fisher, who was ten years her junior and especially skilled at courting publicity and manipulating the press, Murray
was an *ingénue* at this new art of self-promotion. Fisher, unlike Murray,
actively drew publicity to herself by personally engaging with the
media – by describing 'the Baseness of little Scribblers', for example, or

remonstrating with the editors of newspapers and *Harris's List*, Fisher maintained her newsworthiness.[6] Unusually for women in the public gaze, Fisher also took a keen personal interest in the representation of her image for the print-shop market. This was particularly true of her portrait by Joshua Reynolds as *Cleopatra dissolving a Pearl* which she reputedly owned and from which, presumably, 'she authorised the creation and sale of a print that became extremely popular'.[7]

As an accomplished equestrian, she might have even engineered a dramatic publicity stunt when, in March 1759, she fell from her horse while riding in St James's Park. Her accident caused a sensation, with reports of her mishap, which played on the notion of the 'fallen woman', instantly flying off the presses. Lampoons such as *The Merry Accident* (*c.* 1759) helpfully illustrated the expanse of leg that had been exposed in her tumble. The amount of attention Fisher's fall received was ridiculed in the satirical *Horse and Away to St James's Park* (1760) where it was remarked that it was 'enough to debauch half the Women in London' for 'who the D[evi]l would be modest, when they may Live in this state by turning [prostitution]'.[8]

Murray's stratagems for holding the public's attention and safeguarding her premier status as a top-class courtesan were less melodramatic, but no less theatrical. Knowing that nothing succeeded like success, Murray lived her public life in a maelstrom of ostentatious display, and for almost a decade she excelled in fashioning herself as the most stylish, exclusive and irresistible object of desire on the market. According to the *Memoirs* (1:147), Atkins furnished her with 'a wardrobe of the most gorgeous apparel, and a casket of --- valuable jewels' so that she would have dazzled when she appeared at fashionable venues such as the pleasure gardens at Vauxhall and Ranelagh, or the theatres in Covent Garden.

Although the *Memoirs* (2:172) liked to present her as 'never gaudy in dress, and but seldom expensive', by 1750, she was the very epitome of extravagance and excess. She might have taken possession of the splendid former royal retreat of Durdans with its beautiful parkland and gardens that Atkins had leased, and, according to the *Derby Mercury*, she owned her own carriage, the last word in status symbols.[9] The *Memoirs* (2:184) fancied her 'rolling in her chariot, with all the splendor of a dutchess' while 'Polly. A new Song', which came out in 1757, recalled the days when 'Fanny Murray's chariot stroll[ed]/ Through clouds of am'rous beaux'.[10]

For the courtesan, such extravagant displays of wealth and material possession were essential to preserving her elite status among the public at large as well as those men who were her potential clients. The more extravagant, wasteful and luxurious her conspicuous consumption, and the more successful she appeared, the more it redounded to her fame, reputation and social power. When Giustiniana Wynne (1737–91), the Anglo-Venetian writer, visited London (1759–60), she pointedly remarked on the fact that Fisher, 'lives in the greatest possible splendour, spends twelve thousand pounds a year, and she is the first of her social class to employ liveried servants'.[11] Wynne's famous lover, Casanova, recalled seeing Fisher shimmering in diamonds which he estimated to have been worth more than 100,000 crowns as she waited to be taken to a ball.[12]

A courtesan's wealth, however, and with it, her sexual power and social standing, could evaporate almost overnight. Such was the fate of Sophia Baddeley who, like Fisher, revelled in unimaginable wealth and was breathtakingly profligate.[13] At the height of her beauty, and under the protection of the indulgent and exceptionally wealthy Peniston Lamb, Lord Melbourne (1745–1828), Sophia was a compulsive and capricious spendthrift. Elizabeth Steele, her companion and biographer, described how Baddeley could easily splash out £4,000 (over £400,000 today) on diamonds, and 3 guineas a day (approximately £300) on flowers.[14] In the end, however, her extravagances spiralled out of control and left her with massive debts which, combined with ill-health and laudanum addiction, cost her her wealthy lovers and her premier position among courtesans.

At the height of their power, however, such dazzling courtesans and actresses lived in rarefied worlds far removed from the mundane rhythms of normal existence. Yet a growing consumerism and demand for luxury goods provided opportunities for those, even on modest incomes, to buy an imagined share in the glamorous lifestyles of these exquisite women. By aping their fashions and imitating their consumer tastes, ordinary individuals could purchase a false sense of intimacy with the most modish women of the day and a sense of status among their own more impressionable friends. Such a style-following could increase the social status of courtesans and actresses alike, and bring them substantial financial rewards in the form of wealthy protectors. Such men were only too eager to improve their own standing among their peers by taking the most expensive and fashionable beauties of the day as their mistresses.

1 *Miss Fanny Murray*, published by Richard Bennet (1754). (© Victoria and Albert Museum, London)

2 *Miss Kitty Fisher*, commissioned by John Bowles and Son (n/d). (© Victoria and Albert Museum, London)

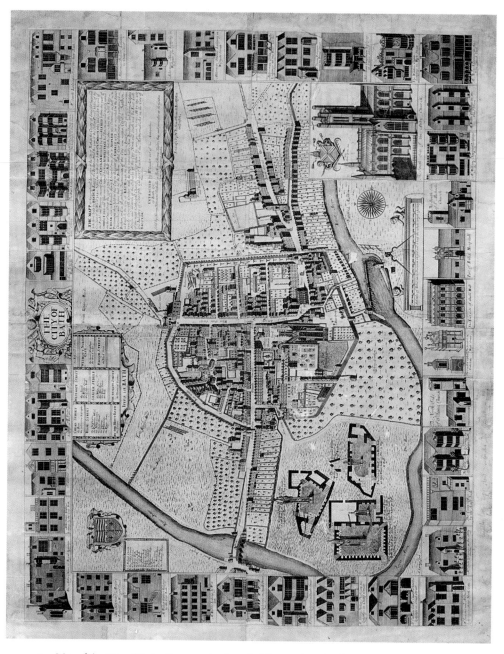

3   *Map of the City of Bath 1694–1717*, by Joseph Gilmore (1717). (© Bath in Time – Bath Central Library Collection)

4 *St John's Court, Bath*, by Henry Venn Lansdown (1858). (© Bath in Time – Bath Central Library Collection)

5 *Richard Nash Esq.*, by A. Walker, after William Hoare (n/d). (© Bath in Time – Bath Central Library Collection)

6 *The Hon. John Spencer with his son on Horseback*, after George Knapton (1746). (From the Collection at Althorp)

7 *John Montagu, 4th Earl of Sandwich*, by Joseph Highmore (1740). (© National Portrait Gallery, London)

8 *Miss Fanny Murray*, by Adriaen Carpentiers
(*c.* 1745). (By kind permission of Sir Edward
Dashwood, Bt)

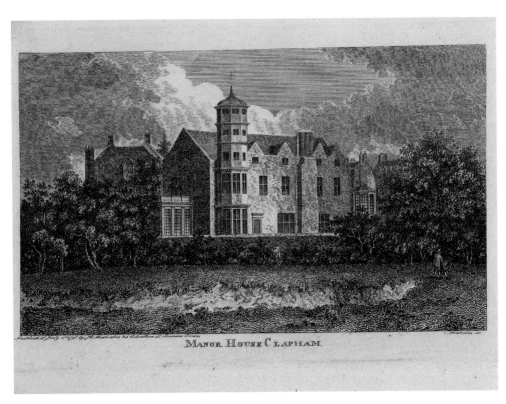

MANOR HOUSE CLAPHAM

9 *Manor House, Clapham*, by James Peller Malcolm (1798). (© National Trust/David Cousins)

Vander Mijn Pinx^t.   R^d Purcell fecit.

Printed for Robt Sayer at the Golden Buck in Fleetstreet.

10   *Lucy Cooper*, by Richard Purcell, after Frans van der Mijn (*c.* 1760). (Author's Collection. Photograph Dan Brown)

11 *Durdans, Surrey*, by Jacob Scmits (or Smits) (1689). (By kind permission of the Berkeley Will Trust. Photograph © the Paul Mellon Centre for Studies in British Art)

J. Reynolds pinx.   *J. Watson fecit.*

Miss Kitty Fischer.

Printed for John = Bowles at the Black Horse in Cornhill.

12 *Miss Kitty Fischer as Cleopatra Dissolving the Pearl*, by James Watson after Sir Joshua Reynolds (*c.* 1760). (Author's Collection. Photograph Dan Brown)

13 'Fanny Murray' song in *Clio and Euterpe: or, British Harmony: A collection of celebrated songs and cantatas* … (1762). (Author's Collection. Photograph Dan Brown)

14　*Shepherdess*, by John Faber the Younger, after Henry Pickering (n/d). (© The Trustees of the British Museum. All rights reserved)

15　*Miss Fanny Murray*, by James McArdell, after Henry Morland (n/d). (© Bath in Time – Bath Central Library Collection)

The Morning Taft; or Fanny M—'s Maid Wafhing her Toes.

16　*The Morning Tast; or, Fanny M----y's Maid Washing Her Toes*, by George Bickham the Younger (*c.* 1751). (Author's Collection. Photograph Dan Brown)

Mezetin comprend bien qu'il luy faut du secours
Devant a sa toillette haranguer une belle
avec privillege du Roi

Du Son d'une Guittare il soutient son discours
Souvent un jnstrument fléchit la plus rebelle

Gillot inv.   Huquier Sculp. ex.
                               J.D.F.

17   *Mezetin Comprend Bien Qu'il Lui Faut du Secours* (*Mezetin Understands He Needs Help*),
by Gabriel Huquier, after Claude Gillot (n/d). (Bibliothèque Nationale de France)

Miss Fanny Murray.

J June sculp.

Sold by Jn.º Smith at Hogarths Head Cheapside.

18   Watch paper
with a portrait of
Fanny Murray by
John June, after
Henry Morland
(n/d). (© The
Trustees of the
British Museum.

19   *Medmenham Abbey*, by James Tingle, after William Tombleson (1840). (Author's Collection. Photograph Dan Brown)

20   *John, 1st Earl Spencer*, by Thomas Gainsborough (*c.* 1763). (From the collection at Althorp)

21   *Georgiana, Countess Spencer*, by Pompeo Batoni (*c.* 1764). (From the collection at Althorp)

22 David Ross as
Kitely, in *Every Man
in his Humour*, by Tilly
Kettle (*c.* 1776–83).
(The Art Archive/
Garrick Club)

Miss Murray.

23 *Miss Murray*, by
Richard Houston,
(*c.* 1760–75). (© The
Trustees of the British
Museum. All rights
reserved)

24 *Female Court Martial*, by Louis Philippe Boitard (1757). (Author's Collection. Photograph Dan Brown)

25 *Miss Fanny Murray, the Fair and Reigning Toast, in her Primitive Innocence* (c. 1764). (© The British Library Board. Shelfmark – HS 74/1659)

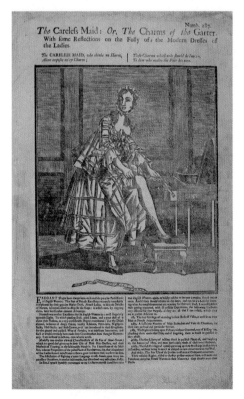

26 *The Careless Maid: or, The Charms of the Garter. With some Reflections on the Folly of the Modern Dresses of the Ladies* (c.1764). (© The British Library Board. Shelfmark – HS 74/1659)

30 *A View of the Dresses at the Late Masquerade given by the King of Denmark*, drawn and engraved by J. Lodge (1768). (© Bath in Time – Bath Central Library Collection)

31 Miniature portrait of Louise de Kéroualle, Duchess of Portsmouth, by Wolfgang William Claret (before 1706). (From the collection at Althorp)

In this milieu, the ultimate accolade for upwardly mobile Cyprian fashion plates was to be identified by name with the fashions they had introduced, and to have their style adopted by the public at large. Thus, when the actress Ann Catley created a signature hairstyle by having her fringe cut down over her forehead 'like a fan', it was soon the fashion to have 'Catlified hair'.[15] Hair 'à la Santlow' in imitation of the actress Hester Santlow (*c.* 1690–1773) was also popular.[16]

Mary 'Perdita' Robinson, when a fashionable courtesan, popularised a number of 'Robinson' hats, as well as the daring 'Perdita' chemise – a soft, fluid muslin dress that 'dispensed with bodice and hoops, panniers and trains'.[17] Around 1777, the courtesan Margaret Caroline Rudd (*c.* 1744–97), who was involved in the forgery trial of the Perreau brothers, started a trend while in Newgate Prison for a 'polonaise' jacket that was still popular among society ladies several years later.[18] Hats, such as the Nancy Dawson 'new kick', the 'Abington cap' and the Kitty Fisher 'fancy' also had their turn as the season's prevailing rage.[19] For a while, shortly after 1748, the headgear *de rigueur* was the Fanny Murray 'cock', giving proof to the claim in the *Memoirs* (1:148) that at the height of her power, whatever Murray wore was 'the law of fashion' and her style 'the only standard' of women's dress. Worn at a jaunty angle, Murray's particular style of straw, or chip hat, which she wore in nearly all her portraits, appears to have been popular with fashion-conscious men and women alike. Mrs Hibbert Ware, in her nineteenth-century novel on the life and times of Richard Nash, described how:

> One fop in an embroidered coat from Paris, for London-made coats were sedulously eschewed, stood erect with his black beaver hat tucked under his arm, a Fanny Murray'd hat, as they called the quaintly cocked hat of the period, and took a pinch of snuff in order to display his white hands.[20]

The compulsion to follow the latest trends, inspired by the celebrated names of the day, created the inevitable fashion victim, and a Miss Bennet was one whose face was not at all flattered by the shape of a Fanny Murray hat. She was said to have 'apparelled her Nob in a frightful Fanny Murray Cap, and looked five and forty'.[21] Indeed, the *Lady's Magazine* in 1785, published seven years after Murray's death, used the particular example of Murray's style of hat to warn its readers against

following the latest fashion trends, recalling how Fanny's contemporaries had followed her into disastrous fashion *faux-pas*:

> The late Fanny Murray whose face was very handsome, though somewhat awry, used to wear a hat of her own contrivance, which was so well judged, that it concealed the imperfection of her face, whence it was called Fanny Murray's cock; and became a general fashion: but the misfortune was, that many who wore this hat did not consult the *traits*, or features, of their faces, did not look near so well, as they had done with any other of a less conspicuous form.[22]

Moralists, however, saw greater perils in celebrity endorsed fashions than merely leading the unwary into sartorial blunder. As suggested by the fop in his Parisian embroidered coat, garments popularised by women of ill-repute could suggest moral degradation in the wearer. This was exemplified by a scene in William Dodd's moral tale, *The Sisters*, in which those who sported Fanny Murray cocks were shown to be duplicitous and untrustworthy. *The Sisters* told the tale of Lucy and Caroline Sanson who were both duped into prostitution. By a twist of fate, Caroline was able to escape and remain virtuous, while her sister Lucy was tricked into a sham marriage and followed a downward path. Her undoer was Leicart, the character modelled on Robert 'Beau' Tracy, who was 'fond of ruining any woman that shall fall in his way'.[23] Lucy had been introduced to him by some newfound, but ultimately false friends who were:

> Well-known ladies, eminently distinguished by their careless air and dress, their long, white, pearly ear-rings, and quaintly-cocked (or, as they have been perhaps not improperly call'd, *Fanny-Murray'd* hats).[24]

Dodd's warning that '*Fanny-Murray'd* hats' signified moral dissipation and perdition inevitably fell on deaf ears as the fashionable put any concern for reputation aside in their scramble to copy the latest fashions worn by the stars of the day. Thus, much to the disapproval of her friend Lady Caroline Fox, the impressionable Lady Susan Fox-Strangways (1743–1827) was so devoted to 'the Kitty Fisher style' that she not only copied Fisher's fashions, but also had her portrait painted by Allan Ramsay in the same pose that Fisher had adopted for Joshua Reynolds.[25]

27 *Theatre Royal, Edinburgh*, by William Wallis, after Thomas Hosmer Shepherd (*c.* 1830). (Author's Collection. Photograph Dan Brown)

28 David Ross in the Character of Essex, in *The Earl of Essex*, by J. Thornthwaite, after James Roberts (1776). (The Art Archive/Garrick Club)

29 *The Celebrated Miss Murray*, by Thomas Johnson, after Thomas Ross (*c.* 1750–60). (© The Trustees of the British Museum. All rights reserved)

As Murray mania took hold in the late 1740s, her influence extended well beyond the world of fashionable clothes and chip hats. Poets, musicians, writers and artists were all eager to extol her charms, and of course, cash in on her popularity. From the beginning of her career, asserted the *Memoirs* (2:83), 'poets, painters and engravers, began to exercise their arts upon our heroine – Scarce a magazine appeared without an ode, or an acrostic upon Fanny'.[26] Whether it was to acknowledge 'the single charms of Fanny Murray' or imagine feasting on her with as much relish as roast beef – 'and sup, in Middlesex, or Surrey,/ On coarse cold beef, and Fanny Murray' – whether it was to liken her to Flora, or revere her as Venus, 'the *Fanny Murray of Olympus*'; poetic references to Murray proliferated.[27] So much so, that Eliza Haywood in her novel *The Invisible Spy* (1754) imagined a scene in which the business of the House of Commons was brought to a standstill by the reading of salacious verses dedicated to Murray. Watching from the gallery, a character named Careless, was:

> Never more diverted in [his] whole life, than to see below how some young members, who had got their heads together and were giggling over a copy of verses inscrib'd to Fanny Murray, were put to silence in an instant, and look'd as silly as a school-boy under the lash of correction, on the Speaker's crying out with an audible and austere voice, – To order, gentlemen, – for shame – to order.[28]

In his 'Ode to Miss Fanny Murray', the poet Thomson had claimed that Murray was 'the Theme of every Song', an exaggeration of course, but Murray was certainly celebrated in popular music. 'Fanny Murray', which was included in a 1762 collection of eighteenth-century songs, paid tribute to her beauty in simple verse:

> What Paint with her Complexion vies
> What Jewels sparkle like her Eyes
> What Hills of Snow so white as Rise
> The Breast of Fanny Murray.[29]

'A Song Wrote by Mr Boyce on Sight of Fanny Murray' which appeared in the November 1755 issue of the *Universal Magazine* was also popular.[30] Written in four verses, the song is attributed to the composer Dr William

Boyce (1711–79), rather than the poet Samuel Boyce (d. 1775) – the author of *Poems on Several Occasions* (1757), to which Murray subscribed.

It was first performed by the celebrated Thomas ('Tommy') Lowe whom Charles Burney described as having 'the finest tenor voice I ever heard in my life'.[31] Lowe was a member of Handel's oratorio company from 1743 until 1751 and principal tenor from 1748. He was better known, however, as a popular theatre and pleasure garden singer and often performed at Vauxhall and at Marylebone Gardens, which he also managed, albeit unsuccessfully, between 1763 and 1768. Undoubtedly, it would have added significantly to Murray's cachet and strengthened her hold on the public imagination to have the mellifluous voice of Tommy Lowe singing her praises in London's most fashionable resorts.[32]

In 1748 the first, and wholly inaccurate, narrative of Murray's life appeared in *The Humours of Fleet-Street*. In the same year, Henry Fielding also recognised the selling power of the very name of Fanny Murray. His play, *The Covent Garden Tragedy*, had 'met with the universal Detestation of the Town' when it was first performed on 1 June 1732 as an afterpiece to *The Old Debauchees*, and it was withdrawn immediately after the first night.[33] Set in Mrs Punchbowl's brothel, the play, which told of the rivalry between two prostitutes, Kissinda and Stormandra, for the love of Lovegirlo, had proved too vulgar for theatre-going tastes. The play fared much better, however, when it was presented in puppet form in May 1748 at Fielding's Panton Street puppet theatre. In this version of the play, the main characters were renamed after well-known celebrities of the day so that Stormandra became Mrs Puppet Fllips – a reference to Constantia Phillips whose outrageous serialised memoirs had begun to appear in instalments in April that year – and Kissinda, Mrs Puppet Morrey, a thinly veiled Murray.[34]

While the idea of a puppet playing the sexiest woman in London might seem incongruous, Murray was also the subject of other equally curious pairings. It has been suggested that gin cocktails were created in Murray's honour with names such as 'Fanny Murray's Pick-Me-Up', 'Fanny Murray's Nettle Juice' and 'Gin and Fanny Sandwich'.[35] At least one ship bore her name, and the *Fanny Murray* made the newspapers in March 1748 when it was reported that she had been retaken by Sir Peter Warren, Admiral of the White, while sailing between Maryland and London.[36]

After her retirement from prostitution, Murray appeared in 'Ship News' of a different kind when the *Centinel* (1757) employed nautical double entendres for the titillation of its readers.[37] Thus, a cargo bound for 'Merryland' was 'consigned over to Mrs Douglas' (the brothel-keeper) while 'the Fanny Murray [was] for the park', a reference, perhaps, to Vauxhall Gardens where, according to the abused wife Lucy Strode, Murray had once taken lodgings.[38]

Several racehorses were named after Murray which, as Faramerz Dabhoiwala has pointed out, was a relatively new practice since horses had rarely been called after individuals before 1700.[39] Mr Hauxby's grey mare, 'Miss Fanny Murray' raced at Carthorpe in North Yorkshire on 30 May 1748, while Mr Hall's black mare 'Fanny Murray' came in fourth in His Majesty's 100-guinea race for 5-year-olds at Hambleton, also in North Yorkshire, on 29 July 1749. The black mare was racing again at Wakefield on 28 August.[40] A year later on 26 September 1750, Mr Blacket's bay mare ran at Morpeth in Northumberland for a subscription purse. Almost a decade later in July 1759, yet another 'Fanny Murray', this time a 5-year-old bay owned by Mr Frankland, was beaten into second place by Mr Ingleby's grey mare 'Kitty Fisher' at a £100 sweepstake held at Durham.[41] The irony of the equine Kitty Fisher's victory would not have been lost on those race-goers who followed the gossip columns and knew that, as the new toast of the town, Fisher had eclipsed Murray, and not only on the racecourse.

In 1757, the racing motif was extended for the amusement of readers of the *Crab-Tree* weekly magazine. It imagined a race at Newmarket for the 'entire stock in trade of honesty and honour' in which Murray was one of the runners. According to the *Crab-Tree*'s light-hearted whimsy, Murray and an unnamed titled lady paid their entrance fee to Mrs Douglas, the brothel-keeper, and 'Miss Fanny protested she could out run her ladyship; upon which several bye standers backed Fanny, five to one against the field, let what would come'.[42]

As the *Crab-Tree* suggests, Murray's name was also to be found in popular jest books, and she was the butt of good-humoured, if smutty, jokes and anecdotes, some of which were still doing the rounds twenty years after her death. The jokes, however, were not specific to Murray since the same comic effect was achieved by referencing any well-known woman with a reputation for sexual rampancy:

Question – Why is Fanny M----y like a Field of new Hay?
Answer – Because she's toss'd about by Rakes.[43]

Question – Why is Fanny M----- like the Serjeant at Arms?
Answer – Because she takes unruly Members into Custody.[44]

As a result, these particular quick-fire question-and-answer-style gags were not only told against Murray but the sergeant-at-arms joke was also told against Fanny D--- (most probably the courtesan Fanny Davies) and the field of hay joke against the actress Peg Woffington. This is a further example of the disposable nature of celebrity, as described by Kevin Jordan Bourque – it was probably printer error, or laziness, in failing to update faded stars with the latest celebrities of the day that explains why some Murray jokes outlived her.

As well as quick one-liners, Murray was also the subject of humorous anecdotes. These were more carefully composed for the humour worked by placing a ribald punch line at the end of a plausible narrative. Thus, in the following 'parrot joke' from 1796, Murray was imagined in her real-life lodgings but the rest of the story was an invention. The passage of time has dulled this particular joke's humour since the double meaning of 'whore's bird' as a debauched fellow or illegitimate child is now lost:

> This lady [Murray] once had lodgings near Dean's-yard, Westminster. It was frequently her practice to amuse herself with a favourite parrot at an open window; in this realm of youthful waggery, she soon became a mark for the Westminster despots of the great seminary; a party of them accordingly took the station before her apartment during one of her conversations with pretty Poll. 'Jack' exclaims the leader of the joke, 'what bird's that?' – 'What bird, why a whore's-bird,' to be sure.[45]

In another droll anecdote, Murray was placed alongside Peg Woffington at the trial of Simon Fraser, 11th Lord Lovat, whose execution on 9 April 1747 for his part in the 1745 Jacobite Rebellion, distinguished him as the last man in Britain to be beheaded on Tower Hill:

> A Gentleman sitting by Mrs W[o]ff[ingto]n at Lord Lovat's trial, took notice to her of Fanny M-----'s being at a little distance from them. O! said she, I suppose Fanny 'has an eye upon the whole house of commons.

And I dare answer for her. Madam, reply'd the Gentleman, if she has, her eye's no bigger than her belly.'[46]

It is, of course, possible that both these anecdotes grew out of quasi-accurate reports which were embellished for comic effect. It was not uncommon, for example, for fashionable ladies to be seen in courtroom galleries during high-profile cases, especially when the defendant was infamous, titled or handsome. Indeed, one of Horace Walpole's beauties, Lady Caroline Petersham *née* Fitzroy, had even spoken for the defence at the trial in September 1750 of Murray's alleged lover, the highwayman James MacLaine.

Murray's name was also appropriated within the private sphere and might have been used as a code name in confidential correspondence. Mrs Gillespie Smyth, in her 1849 edition of the letters and memoirs of the soldier and diplomat Sir Robert Murray Keith (1730–95), claimed that references by the politician Thomas Bradshaw (1733–74) to 'Miss Fanny Murray' was a private cipher for Henry Howard, 12th Earl of Suffolk.[47] This view has been challenged, however, by Bradshaw's recent biographer, Richard Lee Bradshaw, who has suggested that the Fanny Murray mentioned in the letters was, in fact, a member of Murray Keith's family.[48] Even so, the idea that Murray's name was used as a cipher, particularly in diplomatic circles, is credible. For example, when Philip Dormer Stanhope, Earl of Chesterfield wrote to his godson, Solomon Dayrolles, who had recently taken up a diplomatic posting at the Hague, it is possible that he was using Fanny Murray as a code name for an unidentified third party – 'Fanny Murray was last night in the Park in perfect health but in very close mourning – for some near relation, I presume, of the illustrious family of the Murrays!'[49]

By the end of the eighteenth century, Murray's name had also been appropriated into the clandestine world of London's gay subculture where homosexuals, known as mollies, commonly used ciphers and christened one another with 'maiden names'. Robert Holloway, in his account of the Vere Street coterie that met at the Swan public house around 1810, was intrigued that as well as 'effeminate delicate beings', the tavern attracted very masculine-looking men who took the names of long-dead stars from the Cyprian world. According to Holloway, 'Fanny Murry [sic], Lucy Cooper, and Kitty Fisher, are now personified by an athletic Bargeman, an Herculean Coalheaver, and a deaf tyre

Smith'.[50] It would seem, therefore, that even thirty years after her death, Murray, and her fellow courtesans, were still acknowledged symbols of beauty and sexual potency.

During her heyday, it must have seemed as if Murray's name was ubiquitous, being heard everywhere from the high seas to the pleasure garden, from the racecourse to the tavern. Yet it was the visual image rather than the printed or spoken evocation of her name that proved the most powerful and effective medium in establishing, and maintaining, Murray as a celebrated public figure. Prints of Murray, which were reproduced in their thousands, brought her to a much wider audience and turned her into a national pin-up.

This biography is the first time that examples of extant prints and satires connected with Murray have been presented together. Where a number of similar versions of prints are available, such as for *Miss Fanny Murray* (c. 1750), discussed below, and *Female Court Martial* (1757), discussed in chapter nine, a representative engraving has been selected for inclusion. In addition, *The Shepherdess* (c. 1750) by John Faber the younger (c. 1695–1756), after Henry Pickering (c. 1720–c. 1771), has also been included even though Murray's identification is tentative. Since sitters are no longer as instantly recognisable as they once were, the model for *The Shepherdess* might be Murray, but she might also be Flora MacDonald, the Jacobite heroine who famously helped Bonnie Prince Charlie to escape after his defeat in 1746 at the Battle of Culloden.[51]

Other visual representations of Murray were also being mass-produced to satisfy an avid public. Samuel Derrick of *Harris's List* fame, who became master of ceremonies at Bath shortly after the death, in 1761, of Murray's early protector Richard Nash, recalled seeing a medal of Murray made out of plaster of Paris during his travels in Ireland in 1760. It belonged to an eccentric and impoverished 63-year-old widower and former lieutenant named Patrick, who lived some 15 miles outside Waterford on the Kilkenny road. The old man's parlour was filled with a miscellaneous collection of paintings, busts and medals which, alongside Murray, included the Duke of Cumberland, Homer, King George III and St Patrick.[52]

The old man's eclectic arrangement of whores, heroes and patron saints reflected what was to be found in any of the numerous print-shops that plied their trade around Covent Garden, the Strand and Holborn, where portraits of notorious whores and persons of quality were indiscriminately 'huddled together in one window'. The humour, novelty and haphazard nature of such displays led one print-shop patron to liken print-shops to graves 'into which we are all at a certain period laid low, without distinction of rank, age, or sex'.[53] In *The Chinese Spy*, Mandarin Cham-pi-pi, a fictional visitor to Europe, offered his observations on English politics and customs and described how:

> In these face-shops you see vice on a level with virtue; for I bought the following, which were all in a string: Fanny Murray, Lady Berkeley, Kitty Fisher, Lady Fortescue, Charlotte Fisch, Lady Waldegrave, Nancy Dawson, Lady Barrington, Nelly O'Brien, the Dutchess of Ancaster.[54]

The first mass-produced prints of Murray began to appear in the early 1750s when, according to the *Memoirs* (2:83), 'every print-shop window presented you with Fanny in metzotinto'.[55] A particularly popular print was *Miss Fanny Murray* which was copied from a portrait, now lost, by the artist Henry Robert Morland.[56] Throughout the 1750s, impressions of Morland's portrait by the Irish engravers James McArdell, Richard Purcell (also known as Charles or Philip Corbutt) and Charles Spooner flooded the market in print runs that might have exceeded 3,000–4,000.[57]

Miss Fanny Murray is an arresting half-portrait of Murray in her prime; her skin appears translucent, and her dark, almond eyes meet the viewer in a deep, alluring gaze. She is richly dressed in a fashionable sack-backed gown, embellished with ruches that continue over the shoulder on either side of a jewelled bodice, and there are striped bows at the elbow. Four intricate arrangements of pearl flowers that complement Murray's large pendant pearl earrings adorn the bodice, while a diaphanous and ruffled muslin *fichu*, arranged over her shoulders, draws attention to her creamy décolletage. A perfect kiss curl rests seductively on her left cheek and she wears her signature chip hat, tied decoratively in a bow beneath her chin, under which can be glimpsed, as was the fashion, a lace cap. The portrait captures a demure quality in Murray, so much so that she could easily pass for a modest and respectable woman.[58] It is only the caption's tell-tale reference to 'sportive Loves' with its suggestion of sexual pleasure that belies the image of innocence:

> Here sportive Loves inviting seem to say,
> Behold this Face, and gaze your Heart away.

There is a similar effect in a full-length 1754 portrait of Murray by the engraver, printer and music seller Richard Bennet (or Bennett), who operated out of the Blue Bell near St Clement's churchyard. Murray's seeming respectability in Bennet's print, also entitled *Miss Fanny Murray*, is counterbalanced by a caption, taken from Alexander Pope's description of Belinda in 'The Rape of the Locke' (1712) that reinforced Murray's fallen status:

> If to her share some Female Errors fall,
> Look on her Face, and you'll forget 'em all.[59]

Murray was once again depicted in fashionable dress with an elaborate bodice, ruched muslin *fichu* and three-quarter sleeves frilled from the elbow and decorated with dark ribbon. She stands with a sheet of music in her right hand, while her left hand rests on a table near to a closed book and fan.

Bennet, in an advertisement that he had placed in the *London Daily Advertiser* on 9 August, offered his print for sale at sixpence and claimed that it had been 'drawn from the life'. The suggestion that Murray had sat for the portrait was disingenuous, for a cursory inspection of the print reveals that Murray's head, including the provocative kiss curl and signature chip hat, had been repurposed from a mezzotint after Morland. Bennet was clearly trying to produce his print as cheaply as possible while at the same time maximising his profits by giving the print a musical theme and using Murray's famous face to promote his business as a sheet-music dealer.[60]

As well as flattering portraits of beautiful women, print-shops also did a roaring trade in satires and caricatures, although satirical prints of courtesans were fairly uncommon. *The Morning Tast; or Fanny M---'s Maid, Washing her Toes* (1751) which showed Murray at her morning toilette was the work of an early caricaturist, the engraver, publisher, and pornographer George Bickham the younger (*c.* 1704/6–71).[61] At one time he had also been a drawing master at the academy at Greenwich which probably accounts for the quality of the engraving. Like Bennet, Bickham also publicised his print by placing an advertisement in the newspapers. The *General Advertiser*, dated 1 February 1751, announced that *The Morning Tast* was available for purchase at 6*d* plain, and 1*s* coloured, from Bickham's own address in May's Buildings in Covent Garden 'and at all the Print shops'.

Bickham's satire reflected the influences of William Hogarth on his work and *The Morning Tast*'s resemblance to the fourth plate of Hogarth's 'Marriage à la Mode' series entitled *The Toilette* (1743–45) is clearly evident. In both prints, Murray and Hogarth's countess are observed at their morning *levée* as they complete their toilette while entertaining their guests. In Bickham's engraving, however, the central figures of Murray and her maid are not borrowed from Hogarth but copied from a print by the French engraver Gabriel Huquier (1695–1772).[62] Entitled *Mezetin Comprend Bien Qu'il Lui Faut du Secours* (*Mezetin Understands He Needs Help*) after the painter Claude Gillot (1673–1722), the print was part of a set of twelve illustrations Huquier completed around 1732 for *Théâtre Italien: Livre de Scènes Comiques Inventée par Gillot*. The woman at her toilette in Huquier's print is harangued by Mezetin, a stock character from the Italian *commedia dell'arte*, while a maid washes her feet and another dresses her waist-length hair.

The Morning Tast is voyeuristic in style, for the onlooker is invited to enjoy, unobserved, a private view into Murray's apartment to watch her at her toilette. Here was an opportunity for the public at large to see Murray in a state of undress and to ogle her naked flesh, in print form at least, that few could afford in reality. Murray is centrally, if inelegantly, seated in a 'grandly panelled' room within a shaft of light that extends left to right from an open door.[63] She warms her right hand before a grate in which a small fire burns, but the print gives no sense of warmth, a motif perhaps for sex without love.

The focus of the print is Murray's exposed leg, which is naked to mid-thigh. It is awkwardly extended over a chamber pot that doubles as a wash basin, while her maid washes her foot. Behind Murray, a barber, the very antithesis of Hogarth's line of beauty, hunches over her long tresses with a curling iron. The maid's gaze directs the viewer to an enervated young man to the right who is seated beneath a portrait of two spotted dogs as they copulate on a tasselled cushion. The canine portrait serves to comment on the youth's relationship with Murray, and perhaps explains his incapacitation.

In contrast to Hogarth's countess, who offered her guests tea out of porcelain cups, Murray's hospitality is basic and the louche young man idly opens an oyster, a staple food among the lower orders that could be bought by the barrel from any street corner. Even in this subsistence food there was, however, a hint of affectation in that the oysters in question were the white and fleshy 'Native Miltons' from Kent, regarded as among the best in the country. Across the expanse of floorboards the young man's leg and gaze signpost the viewer toward a lawyer who holds a rolled up deed of settlement under his arm, suggesting Murray was once more in negotiation with a prospective protector. Even with a wealthy keeper on the horizon, so the print suggests, Murray was unwilling to give up her nightly pleasures with dubious men of her own choosing.

The room itself in *The Morning Tast* reinforces the notion of Murray's moral abandonment, her sexual availability and her lowbrow tastes. Clearly, the canine portrait and the decoration over the chimney breast, with its urn, dog's head and loose arrangement of swags, would not be found in refined households. Murray's uncultured tastes were further suggested by her choice of reading material for she holds in her left hand, a copy of one of the Ordinary of Newgate's regular publications, the sensationalist *Accounts of the Last Dying Speeches* of criminals condemned to hang at Tyburn. Given her fondness for rough-edged lovers and that the highwayman MacLaine had been executed only four months before the print's issue, *The Morning Tast* hinted that Murray might have had more than a passing interest in the ordinary of Newgate's publication.

If Murray was unattainable to all but the wealthy, there was still a way for gentlemen to enjoy an intimacy with her and to press her to their hearts. Watch papers, which were decorated with a range of miniature engravings and inserted inside pocket watches, were available for as little as threepence. These roundels of fabric or paper served the practical purpose of protecting watch cases against dust, but they also provided an opportunity for gentlemen to enjoy privately and, at will, the print of their choice simply by springing open the cover of their pocket watches.

Watch papers covered a bewildering number of themes from the depiction of epic battles and scenes from antiquity, to portraits of national heroes, clerics and statesmen as well as members of the royal family and aristocracy. Even relatively obscure characters like the grocer, Edward Bright, 'the fat man of Malden', could be found on a watch paper. There were also a large number of images available for those looking to share intimate moments with fashionable beauties, courtesans and actresses. In 1774, four years before Murray's death, Robert Sayer was advertising for sale 'designs in miniature for watch-cases' from his premises at 53 Fleet Street at threepence for plain, and sixpence for the 'neatly coloured' versions. Designed and engraved by Louis Philippe Boitard, the watch paper bearing Murray's image belonged to a set known collectively as 'The Four Seasons' – Miss Wilson appeared as spring, Murray as summer, Constantia Philips as autumn and Frances, Lady Vane as winter.[64] John June (fl. *c.* 1740–70) whom Joseph Strutt described in his 1786 biographical dictionary of engravers, as 'an English artist of no great eminence', also produced a watch paper design of Murray. This was copied from McArdell's mezzotint after Morland, and was decorated with a circlet of hearts 'burning ardently' around her.[65]

Murray enthralled a nation for almost a decade: she was known from the race tracks of Durham to the brown-stained parlours of threadbare soldiers near Waterford. She was glorified in poetry, prose and portraiture, and fashionable society slavishly followed her taste and copied her style. Indeed, Murray's celebrity lifestyle was such that she was said to have 'made more Whores than all the Rakes in *England*' out of women who were willing to turn prostitute in the hope that they, too, might emulate her wealth and 'grandeur'.[66]

Her assiduous cultivation of her persona as an elite courtesan kept her at the top of her profession and in demand by the wealthy few who could afford her. Her very exclusivity and unattainability fuelled an obsession with her among the public at large and the desire to possess her in some form, be it as a mezzotint, a watch paper or a Fanny Murray cock.

It was the kudos attached to her name that no doubt prompted Sir Francis Dashwood, so tradition has it, to introduce her to the most scandalous secret gentlemen's club of the eighteenth century. The exact name of the club is unknown and it has been variously described as the Order, Society, Knights, Brotherhood or Friars of St Francis in honour of its founder.[67] Today, it is known simply as the most infamous of the hell-fire clubs.[68] It was there, so it is said, that Murray enjoyed her carnal pleasures as one of Dashwood's 'Nuns of Medmenham'.

Notes

1 George Alexander Stevens, *The History of Tom Fool*, 2 vols (1760), vol. 2, p.178.
2 'The Connoisseur' in Alexander Chalmers (ed.), *The British Essayists ...* (1817), vol. 31, p.4 (no. 47 for 19 December 1754).
3 *The Centinel*, 2nd ed., 2 vols (Dublin: 1758) vol. 1, p.169 (no. 36 for 30 July 1757).
4 Archenholz, *Picture of England*, vol. 1, p.109.

5 *The Westminster Magazine: or, the Pantheon of Taste* (February 1785 issue), vol. 13, p.78.

6 *Public Advertiser*, 24 March 1759. See also, *Harris's List* (1761), p.49.

7 Pointon, 'Lives of Kitty Fisher', p.79.

8 *Horse and Away to St. James's Park* ... [1760], p.1. See also, *N&Q*, 3 Ser. VIII (29 July 1865), p.82; McCreery, *Satirical Gaze*, pp.86–91.

9 *The Derby Mercury*, 18 October 1781.

10 'Polly. A new Song', in the supplement to *The Universal Magazine* (1757), vol. 20, p.330. See also, *Memoirs*, vol. 2, p.80. Mary Robinson's carriage was famous for its cipher which was designed to suggest a royal coronet and thereby, her royal connections. Byrne, *Perdita*, p.132; *Vis à Vis of Berkley Square*, p.24 (footnote).

11 Quoted in Andrea Di Robilant, *A Venetian Affair, A True Story of Impossible Love in the Eighteenth Century* (& New York: Fourth Estate, 2004) p.215.

12 Casanova, *History of My Life*, p.933.

13 For the life of Sophia Baddeley, see Hickman, *Courtesans*, pp.29–81.

14 Elizabeth Steele, *The Memoirs of Mrs Sophia Baddeley* ..., 6 vols (1787), vol. 2, pp.146–47.

15 Ambross, *Life and Memoirs of the Late Miss Ann Catley*, p.51.

16 Jessica Munns, 'Celebrity Status: The Eighteenth-Century Actress as Fashion Icon', in Tiffany Potter (ed.), *Women, Popular Culture, and the Eighteenth Century* (Toronto: University of Toronto Press, 2012), p.74.

17 Byrne, *Perdita*, pp.203 and 208. The large bead at the bottom of a lacemaker's bobbin is still known as a 'Kitty Fisher Eye'.

18 Sarah Bakewell, *The Smart: The True Story of Margaret Caroline Rudd and the Unfortunate Perreau Brothers* (Chatto & Windus, 2001), p.153.

19 *The European Magazine and London Review* ... (James Asperne, June 1804 issue), vol. 45, p.413. Nancy Dawson (*c.* 1728–67) was particularly famous for her hornpipe dance which she performed in *The Beggar's Opera*.

20 Mrs Mary Clementina Hibbert Ware, *The King of Bath: or, Life at a Spa in the Eighteenth Century* ..., 2nd ed., 2 vols (Charles J. Skeet, 1879), vol. 2, p.292.

21 *The Complete Letter-Writer* ..., 2nd ed. (1756), p.170.

22 *Lady's Magazine* (April 1785 issue), vol. 16, p.191.

23 William Dodd, *The Sisters: or, the History of Lucy and Caroline Sanson, Entrusted to a False Friend*, 2 vols (1754), vol. 1, p.75.

24 Dodd, *Sisters*, vol. 1, pp.74–75.

25 Stella Tillyard, *Aristocrats: Caroline, Emily, Louisa and Sarah Lennox 1740–1832* (Chatto & Windus, 1994), p.155. Bourque, 'Blind Items', p.77 has illustrations of nine other portraits that were painted in the Kitty Fisher style.

26 Pages are misnumbered in this part of the text. This quotation is to be found in vol. 2, Ch. 9.

27 See David Mallet, 'The Reward: or, Apollo's Acknowledgements to Charles Stanhope' (written 1757), and 'Cupid and Hymen: or, The Wedding-Day', in Samuel Johnson, *The Works of the English Poets* ..., 58 vols (1779), vol. 53,

pp.299 and 185 respectively. This is not to be confused with the tract by Henry Carey entitled 'Cupid and Hymen: or, a Voyage to the Isles of Love and Matrimony ...' (1742). When the poem was republished in 1748, an advertisement in the *General Advertiser* dated 13 October added that 'Cupid and Hymen' was 'Address'd to that irresistable [sic] Charmer Miss Fanny M----y'. The 'Flora' reference is in *The Adulteress* (1773), p.vii. The 'Venus' reference is in *British Worthies: or Characters of the Age ...* (1758), p.14 (footnote). See also, Hill, *The Inspector*, vol. 2, p.300.

28 Eliza Fowler Haywood, *The Invisible Spy by Exploralibus*, 4 vols (1755), vol. 2, p.285.

29 *Clio and Euterpe: or, British Harmony: A collection of celebrated songs and cantatas ...*, 3 vols (1762), vol. 2, p.104.

30 *Universal Magazine* (November 1755 issue), vols. 16–17, pp.223–24. According to copies held in the British Library, the song might have first appeared in 1750. (Ref: BL – Music Collections G.313. (205) and H.1601.a(48)).

31 Charles Burney, *A General History of Music, from the Earliest Ages ...*, 4 vols (1776–89), vol. 4 (1789), p.667.

32 Murray might also have been the subject of 'Salute to Miss Fanny Murray', a piobaireachd composed for the Highland bagpipes by John MacGregor, piper to Lt Col John Campbell of Glenlyon, which was entered in a piping competition at Edinburgh in 1786. It is more likely, however, that the salute was intended for a member of the family of Atholl. See Iain I. MacInnes, 'The Highland Bagpipe: The Impact of The Highland Societies of London and Scotland 1781–1844' (unpublished M.Litt. thesis: University of Edinburgh, 1988), p.336.

33 *Gentleman's Magazine: or, Monthly Intelligencer* (July 1732 issue), vol. 2, no. 19, p.856.

34 Martin C. Battestin, 'Fielding and "Master Punch" in Panton Street', in *Philological Quarterly* (1966), vol. 45, no. 1, pp.191–208; Martin C. Battestin with Ruthe R. Battestin, *Henry Fielding: A Life* (& New York: Routledge, 1989), p.439.

35 McCormick, *Hell-Fire Club*, p.147. See also, Fergus Linnane, *The Lives of the English Rakes* (Piatkus, 2010), p.135 (footnote). It has not been possible to verify this claim from contemporary sources.

36 *General Advertiser*, 9 March 1748.

37 Prostitutes were often described, to humorous effect, as ships. See, for example, *Harris's List* (1761), p.80 where Miss Lee was described as 'a Dutch built, squab vessel [who] stores a great deal in the hold'.

38 *Centinel*, vol. 1, p.102 (no. 22 for 2 June 1757).

39 Dabhoiwala, *Origins of Sex*, p.312.

40 *The Newcastle Courant*, 2 July 1748; William Pick, *An Authentic Historical Racing Calendar ...* [York: 1785], p.47. See also, *Whitehall Evening Post*, 5–7 September 1749.

41 John Cheny, *An Historical List of Horse-Matches Run ...* (1751), p.55; Reginald Heber, *An Historical List of Horse-Matches Run ...* (1760), vol. 9, p.39.

42 *The Crab-Tree* (1757), p.84 (no. 14 for 26 July 1757).

43 *The Witling …* (1749), p.3; *A Key to the Witling …* (1750), p.3.

44 *Ben Johnson's Jests …*, 3rd ed. [1755], pp.92 and 115.

45 *The Monthly Mirror Reflecting Men and Manners …* (April 1796 issue), vol. 1, p.337.

46 *Joe Miller's Jests …*, 7th ed. [1744], p.93.

47 Mrs Gillespie Smyth (ed.), *Memoirs and Correspondence … of Sir Robert Murray Keith …*, 2 vols (Henry Colburn, 1849), vol. 1, pp.370 (and footnote), 374 and 377.

48 See also, Richard Lee Bradshaw, *Thomas Bradshaw 1733–1774: A Georgian Politician in the Time of the American Revolution* (Bloomington, Indiana: Xlibris, 2011), p.128.

49 Lord Mahon (ed.), *The Letters of Philip Dormer Stanhope, Earl of Chesterfield …*, 4 vols (Richard Bentley, 1845), vol. 3, p.216. Letter dated 31 July 1747. In this context, the anecdote, related by Richard Rigby, of a row between Murray and the diplomat Thomas Robinson might have been a coded reference to an unnamed third party. See Introduction, above, p.24.

50 [Robert Holloway], *The Phoenix of Sodom: or, the Vere Street Coterie …* (J. Cook, 1813), p.13. See also, Rictor Norton, *Mother Clap's Molly House: The Gay Subculture in England 1700–1830*, 2nd rev. ed. (Stroud: The Chalford Press, 2006), p.148.

51 See http://www.britishmuseum.org/collection. A note on *The Shepherdess* under the heading 'Inscriptions' explains that the museum's copy of the print was 'annotated in pencil on the verso Mrs Flora Macdonald? Fanny Murray'. Another print of *The Shepherdess* which was for sale in Oxford's print-shop at the time of writing, is similarly annotated in pencil and the sitter claimed as Princess Louisa, James II's daughter who died in 1712, eight years before the painter Henry Pickering was born. See also, McCreery, *Satirical Gaze*, p.98.

52 Samuel Derrick, *Letters written from Leverpoole, Chester, Corke …*, 2 vols (Dublin: 1767), vol. 2, p.8. Letter from Dublin dated 17 November 1760.

53 *Westminster Magazine* (February 1785 issue), vol. 13, p.79.

54 [Ange Goudar], *The Chinese Spy …*, 6 vols (1765), vol. 6, p.209.

55 Pages are misnumbered in this part of the text. This quotation is to be found in vol. 2, Ch. 9.

56 See http://www.britishmuseum.org/collection for various impressions of 'Miss Fanny Murray'. See also, John Chaloner Smith, *British Mezzotinto Portraits …*, 2nd part (Henry Sotheran & Co., 1879), p.884.

57 [Goudar], *Chinese Spy*, vol. 6, p.208.

58 McCreery, *Satirical Gaze*, p.83 (footnote 9).

59 Alexander Pope, 'The Rape of the Locke. A Heroi-Comical Poem', in *Miscellaneous Poems and Translations. By Several Hands* (1712), p.357.

60 http://www.bookhistory.blogspot.com/2007/01/berch-b.html – Ian Maxted (ed.), with newspaper extracts compiled by Victor Berch, *Exeter Working Papers in British Book Trade History*; 10 – 'The London Book Trades of the Later

Eighteenth Century: Names: B' (2007). See also, Bourque, 'Blind Items', p.13 and Introduction, above, p.28.

61 Frederic G. Stephens (ed.), *Catalogue of Prints and Drawings in the British Museum*. Division 1. Political and Personal Satires, 4 vols (1870–83), vol. 2 (1873), pp.866–67 and vol. 3, part 2 (1877), p.844; O'Connell, *London 1753*, pp.141–42.

62 See http://www.britishmuseum.org/collection – curator's comments for *The Morning Tast*.

63 O'Connell, *London 1753*, p.141.

64 *Robert Sayer's New and Enlarged Catalogue for the Year 1774* ... [1774] pp.79–80.

65 Joseph Strutt, *A Biographical Dictionary Containing an Historical Account of all the Engravers* ..., 2 vols (1785–86), vol. 2 (1786), p.57; O'Connell, *London 1753*, p.139.

66 *Congratulatory Epistle from a Reformed Rake*, p.12. See also, *Harris's List* (1789), p.58; *Juvenile Adventures*, vol. 1, pp.109–10.

67 Towers, *Dashwood*, p.148.

68 *T&C* (May 1773 issue), p.245 contains one of the earliest references to the Order of St Francis as a hell-fire club.

7

The Nuns
of Medmenham

The beauteous Murray has been here,
To shed the mournful lover's tear
On Dashwood's sad remains;
She brought Sir Archibald along,
And while the Muse inspir'd her song,
He listen'd to the strains

'Gods! (she exclaim'd with frantic start)
The urn contains the guilty heart
Of Whitehead, vile seducer!
Oh! But for him I'd been a Nun!
Except the affair with I-----n,
Unknown by Lords, and you, Sir.' [1]

On the evening of 25 May 1751, Murray attended a dinner party at one of the homes of Sir Francis Dashwood's close friend and political ally, George Bubb Dodington (1691–1762) and his wife, the former Mrs Beaghan.[2] The dinner took place either at Bubb Dodington's mansion in Pall Mall that adjoined Carlton House, or at his magnificently ostentatious villa in Hammersmith, known as 'La Trappe'.

At La Trappe, Bubb Dodington would have undoubtedly shown off his home's opulence by taking his guests on a tour that led 'through two rows of antique marble statues ranged in a gallery floored with the rarest marbles, and enriched with columns of granite and lapis lazuli'.[3]

Besides Murray, the other dinner guests that evening were Dashwood; Sir Charles Tynte, a Somersetshire MP; Sir Charles Mordaunt, MP for Warwickshire; and a Miss Benett, who might have been an actress.[4] Murray's dinner invitation was further proof of her entrées into the most costly, if garish, surroundings, equally at ease 'under painted ceilings and gilt entablatures' as in the company of wealthy landowners and politicians.[5]

The dinner invitation also suggests that Murray had remained in Dashwood's orbit after the Divan Club had disbanded in 1746. Even so, the scandalmongers did not speak of them as lovers. When, for example, Dashwood's amour with Miss Barry was exposed in a 'tête-à-tête' feature for January 1774, it was claimed that, in his youth, he had been involved with some of Murray's contemporaries, namely Constantia Phillips, Lucy Cooper (named Cowper in the article), Kitty Fisher and Francis Delaval's long-term mistress Elizabeth Roach (b. *c.* 1736). Murray, however, was not included in the list of Dashwood's paramours.[6]

Even before the demise of the Divan Club, Dashwood had been devising a new and altogether more exclusive and secret gentlemen's club for the entertainment of select friends, family and West Wycombe neighbours. The resulting 'Order of St Francis' probably held its earliest meetings at a variety of locations, including the private homes of the original members and the newly opened George and Vulture Inn, at Castle Court near Lombard Street.[7] It had always been Dashwood's intention, however, to move his club to a permanent, secluded venue, far from the prying eyes of London's gossip-mongers.

By the time he sat down to dinner with Murray and Bubb Dodington in 1751, Dashwood might have all but completed negotiations with his Buckinghamshire neighbour, Sir Francis Duffield, on the lease of a small twelfth-century Cistercian monastery called Medmenham Abbey (pronounced 'Mednam') that had been in the Duffield family for over 200 years.[8] The abbey was conveniently situated 6 miles from Dashwood's home at West Wycombe Park and only a five-hour drive from London.[9] As Dashwood gazed on Murray's beauty across Bubb Dodington's candlelit dining table, he might have considered the beautiful courtesan perfect for some of the lewder activities he envisaged within the cloisters at Medmenham.

Several claims, all unsubstantiated, have been made for Murray's involvement at the abbey, including that she boasted she had 'waited on the monks at Mednam' and that she was first introduced to Dashwood's 'Franciscan Order' by Lord Sandwich.[10] This might be true, but since Sandwich had first sampled Murray some five years previously, it seems more likely that, in pursuit of variety, he would have preferred newer, fresher faces to entertain him at Medmenham.

In any case, the dinner at the Bubb Dodingtons' shows that Murray needed no intermediary to reintroduce her to Dashwood after their Divan Club days, and is rare proof of a link between Dashwood and Murray at the time he was establishing his mock-religious order at Medmenham. A further indication of Murray's connection with Medmenham is to be found in a short poem entitled 'LINES written some Time ago upon FANNY MURRAY' subtitled 'Mausoleum, West-Wycome [sic] Hill' which appeared in the *Public Advertiser* in 1784, and is reproduced at the head of this chapter. The poem not only linked Murray with Medmenham but also alleged that her Medmenham *amours* had included an unidentified Sir Archibald, another unnamed lover, and Paul Whitehead, a minor poet and the Order's loyal secretary and steward. Allowing for poetic licence (Murray is depicted mourning over the body of Dashwood who died in 1781, when she actually predeceased him by three years), the poem is significant in reflecting contemporary perceptions of Murray's involvement with the Order.

Medmenham Abbey lies in the heart of the Buckinghamshire countryside, on the banks of the River Thames, between Henley and Great Marlow where the 'circling meanders' of the Thames form 'an inverted crescent' in front of what was, in Dashwood's time, a dilapidated monastery and adjoining derelict Elizabethan mansion.[11] The abbey's scenic location and its ruined appearance lent itself perfectly to Dashwood's vision of transforming Medmenham into a gothic fantasy and private retreat for friends and neighbours whom he had invited to join his Order.[12] It was there, at regular intervals throughout the year, that club members, known as 'friars' or 'monks', and their guests, gathered together to enjoy monastically themed revelries and participated in the mock-religious ceremonies and rituals, the banquets and carnal amusements that Dashwood had devised for their entertainment.[13]

Dashwood's inspiration for Medmenham was the utopic Abbey of Thélème, set in the Loire valley, as envisioned by François Rabelais in

Gargantua (*c*. 1535). The monastery of Rabelais's imaginings overturned traditional monastic values by creating, as he termed it, 'an institution of enlightenment' where monks and nuns, chosen for their handsomeness and amiability, lived together according to their own free will and pleasure, unfettered by law.[14] Rabelais took as his motto for Thélème, '*Fay Ce Que Voudras*' ('Do What You Will'), redacted from St Augustine's injunction '*Ama Deum et fac quod vis*' ('Love God and Do What You Will'). Rabelaisian free will was not, therefore, a prescription for unbridled licentiousness, indeed Thélèmites lived chastely together, but taught that right actions derived from the desire to love God and fulfil the Divine will.[15]

Rabelais's motto was inscribed over fireplaces and on chimney breasts throughout Medmenham, but most significantly over the porch of the main entrance. Dashwood, however, intended Medmenham to be the very antithesis of Rabelais's monastic utopia as his 'adolescent fondness for mockery and blasphemy' turned Christianity on its head and fused irreverence toward its religious rites with an unholy quest for illicit sexual pleasure.[16]

Dashwood began work immediately on converting his newly leased property to suit his purposes. He enhanced the abbey's gothic atmosphere by adding an ivy-clad cloister and a newly built 'ruined' square tower to the south-east corner of the frontage facing the river. Within the abbey itself he added new rooms to create a 'number of convenient apartments'. All the rooms, hallways and staircases were embellished with inscriptions and mottoes and, according to the radical politician John Wilkes's later jaundiced view, hung with Catholic prints and caricatures 'of a ludicrous turn'.[17]

Windows were reglazed with stained glass to add to the darkly ecclesiastical ambience, so that the abbey offered lovers enticingly gloomy rooms and recesses for sexual dalliance.[18] The gardens, too, reflected the Order's emphasis on sexual gratification over Christian ideals of righteousness and virtue. Maurice-Louis Jolivet, Dashwood's gardener at West Wycombe Park, created sexualised spaces for erotic pleasure at Medmenham, complete with obscene statuary and phallic symbols. If Wilkes is to be believed, a statue of Venus stood at the entrance to a cave with her buttocks, 'the two nether hills of snow', facing the onlooker and her back bent to remove a thorn from her foot. Inside the cave, according to Wilkes, the inscription on a mossy couch encouraged energetic fornication:

Ite, agite, o juvenes; pariter sudate medullis
Omnibus inter vos; non murmura vestra columbae,
Brachia non hederae, non vincant oscula conchae

Go into action, you youngsters, put everything
You've got into it together, both of you; let not doves outdo
Your cooings, nor ivy your embraces, nor oysters your kisses.[19]

The abbey's transformation was probably sufficiently advanced by the summer of 1752 for Dashwood to host an inaugural meeting of his 'Franciscan monks'. The covert nature of the Order, with its secretive mock-religious rituals, initiation ceremonies and 'sacred rites' that took place behind the locked doors of the chapel and chapter room, invited intense speculation and lurid gossip. By the time Duffield sold Medmenham in 1778, the Order was already associated with the most outrageous of the so-called hell-fire clubs.

Many of the rumours originated in 1763 when Wilkes, who probably joined the Order in 1760, broke with his former friends at Medmenham and exposed their secret activities to public scrutiny. This followed an acrimonious rift that divided the Order along political lines, with Wilkes, and the poets Charles Churchill and Robert Lloyd on one side, and Dashwood, Sandwich and other members of the Order on the other. The bitter quarrel, which played out at Westminster, caught Murray in its tailwind and is discussed in chapter nine.

The political rift saw Wilkes follow William Pitt, 1st Earl of Chatham and Thomas Pelham-Holles, 1st Duke of Newcastle into opposition on the appointment of John Stuart, 3rd Earl of Bute as prime minister (1762–63). Dashwood served in Bute's ministry as Chancellor of the Exchequer. It culminated, in 1763, in Wilkes's prosecution for seditious and obscene libel, engineered in large part by Sandwich.

Wilkes's first salvo, which was published in the *Public Advertiser* on 2 June 1763, directed a blow at Dashwood's reputation by describing the eroticism of his garden at West Wycombe Park, and hinting at 'the English Eleusinian Mysteries' of Medmenham. A detailed description of these mysteries appeared as an explanatory note to Churchill's poem *The Candidate* (1764), and was republished (without the poem) in a collection of Wilkes's letters in 1769.[20] Wilkes's politically motivated account turned Medmenham's erotic landscapes, statuary and inscriptions into emblems of 'monastic debauchery and intemperance' and aimed to discredit both Dashwood and Sandwich by association.[21]

His partisan revelations prompted further scurrilous and conjectural exposés. The most significant of these was Charles Johnstone's four-volume novel entitled *Chrysal; or The Adventures of a Guinea*, which followed the coin as it passed from hand to hand and into the pocket of one of the Medmenhamites. *Chrysal* had first appeared in 1760 but was republished in 1765, in a revised and larger edition, to take account of Wilkes's disclosures. Although highly fictionalised and sensationalist in nature, the novel became an influential and quasi-authoritative account of Medmenham, and the source of many of the subsequent claims for its excesses.

As a result, Dashwood's Order has been linked to the practice of everything from witchcraft, Satanism and human sacrifice, to freemasonry and political conspiracy, from black arts and black masses, to lesbianism, orgies and incest.[22] In reality, however, the activities of the Order were far less lurid. It might not have been the respectable gentlemen's country club suggested by Dashwood's biographer, Betty Kemp, but the immorality of the monks of Medmenham appears to have extended no further than the pursuit of conviviality, sexual pleasure, and a mischievous enjoyment of religious mockery.[23]

There was no sign of the gathering storm clouds in the meetings that Murray was likely to have attended between 1752 and 1754, when the club's novelty, the cheerful company of the monks and nuns, the scenic location and extravagant entertainments, combined to create a self-contained clandestine world of pleasure and fantasy. Members entered into the spirit of the Order by adopting pseudonyms so that Wilkes, who was MP for Aylesbury, became John of Aylesbury, and Dashwood, Francis of Wycombe. They also dressed up in the clerical vestments of the Order, and while this might conjure erotic images of Murray in a nun's habit, the garments worn by the monks and nuns of Medmenham were sexless, white-trousered ensembles. According to Walpole, who looked round the abbey in 1763 after he had tipped the housekeeper to gain entrance, the habits looked 'more like a waterman's than a Monk's, & consist[ed] of a white hat, a white jacket & white trousers'.[24]

The Order's emphasis on the pursuit of pleasure and heterosexual gratification demonstrates the centrality of women to Dashwood's vision at Medmenham. As Walpole expressed it, 'whatever their doctrines were, their practice was rigorously pagan: Bacchus and Venus were the deities to whom they almost publicly sacrificed'.[25] In a similar vein, Whitehead's biographer, Edward Thompson, described Medmenham's monks as 'happy disciples of *Venus* and *Bacchus*, got occasionally together, to celebrate Woman in wine'.[26]

The fullest account of the role of women at Medmenham is to be found in *Nocturnal Revels*, a gossipy two-volume survey of London's sexual underworld, written anonymously by a 'Monk of the Order of St Francis'.[27] It has been suggested that this was Agnes (real name Mary) Perrault, who was rumoured to have been Dashwood's mistress, and whom Whitehead was said to have introduced to Medmenham as 'St Agnes'.[28] Some of the claims in *Nocturnal Revels* were clearly exaggerated, such as the assertion that there were lying-in facilities and obstetric services at Medmenham.[29] Equally overstated were suggestions that the offspring of women made pregnant by the monks were cared for, in perpetuity, by the Order and suitable work found for them within the abbey. In reality, the Order was too short-lived to service any children in this fashion and, as Walpole observed in 1763, there was only one 'Maid to dress their dinner & clean the house, but no other Servants'.[30]

According to *Nocturnal Revels*, only women 'of a Chearful, lively disposition, to improve the general hilarity' were invited to join the sisterhood – in other words, the nuns of Medmenham were expected to be convivial company and, in contrast to the nuns of Thélème, enthusiastically promiscuous. They did not disappoint – when John King from Ashby in Lincolnshire, sent his apologies to Dashwood for missing a meeting, he also sent his 'Mirth to the Sisterhood'. In his letter dated 3 September 1770, he referred to the nuns as those 'who are determined to exert their spiritualities there … for I assure your Lordship their spirits are willing but the Flesh is weak'.[31]

The licentiousness of the nuns has given rise to speculation that consignments of whores and virgins were delivered to Medmenham, as required, from the brothels of London, and especially Charlotte Hayes's superior establishment at King's Place in Pall Mall.[32] Dashwood's biographer, Eric Towers, found this improbable, arguing that the monks would have preferred whores of their own choosing rather than taking 'pot-luck on an assorted group sent down to the country'.[33] Donald McCormick, however, claimed the existence of a diary belonging to Hayes, entitled *Memoirs of a London Abbess*, in which she had noted for 19 June 1759 that she would provide 'Twelve Vestals for the Abbey. Something discreet and Cyprian for the Friars'.[34] The diary has proved untraceable, but Hayes's connection with Medmenham was noted by an anonymous poet in 1775:

> A lady abbess, Charlotte Hayes retires,
> And pimps are metaphos'd into Friars.[35]

According to *Nocturnal Revels*, each monk was permitted by the rules of the Order, to invite a female guest. The names of these women are a matter of guesswork, if only because the monks were scrupulous about safeguarding the identities of their nuns. Even Wilkes maintained discretion on this point.[36] The author of *Nocturnal Revels* claimed that there was a 'rite' which was designed specifically for the nuns' protection and which was performed shortly after the monks and their guests arrived at Medmenham. The monks were said to pass 'in review' before the nuns, who were disguised with masks. Any nun who recognised 'an unwelcome acquaintance', presumably a brother, father, husband or lover, could 'retire without making any apology, or revealing themselves to any but their temporary husband'.

Aside from Murray, Hayes and Perrault, the only other Cyprians to have been speculatively connected to Medmenham are Lucy Cooper, Betsy Wemyss, Elizabeth Roach and the procuress Elizabeth Dennison, who might have been wrongly associated with the Order on account of her 'Hellfire Dennison' nickname.[37]

Women from the same social class as the monks might also have formed part of the sisterhood, since Medmenham offered adulterous wives the opportunity for private dalliances with their monkish lovers away from the prying eyes of cuckolded husbands. The presence of higher-class women at Medmenham was underlined in *The Candidate* where Churchill noted that some of the nuns had reputations that stood to be compromised or 'undone' by the monks:

> Whilst Womanhood, in habit of a Nun,
> At M[edmenham] lies, by backward Monks undone.[38]

Evelyn Lord's suggestion in *The Hell-Fire Clubs*, that Dashwood extended invitations to married gentlewomen of his acquaintance, some of whom might have accepted the opportunity for sexual variety and intrigue, adds weight to the premise.[39] Of the elite women whose names have been connected with the Order, only Frances, Lady Vane, author of the scandalous *Memoirs of a Lady of Quality*, seems a likely candidate. Of the others, Lady Betty Germain (1680–1769), the daughter of the 2nd Earl of Berkeley, was in her seventies by the time the Order was meeting at Medmenham, while Dashwood's favourite half-sister Mary Walcot was dead by 1741. It has been suggested that Lady Mary Wortley Montagu, who was in her sixties and living abroad for most of the 1750s, might have been accorded an honorary membership, but as with most of the claims for the nuns of Medmenham, this too is unsubstantiated.

The primary duty of the nuns, as noted in *Nocturnal Revels*, was to provide jovial company and to participate enthusiastically in the revelries. As the premier courtesan of the day, it probably fell to Murray to head the evenings' lascivious entertainments. Geoffrey Ashe, in his study of the Order, suggested that some of the diversions at Medmenham included group sex, as well as the public or private enjoyment of sex toys provided by the Order. He described an '*Idolum Tentiginis*, a sort of hobby horse in the shape of a cock, with a phallus-beak turned backwards so that a woman bestriding it could stimulate herself'.[40] Other commentators agreed that bacchanalian orgies were a central feature of Medmenham's diversions. Militating against this view, however, was the claim in *Nocturnal Revels* that nuns were regarded as the 'lawful wives of the brethren' for the duration of their stay, and that monks were 'religiously scrupulous not to infringe upon the nuptial alliance of any other brother'. The only exception to this rule was the abbot who was elected for the day, wore a red hat to denote his office, and had first choice of the nuns.

Daytimes at Medmenham were heavily punctuated by compulsory attendance at communal meals which were taken in the newly built refectory. These were extravagant affairs that aimed at 'the improvement of mirth' and where there was 'no constraint with regard to the circulation of the glass'. Outside mealtimes, monks and their temporary wives were at liberty to amuse themselves. The author of *Nocturnal Revels* painted a rather improbable picture of the nuns, prostitutes and high-born ladies alike, withdrawing together, perhaps to the opulent drawing room which was furnished with 'two or three long drinking sofas, covered with green silk damask' to make 'select parties among themselves, or entertain one another, or alone, with reading, musick , tambour-work, &c'.[41]

The public rooms were well equipped with musical instruments, back-gammon tables, chessboards and cards, while the library was stocked with a range of titles, from novels and religious works to a selection of erotica and pornographic literature.[42] It was the wish of Sir William Stanhope, Dashwood's neighbour at Eythrope and fellow Medmenhamite, that such works would 'now and then occasion an extraordinary ejaculation to be sent up to heaven'.[43] At Medmenham, the very acts of 'reading, writing, play, or conversation' were sexually charged and when discussions 'unexpectedly become too warm and passionate, the use of fans is allowed, to prevent the appearance of the Ladies' blushes; and under these circumstances, some females seize this opportunity for a temporary retreat with their paramours'.

Lovers might have retired to the gardens or to their bedrooms where, Walpole noted, 'each [monk] is to do whatever he pleases in his own cell, into which they may carry Women'. In contrast, however, to the luxury of the public rooms and despite the Order's emphasis on sexual pleasure, the bedrooms to which lovers retreated were cramped, spartan and win-dowless, containing 'little more than a bed', as if nothing should distract from amorous intent.[44]

Meanwhile, back in London, what of Murray's protector, Sir Richard Atkins? He was presumably left to kick his heels about town or in Clapham while Murray disappeared to Medmenham for days at a time in the intimate company of other men. Despite having been High Sheriff of Buckinghamshire (1750–51), Atkins was never associated with Medmenham, either as member or guest. Indeed, if Murray kept to the Order's pledge of silence, he might have been wholly ignorant of her involvement with the Order.

Little is known of their life together during the early 1750s. It seems likely, however, that during 1750, when Murray was conducting her affair with Robert Tracy, that Atkins and Murray spent time at Durdans, the country retreat that Atkins had leased. They might have also attended the races at Epsom, where Atkins's 6-year-old black horse 'Surley' ran on 18 May 1750.[45]

By May 1751, however, Murray was involved with Edward Strode. The *Memoirs*, perhaps not wishing to tarnish their portrayal of Murray as naturally virtuous, did not mention her affair with this new and violent lover. Rather, and in the absence of anything more newsworthy, her biographer conjured up two continental adventures for Murray and

Atkins. The first was a trip to Paris which, as a piece of journalistic fancy, aimed at ridiculing the mincing ways of the French and puffing Murray as internationally irresistible.[46] Contriving to delay Atkins in London with business, the *Memoirs* (1:154) imagined Murray, unfettered by her protector, taking Paris by storm as '*l'ange Angloise*'. In a storyline that even the *Memoirs* (1:167) admitted was 'beyond the bounds of reason', Murray's finest moment came during a hunt at Fontainebleau when she attracted the attention of none other than the King of France.

The second trip, arranged for the summer of 1756, was purportedly a cruise to Genoa with a party of friends. The plan for the voyage, claimed the *Memoirs*, had been hatched over dinner at the Shakespear's Head Tavern, perhaps two years previously, by Atkins and Murray, and their friends Frank Delaval and his mistress Elizabeth Roach, Dashwood's one-time lover.[47] According to the *Memoirs*, the planned cruise was cancelled, but it is possible that a less ambitious trip to Paris went ahead, for it has been claimed that George Bodens, gentleman usher to the king from 1738 to 1779, saw Murray and her friends while he was in Paris. A 'tête-à-tête' for April 1781, subtitled 'The Memoirs of Colonel Witwou'd and the Bird of Paradise' ran an exposé of Bodens's affair with the courtesan Gertrude Mahon (1752–*c.* 1808), whose love of colourful clothes had earned her the 'Bird of Paradise' sobriquet. She once had an affair with Captain Ned Harvey, who had seduced Murray as a young girl in Bath. Given the unreliable nature of the 'tête-à-tête's' style of reporting, it is always possible that the columnist was simply rehashing what he had read in an old copy of the *Memoirs*, or was relying on gossip that had circulated in the early 1750s. Nevertheless, 'The Memoirs of Colonel Witwou'd' claimed that while in Paris, Bodens 'met with a number of acquaintance, amongst whom were Sir Richard Atkins, Sir Francis Delaval, Mr Foote, Lady Echlin [Elizabeth Roach], and Fanny Murray'.[48]

The anticipated sea voyage to Genoa was aborted, so the *Memoirs* claimed, just before the friends were due to sail when Atkins 'fell ill of a violent fever' and died three days later. He was 28 years old. The *Memoirs* (2:158) portrayed Murray as exhausting herself in the care of her protector during his last hours and inconsolable at his death, choosing to 'shut herself from the world for some weeks'. Murray's plight, so the *Memoirs* claimed, was exacerbated by the fact that the sudden onset of Atkins's final illness had prevented him from making a will and providing for his lover's financial security.

This account of Atkins's sudden death and intestacy, Murray's bereavement and subsequent penury, has been adopted in successive retellings of her story. It is, however, largely untrue, since Murray and Atkins had been estranged for up to two years by the time of Atkins's death on 10 June 1756. Indeed, and as will be discussed in the following chapter, Murray had married the handsome actor David Ross just three weeks before Atkins died. Atkins gave little outward appearance of being wounded by his break with Murray. At the end of August 1754, he had been spotted at a grand ball at the Assembly Rooms in York where over 500 nobility and gentry were in attendance.[49] Six months later he might have been with a new lover, for when his coach overturned in Pall Mall the newspapers reported that the occupants of the coach were Atkins, a gentleman and two ladies.[50] It was also in March 1755, probably to celebrate his 27th birthday, that Atkins 'gave a great Entertainment, at which a young Bear, which had been kept on Bread and Milk and Sugar, was roasted, and served up whole'.[51]

By the end of the year, however, Atkins's health was deteriorating, and he would have realised that he was seriously, if not terminally, ill at least six months before his death. On 1 January 1756 he signed a long and detailed last will and testament which stated that while of sound mind, he was 'in bad health of body'. Two further codicils followed on 19 January and 29 May.[52] Not surprisingly, Murray was not a beneficiary in her former lover's will, although he did leave £1,000 to a mysterious Ann Reynolds of Queen Street in Mayfair, described only as a spinster. Was she, perhaps, Atkins's new lover and one of the occupants of the overturned coach?

Atkins died at Arlington Street in Piccadilly and, in accordance with his instructions, his body was returned to Clapham for burial. On 17 June, he was interred in the Atkins's family vault in the churchyard of the crumbling twelfth-century parish church of St Mary's.

The end of Murray's turbulent eight-year relationship with Atkins coincided with the fact that her days as a top-ranking courtesan were numbered. By the summer of 1754, Murray had been doing the rounds of London for almost a decade and, at the age of 25, she was already old for a courtesan. As *Harris's List* expressed it for Kitty E[mer]son in 1773: 'all things wear out. Brooms will wear to the stumps. Seven years in constant use is a long time.'[53] Newer, fresher faces, and Kitty Fisher in particular, were a constant challenge to Murray's primacy. As Murray took stock of her perilous situation, the case of her friend Elizabeth Roach was a harsh reminder of the precarious and vulnerable status of the kept woman.

Roach and her sister Deodata were the illegitimate daughters of Major John Roach and Mrs Mary Anne Raworth, and both girls had been born and brought up in India. Their father died when the girls were about 12 years old, and in November 1748, John Potter, the under-secretary of state for Ireland and husband of Delaval's cousin, Susanna, agreed to be their legal guardian until their coming of age.[54] It was on a visit to Seaton Delaval Hall when Roach was perhaps 19 that her long-term liaison with Atkins's friend, Delaval, began. Some accounts insist that the young heiress was tricked into her affair by a secret marriage which turned out to be a mock ceremony.[55]

Roach was exceptionally beautiful, yet she was fiery tempered and had an unfortunate manner that often gave offence. The actor/man-ager Tate Wilkinson called her 'the goblin Miss Roach, a horrid spectre' while the actress Eliza Baker who had heard that Roach 'was indelicate in conversation', was determined to avoid her 'like a viper'.[56] Delaval, by contrast, was drawn to Roach: her foul language, and the feistiness that led her to challenge a rival to a pistol duel in Hyde Park, served only to amuse him. In addition he shared with her a disregard for convention, so much so that Lord Chesterfield was deeply offended by their scandal-ous conduct: 'Miss Roach exhibits to the public [a great belly] of seven months by the eldest Delaval, and neither of the *belligerent* or contracting parties seems to care who knows it.'[57]

As well as her beauty and fiery temperament, one of Roach's undoubted attractions for Delaval was her inheritance, small though it was. When Roach came of age, Delaval quickly ran through her legacy and she was left in a penurious state by his and her own profligacy. In August 1758, Roach acknowledged receipt of £1,558 12s 6d from Delaval's brother, John, who managed the Seaton Delaval estate, in part settlement of her personal debts amounting to £2,000. She owed money to at least twenty-five creditors including £66 19s 2d to Mr William Wright a coach maker in Longacre, and £150 8s 0d to Mr Robinson, a jeweller in Leicester Fields.[58]

Any hopes that Roach might have harboured of marriage to Delaval were dashed when, on 8 March 1750, he married Atkins's step-aunt, the middle-aged, 'monstrously fat' and dull-witted Lady Isabella Powlett (or Paulett), (d. 1764) in order to repair his squandered fortune.[59] Nevertheless, Roach remained his mistress, and by 1754 had borne him two children, purposely named Francis and Frances, and had endured the ignominy of a court case when Lady Delaval instituted divorce proceedings against her husband on the grounds of his adultery with Roach.[60]

By 1758 Roach had left Delaval and was living in Curzon Street in Mayfair. In September, she married an 18-year-old Irish baronet, Sir Henry Echlin but was soon back with Delaval, despite knowing that 'neither his attention nor his honour in any thing that relates to me or indeed to himself can be relied on'.[61] It is unclear how long Roach remained with Delaval, who died in 1771, but by the 1760s she had sunk to the level of a 'drab provincial actress'.[62]

A similarly miserable fate could have easily awaited Murray now that she was without a wealthy keeper or any long-term financial settlement. Thrown back on her own devices, she would need to muster all her talents and resourcefulness to support herself as she considered her options. At worst, she could return to the streets and the brothels which she had patrolled some ten years earlier, or she could, as Charlotte Hayes had done, once her looks began to fade, set herself up as an upmarket brothel-keeper with a nunnery of girls to work for her. Alternatively, she could, as both Constantia Phillips and later Harriette Wilson chose to do, publish her memoirs and blackmail her former lovers by offering to excise their names for a fee.

Murray chose none of these alternatives. In 1755 she took a momentous decision that would change the course of her life. She wrote a letter to the son of the man who had first seduced her to beg his assistance, and John Spencer of Althorp heeded her plea.

Notes

1 *Public Advertiser*, 27 September 1784.
2 Walters, *Royal Griffin*, p.76 suggested that Bubb Dodington was one of Murray's lovers.
3 Richard Cumberland, *Memoirs of Richard Cumberland. Written by Himself ...*, 2 vols (1807), vol. 1, p.185.
4 John Carswell and Lewis Arnold Dralle (eds), *The Political Journal of George Bubb Dodington* (Oxford: Clarendon Press, 1965), p.122 (and footnote 3 where Murray is described as a courtesan and actress), entry for 25 May 1751.
5 Cumberland, *Memoirs of Richard Cumberland*, vol. 1, p.185.

6 *T&C* (January 1774 issue), pp.9–10. See also, *T&C* (June 1773 issue), pp.289–90.

7 Dashwood, *The Dashwoods*, pp.27–28; McCormick, *Hell-Fire Club*, p.59.

8 The exact date that Dashwood signed the lease on Medmenham is unknown. Towers, *Dashwood*, p.144 and Gerald Suster, *The Hell-Fire Friars* (Robson Books, 2000), p.98 suggest 1751, which would mean Dashwood began using Medmenham around 1752. Burgo Partridge, *A History of Orgies* (Anthony Blond, 1958), p.151 and Ronald Fuller, *Hell-Fire Francis* (Chatto & Windus, 1939) pp.87, 93 and 271 suggest that Dashwood began using Medmenham in 1752 or 1753. George Martelli, *Jemmy Twitcher: A Life of John Montagu 4th Earl of Sandwich 1718–1792* (Jonathan Cape, 1962), p.44 puts the date later again, as 1755. If Murray, who had retired from prostitution by 1755, was one of the nuns, this would suggest the earlier date for the club's first meetings is correct.

9 Carswell and Dralle (eds), *Political Journal of George Bubb Dodington*, p.133, entry for 19 September 1751 – 'set out from Wycombe at half past ten: arriv'd at Hammersmith at half past three'.

10 See, for example, Geoffrey Ashe, *Do What You Will: A History of Anti-Morality* (& New York: W.H. Allen, 1974), p.130; Linnane, *English Rakes*, p.135; Daniel P. Mannix, *The Hell-Fire Club* (New English Library, 1970), p.37; Suster, *Hell-Fire Friars*, p.90. Towers, *Dashwood*, p.168; Walters, *Splendour and Scandal*, p.73. Both Burford and McCormick are sceptical about Murray's involvement at Medmenham. See E.J. Burford (ed.), *Bawdy Verse: A Pleasant Collection*, (Harmondsworth: Penguin, 1982), p.272; McCormick, *Hell-Fire Club*, p.153.

11 *T&C* (May 1773 issue), p.245, reprinted in the introduction to *Nocturnal Revels*.

12 The identities of the members and their guests, including the inner circle of thirteen monks, is discussed in Ashe, *Do What You Will*, pp.119–24; Dashwood, *The Dashwoods*, pp.37–38; Linnane, *English Rakes*, p.130; McCormick, *Hell-Fire Club*, pp.94–112; Suster, *Hell-Fire Friars*, pp.239–41; Towers, *Dashwood*, pp.146–47.

13 Ashe, *Do What You Will*, p.125; Jones, *Clubs of the Georgian Rakes*, p.125.

14 Towers, *Dashwood*, p.149. See also, Ashe, *Do What You Will*, pp.9–24.

15 Elizabeth Chesney Zegura (ed.), *The Rabelais Encyclopedia* (Westport, Connecticut: Greenwood Press, 2004) p.74.

16 Ashe, *Do What You Will*, p.99.

17 *T&C* (May 1773 issue), p.246.

18 Thomas Langley, *The History and Antiquities of the Hundred of Desborough …* (1797), p.343.

19 *Letters between the Duke of Grafton---and John Wilkes, Esq …*, 2 vols (1769), vol. 1, p.38; Dashwood, *The Dashwoods*, p.31.

20 *Letters between the Duke of Grafton …*, vol. 1, pp.34–40. See also, John Almon (ed.), *The New Foundling Hospital for Wit … Part the Third* (1769), pp.71–75; Jones, *Clubs of the Georgian Rakes*, p.120.

21 *T&C* (May 1773 issue), p.245. See also, Wendy Frith, 'Sexuality and Politics in the Gardens of West Wycombe and Medmenham Abbey', in Michel

Conan (ed.), *Bourgeois and Aristocratic Cultural Encounters in Garden Art, 1550–1850* (Washington DC: Dumbarton Oaks, 2002), pp.285–309. The view that Wilkes aimed at discrediting his former friends by exposing the activities at Medmenham is disputed by Audrey Williamson, *Wilkes: 'A Friend to Liberty'* (George Allen & Unwin Ltd, 1974), pp.39–40.

22 See, for example, Mannix, *Hell-Fire Club*, pp.25–32; Suster, *Hell-Fire Friars*, pp.4–13. Ashe, *Do What You Will*, p.131 discussed Medmenham as a cover for political scheming and Towers, *Dashwood*, p.151 for freemasonry. Henry Blyth, *Old Q: The Rake of Piccadilly: A Biography of the Fourth Duke of Queensbury* (Weidenfeld & Nicholson, 1967), p.85 mentioned lesbianism. Ronald Paulson, *Hogarth's Harlot: Sacred Parody in Enlightenment England* (& Baltimore, Maryland: The John Hopkins University Press, 2003), pp.153–58 and Askham, *Gay Delavals*, p.75 described Black Masses, while Partridge, *History of Orgies*, p.156 suggested Satanism. Incest was suggested in John Hall-Stevenson, 'The Confession of Sir Francis of Medmenham, and of the Lady Mary his Wife', in *The Works of John Hall-Stevenson, Esq* ..., 3 vols (1795), vol. 3, p.270. See also, McCormick, *Hell-Fire Club*, pp.155–59.

23 Betty Kemp, *Sir Francis Dashwood: An Eighteenth-Century Independent* (Macmillan, & New York: St Martin's Press, 1967), p.132; Martelli, *Jemmy Twitcher*, p.47; Clement Shorter, *Highways and Byways in Buckinghamshire* (Macmillan & Co. Ltd, 1910), p.146.

24 Horace Walpole, *Journals of Visits to Country Seats, etc.* (Oxford: Oxford University Press, 1928), vol. 16 of *The Walpole Society*, pp.50–51; Towers, *Dashwood*, p.158

25 Horace Walpole, *Memoirs of the Reign of King George the Third*. First published by Denis Le Marchant, Bart, and now re-edited by G.F. Russell Barker, 4 vols (Lawrence & Bullen, 1894), vol. 1, p.138.

26 Edward Thompson, *The Poems and Miscellaneous Compositions of Paul Whitehead* ... (1777), p.xxxviii.

27 Medmenham is described in the unpaginated introduction to volume one of *Nocturnal Revels* and all further quotations from *Nocturnal Revels* refer to this introduction.

28 Ashe, *Do What You Will*, p.130; Blyth, *Old Q*, p.85; McCormick, *Hell-Fire Club*, pp.65–67 and 154. Williamson, *Wilkes*, p.42 claimed that as Perrault died in the middle of the nineteenth century, she was too young to be concerned in the early activities at Medmenham.

29 See also, Martelli, *Jemmy Twitcher*, p.45.

30 Walpole, *Journals of Visits to Country Seats*, p.50.

31 Quoted in Dashwood, *The Dashwoods*, pp.25–26. See also, Lord, *Hell-Fire Clubs*, p.102 who gives the date as 3 September 1758.

32 Linnane, *English Rakes*, p.122; Martelli, *Jemmy Twitcher*, p.48; Suster, *Hell-Fire Friars*, p.87.

33 Towers, *Dashwood*, p.150.

34 McCormick, *Hell-Fire Club*, p.153.

35 'The Boat-Race, a Poem', quoted in *London Magazine* (November 1775 issue), vol. 44, p.594.

36 Unusually, John King named a 'Curtois Novice' in his letter to Dashwood dated 3 September 1770. The 11th Baronet suggested that this was probably Mary, the daughter of the Reverend John Curtois of Branston. See Dashwood, *The Dashwoods*, p.26.

37 Blyth, *Old Q*, p.86; Ashe, *Do What You Will*, pp.129–31; Linnane, *Lives of the English Rakes*, pp.134–36. See also, McCormick, *Hell-Fire Club*, pp.148–63 and 197–98; Suster, *Hell-Fire Friars*, pp.87–91.

38 Charles Churchill, *The Candidate. A Poem* (1764), p.33.

39 Lord, *Hell-Fire Clubs*, p.102. Williamson, *Wilkes*, p.38. See also, C.F. Lascelles Wraxall, *Life and Times of Her Majesty Caroline Matilda …*, 3 vols (W.H. Allen & Co., 1864), vol. 1, p.9.

40 Ashe, *Do What You Will*, p.129. According to John Hall-Stevenson, in ancient times such sexual aids were used in religious ceremonies. See John Hall-Stevenson, *Crazy Tales* (1762), p.80 (footnote).

41 *T&C* (May 1773 issue), p.246.

42 Dashwood, *The Dashwoods*, pp.29–30; Towers, *Dashwood*, p.153.

43 Quoted in Dashwood, *The Dashwoods*, p.30. The 11th Baronet claimed the letter was written by Sir William Stapleton on 5 September 1761. Stapleton died, however, in January 1740. Ashe, *Do What You Will*, p.126, Linnane, *Lives of the English Rakes*, p.133 and Suster, *Hell-Fire Friars*, p.104 are among those who have claimed that the letter was written in 1758 by Sir William Stanhope. Hinde, in *Tales from the Pump Room*, p.40 has claimed that Murray was mistress to Stanhope (and Lord Chesterfield). Peakman in *Whore Biographies*, vol. 3, p.4 also suggests that Murray was mistress to Stanhope, but it has not been possible to verify this.

44 Walpole, *Journals of Visits to Country Seats*, p.50.

45 *London Evening Post*, 5–8 May 1750.

46 See Peace, '1759 and the Lives of Prostitutes', pp.86–87.

47 Askham, *Gay Delavals*, p.75. See also, Bleackley, *Ladies Fair and Frail*, p.23; Burford, *Wits, Wenchers and Wantons*, p.83.

48 *T&C* (April 1781 issue), p.177.

49 *Public Advertiser*, 31 August 1754.

50 *Whitehall Evening Post*, 6–8 March 1755.

51 *Newcastle Courant*, 22 March 1755.

52 National Archive – Prob/11/823/177. The main business of the will was to safeguard the Clapham estate and ensure that it was not simply subsumed into the estates of Atkins's brother-in-law, George Pitt. The estate was devised to Atkins's sister, Penelope, and on her death in 1795, to Atkins's godson Richard Bowyer (1745–1820), on condition that he take the Atkins's family name. Richard Bowyer was the son of William Bowyer, 3rd Baronet of Denham Court in Buckinghamshire, and his wife, Atkins's aunt Anne Stonhouse (d. 1785). When Bowyer became Richard Atkins Bowyer by private Act of

Parliament, Atkins had ensured, from beyond the grave, that the family name lived on.

53 *Harris's List* (1773), p.76.
54 WNA – 'Order of the Court of Chancery' dated 16 November 1748. (Ref: 2DE/42/3/1).
55 William Parson and William White, *History, Directory, and Gazetteer of the Counties of Durham and Northumberland ...*, 2 vols (1827–28), vol. 2 (1828), p.410.
56 Tate Wilkinson, *Memoirs of his Own Life ...*, 4 vols (York, 1790), vol. 2, p.10 and vol. 4, p.250.
57 Lord Mahon (ed.), *Letters of ... Earl of Chesterfield*, vol. 3, pp.451–52.
58 WNA – (Ref: 2/DE/42/3/6 and 2/DE/42/3/5).
59 The amusing story of Delaval's marriage is told in Askham, *Gay Delavals*, pp.50–54.
60 See *The Trial of Sir Francis Blake Delaval ... for Committing Adultery with Miss Roach, alias Miss La Roche ...* [1782].
61 WNA – (Ref: 2/DE/42/3/7). Letter from Elizabeth Roach to John Delaval, dated 4 May 1759.
62 Ambross, *Memoirs of the late Ann Catley*, pp.23–25; Askham, *Gay Delavals*, p.118; *N&Q*, 10 Ser. XI (26 June 1909), pp.501–2. See also, William Worthen Appleton, *Charles Macklin: An Actor's Life* (& Cambridge, Mass.: Harvard University Press & Oxford University Press, 1961), p.131; *The Leeds Intelligencer*, 10 September 1771.

8

'A New Born Creature'

A much fam'd nymph who lately led the fashion,
And prov'd that love's her universal passion:
But M---y pr'ythee why so strangely alter'd:
You've said, that before marry'd, you'd be halter'd.
But laudable however is your plan,
You've lost the town, and gain'd an honest man.
Honour to you, who've known all scenes of life,
To make an honest, sober, virtuous wife:
Take care, your new-gain'd virtue safely keep,
No more let titles lull that gem asleep;
Never let one false step your marriage cross,
But rest in safety with the name of Ross.[1]

Murray's seducer, the alcoholic John Spencer, died at his Wimbledon home at the age of 37 on 19 June 1746 'merely because', as Horace Walpole expressed it, 'he would not be abridged of those invaluable blessings of an English sub-ject, brandy, small-beer, and tobacco'.[2] As already noted, he had suffered bouts of illness since at least 1738 and recurrent episodes of venereal disease had also taken its toll on a man who refused to compromise his pleasures for the sake of his health.

In the event, he only outlived his grandmother, Sarah, dowa-ger Duchess of Marlborough, by twenty months, for she died 'very little regretted, either by her own family, or the world in general' on 18 October 1744.[3] Before her death and after much vacillation, she had finally made Spencer her sole heir and willed to him her vast fortune. There was, however, a double irony to Spencer's inherited wealth, for not only did he not live long to enjoy it, but his domineering grand-mother managed to control his fortune from beyond the grave. Spencer could not so much as settle his debts, estimated in 1738 to have been over £20,000, since his grandmother had tied up most of his inheri-tance in trusts. In addition, by the terms of her will, Spencer and his descendants were prevented from holding any court or government office apart from the honorary title of Ranger of Windsor Great Park.[4] This exclusion from public service and political power, while intended to protect Spencer and his heirs from political corruption, had the dis-abling effect of locking Spencer and John (1734–83), his only son and heir, into a frustrated aimlessness.

On his father's death, the 12-year-old John, created 1st Baron Spencer of Althorp in 1761 and 1st Earl Spencer in 1765, became 'probably the wealthiest schoolboy in the land'.[5] Brought up with minimal parental control and hidebound by his great-grandmother's will, the heir grew up to be a great patron of the arts, but otherwise without direction, addicted to gambling and profligate like his father.

His saving grace, however, was that on 20 December 1755, the day after his 21st birthday, he followed his heart and married Margaret Georgiana Poyntz (1737–1814), the youngest daughter of the diplomat Stephen Poyntz, in a secret ceremony at Althorp.[6] Lord Spencer's bride was a well-educated young woman with 'a most sensible, generous, deli-cate mind': she was also deeply philanthropic and it was for her 'offices of benevolence and piety' that she was particularly remembered follow-ing her death in 1814.[7]

A letter dated 21 October 1758, from Anne Donnellan to her friend the bluestocking Elizabeth Montagu, spoke of Lady Spencer as 'a natural good young woman, no airs, no affectation, but seems to enjoy her great fortune by making others partakers, and happy with herself'.[8] In simi-lar tones, Lady Stafford commented on her skill in 'the Art of leading, drawing, or seducing People into right ways'.[9] Only a waspish Fanny Burney detected conceitedness in Lady Spencer's philanthropy. On her reacquaintance with the countess in Bath in 1791, Burney commented that in terms of her 'active charity and zeal, that she would be one of the most exemplary women of rank of the age, had she less of show in her exertions, and more of forbearance in publishing them'.[10] Lady Spencer's supposed pretentions aside, she and her husband proved a redemptive force for Murray and changed the course of her life.

Among her many papers – for Lady Spencer was a prolific letter writer – is a collection of over 2,500 letters related to her charitable works, dating from the 1750s until the time of her death, which are now preserved in the British Library.[11] After the death of her husband in 1783, Lady Spencer painstakingly arranged the correspondence in approximate alphabetical sequence, with each batch of letters from individual petitioners placed in chronological order. Some of the letters are annotated in Lady Spencer's own hand as she made brief summaries, usually on the backs of letters, of actions taken and amounts disbursed. Lady Spencer explained, in tones that would have irked Burney, that her careful record of her own philanthropic deeds and those of her late husband, were intended as a tribute to his memory and as 'a Cordial – to remind me of my Lord's never failing Generosity and Humanity and of the earnestness with which I executed and sometimes endeavoured to imitate his benevolence'.[12]

Lady Spencer's letters include fifteen that relate to Murray's petition – nine were written by Murray herself, one by the Spencers and five by the man who became Murray's husband in 1756, the actor David Ross. Murray's letters, which allow her own authentic voice to be heard for the first time, are formal rather than intimate, being addressed principally to her aristocratic benefactors. Even when she wrote to cheer Lady Spencer during an illness, Murray was reserved and offered no personal insights – 'I have no news to tell you', wrote Murray, 'nor is there any thing I know worth troubling you with'.[13] Nevertheless her letters are invaluable in casting a revelatory new light on her life from the watershed period when she turned her back on prostitution to the time of her death in 1778.

During 1755, keen observers of the *haut ton* would have noticed that Murray had withdrawn from the demi-monde and from prostitution. If rumours were circulating about her retreat from London's social scene, they were not generally reported in the newspapers. Only *Jackson's Oxford Journal*, dated 25 January 1755, suggested a change in Murray's circumstances. Sixteen months before she married Ross, it carried an erroneous report that 'the celebrated Fanny Murray was married a few Days since, to a Foreigner of Distinction'.

By the late autumn of 1755, Murray was endeavouring to give up prostitution and to live respectably. To this end, she petitioned Lord Spencer,
the son of her seducer, in the hope that he would offer his charitable
assistance. Her letter is now lost, but according to the *Memoirs* (2:185–8),
Lord Spencer (who was not referred to by name but only as 'one of the
best men living') informed her that she should hear from him once he
had looked into her background and the veracity of her claims. There
is no record of such an exchange, but by mid-December, Lord Spencer
had instructed a Captain Smith to visit Murray at her New Palace Yard
home to inform her of his decision to grant her petition. Believing Lord
Spencer to be in the country, Murray delayed sending her 'unfeined
thanks' until 20 December. Unbeknown to Murray, she had chosen to
write to her newly acquired benefactor on his wedding day.

Along with Murray's original petition, any account of the process that
led her to approach the Spencer family is now lost. The only source for
this period of her life is the *Memoirs* which, as usual, must be treated
with caution. Murray's biographer claimed that the threat of Newgate
Prison, following her arrest for debt and a spell in a sponging house, first
prompted Murray to approach Lord Spencer. Murray's biographer also
claimed to have seen a copy of her original petition, which he reproduced in the *Memoirs* (2:186–7). The letter, like other 'original' documents
presented in the biography, is undoubtedly an invention. Nevertheless, its
emphasis on Murray's impecuniosity and her determination to renounce
her former life reinforced the themes of Murray's authentic letters to the
Spencers in which she stated her desire to begin life afresh, unencum-
bered by debt and released from the necessity of prostitution:

Sir,

Without being able to claim any personal acquaintance with so truly
exalted a character as yours; prompted by the universal opinion of your
beneficence, I have dared pen these lines to you, to demand your aid.

The small pretence I can make to your attention, would but disturb the
ashes of your honoured father, whom you resemble in all his great deeds,
without one of his faults. I have long endeavoured to quit that vicious
path, which a first false step hurried me into. All my efforts have been
frustrated, and yet my disposition for penitence is more fervent than ever.

I am now upon the very brink of ruin, – my inhuman creditors have
been prevailed upon (by a wretch who proposed sinister and cruel

advantages to himself from my detention) to make all their demands at once; and without I can immediately raise the money, I shall be conducted to a loathsome prison, where, perhaps, I may remain for life.

This, Sir, is my present situation, and if it claims your pity, it will procure your beneficence; which the most unkind treatment of all my pretended friends has forced me to supplicate.

I am, Sir, with a thorough sense of your many virtues, your most obedient humble servant,

Fanny M———

Sceptics could argue that Murray's abrupt rejection of her former life was politic rather than genuine. After all, she might have only ceased to appear in public because her debts precluded her from the carriages and finery required of a top-ranking courtesan. According to the *Memoirs* (2:176), she was 'scarce able to support the appearance of a gentlewoman'. It is also true that she had given every indication of enjoying prostitution, faithlessly abandoning Atkins on numerous occasions to consort enthusiastically with a variety of often ill-chosen rakes and libertines. In addition, Murray would have been well aware that any assistance from the Spencers was contingent upon convincing displays of repentance and reformation. Murray's change of heart might indeed have been driven by expediency, especially if she had noticed a dropping off in trade, a fading of her beauty and a new breed of Cyprian poised to depose her. What is undeniable, however, is that from the day she wrote to the Spencers until the day of her death, Murray kept faithfully to her promises of exemplary conduct and never returned to her former way of life.

Lord Spencer's dilemma in coming to Murray's assistance was to ensure that his relief of her financial distress acted not as an aid to further vice but as an encouragement to her moral reclamation and future good behaviour. His solution to the problem of Murray's long-term reformation proved a judicious, if unusual, one. Lord Spencer determined to settle a lifetime annuity upon her, and pay off her current debts on condition that she agreed to an arranged marriage and promised exemplary behaviour. His decision was dutifully summarised by Lady Spencer on the back of Murray's letter dated 20 December, in which she had gratefully accepted Lord Spencer's proposition – 'My Lord granted her a sum of £160 a yr for her life to enable her to quit the way of life she was in & to marry Ross the actor'.[14]

How David Ross first came to Lord Spencer's attention as a potential husband is unknown. Captain Smith, whom Murray addressed affectionately in one of her letters as 'my good Friend Captn Smith', might have had a part to play.[15] He was certainly the go-between, acting on behalf of Lord Spencer in the marriage negotiations that followed. If Smith knew of Ross as an eligible bachelor, he might have made the initial approach and taken informal soundings from Ross at his Bow Street lodgings in Covent Garden, before making his recommendation to Lord Spencer.

Ross certainly had much to commend him as a prospective groom – he had received a gentleman's education at Westminster School and was an established actor on the Drury Lane stage. He earned enough, therefore, to provide for Murray in a modest way, but without being able to afford any of the corrupting extravagances of her former life. The couple's future comfort would depend on their honest hard work and sensible economy. Among Ross's other qualities, Murray's intended husband was convivial, easy-going and, fortunately for Murray, handsome. Indeed, one drama critic, writing in 1757, at the time of Ross's transfer from Drury Lane to Covent Garden Theatre, said that 'the smoothness of his complexion, and the softness of his looks' made Ross almost too handsome for the stage.[16]

Affable and genial though he was, Ross was not weak and compliant in the way that Atkins had been, but combined an easy confidence around women with a commanding authority. If it is possible to believe the following rare anecdote which featured the actress and dancer Nancy Dawson, Ross would have been equal to the task of managing the petulant temper tantrums for which Murray was well known:

Some years ago when Mr Ross (the player, was a young man) he happened to be in the stage box of one of the theatre's royal. Nancy Dawson came on the stage, he addressed her in a free manner, saying, 'on my soul Nancy, you look charmingly to-night.' The lady made no answer, but immediately gave him a slap on the face; fired with resentment, at such a piece of impoliteness, he did not know how to revenge himself; he considered she was a woman – and yet to return a blow in public. – However, he soon recovered from his confusion, and stepping up to the lady, took her round the waist and fairly turned her upon her head, then gently setting her on *her legs again*, he bowed to the audience saying, 'my countrymen will, I hope, be satisfied that it was not a *man* who struck me.'[17]

Murray's proposed husband showed much theatrical promise, and his early career augured well for the future. He had made his debut at the Smock Alley Theatre in Dublin on 8 May 1749 as Clerimont in Henry Fielding's *The Miser*. A couple of years later he transferred to Drury Lane where he was engaged for the 1751–52 season by the theatre's actor/ manager, David Garrick. Making his acting debut on an English stage on 3 October 1751 playing Young Bevil in Richard Steele's popular comedy *The Conscious Lovers*, his performance was well received 'by a polite and distinguishing audience'.[18] According to Ross's good friend, John Taylor, Colley Cibber, the famous actor/manager, once told Ross that he was the best Young Bevil that Cibber had seen on stage since the days of the actor Barton Booth (1681–1733).[19] Murray had every reason to be pleased with the man who had been chosen for her as her husband.

In Murray's reply to Lord Spencer, dated 20 December, she grasped with both hands the new life he offered her. After a career that had placed Murray on intimate terms with members of the lesser nobility, powerful politicians and even royalty, she was now eager to proceed as expeditiously as possible with marriage to a middling actor of modest means whom she might only have seen on the stage or known by reputation. She offered profuse thanks to her 'generous Benefacter' for his willingness to relieve her 'from an unhappy situation which necssity [sic] might plunge [her] into'.[20] His proposal, it would seem, had arrived in the nick of time before poverty and fear of debtors' prison had forced her back into prostitution. The speed with which Murray accepted Spencer's proposition was a measure of her resolve, or perhaps desperation, to 'begin the world as a new Born Creature', free from debt and unobligated to lovers.[21]

Murray did not have to wait long for Ross's response to Lord Spencer's offer – within days she received a letter from him agreeing to the match. Ross had just made himself the most envied man in England, yet he was aware that there were disadvantages to bedding the most desirable woman of the age. Murray's beauty aside, Ross's motives for agreeing to the match are unknown – it is possible that he felt pressured into agreeing to Lord Spencer's proposition, and judged that the advantages to his career and reputation of a connection with this powerful aristocratic family outweighed any damage that could be inflicted by the sudden acquisition of a notorious wife with a disreputable past.

It is clear, however, from one of the conditions he placed on his acceptance, that he was concerned to protect his reputation should his intended bride renege on her earnest assurances of reform and bring the reckless lifestyle of the courtesan to his door. Understanding too well that any lapse in her behaviour would cost him his name and his credit-worthiness, and render him a laughing stock, Ross asked that the marriage be kept secret until Murray had had time to prove herself.

There was a touch of sardonic humour in the suggestion, in the *Caledonian Mercury* dated 9 November 1767, that Ross's motives for marrying Murray were mainly economic, 'especially when it is considered', reported the newspaper, 'that his finances have been improved by a fortunate marriage with Miss Fanny Murray, whose *friends* had placed her in a state of affluence'. After Ross's death in 1790, retrospectives on his life also mooted that financial expediency and a desire to gain possession of her annuity had been Ross's sole purpose in marrying Murray. The *Edinburgh Magazine* was typical in suggesting that 'Ross's dissipations demanded such an addition to his fortune, and as the lady retained nothing of her former situation but her charms, the contract was signed, and the marriage celebrated'.[22]

Such claims were dismissed by loyal friends like Taylor who insisted, in his memoirs, that at the time of his marriage, Ross was in possession of a good salary.[23] Ross did, however, have financial problems. These stemmed from a difficult relationship with his father, Alexander, and were exacerbated by a lifelong mismanagement of his personal finances that was less apparent at the time of his marriage. His father had been a writer to the signet in Edinburgh before moving to London in 1722 to become a solicitor of appeals. Ross was born in London six years later on 1 May 1728. At the age of 13 a permanent rift developed between father and son, which was probably caused by Ross's theatrical ambitions. Alexander Ross was never reconciled to his son's chosen profession and when he died at Gray's Inn in March 1753 he disinherited Ross by bequeathing his lands 'of Little Daan and Muyblairie, in the shire of Ross, together with several heritable bonds on lands in Scotland' to Ross's sister, Elizabeth. To add insult to injury, by the terms of the will, Elizabeth was to pay Ross 'the sum of one shilling, on the first day of every month of May yearly, that being his birth-day, thereby to put him in mind of the misfortune he had to be born'.[24]

As a consequence, Ross was completely dependent upon his earnings from the theatre which, during the 1761–62 season, totalled £287. At the time of his marriage, Ross had been augmenting his earnings by undertaking summer seasons at the Jacob's Well Theatre in Bristol in 1752, 1754 and 1755, and gross receipts for Ross's benefits on 31 March 1752 and 8 April 1755 show that he added £200 and £150 respectively to his earnings on these occasions.[25] Murray's annuity, as the equivalent of just over half a basic season's work was, at first glance, an attractive proposition, but Ross was astute enough to realise that marriage to a former courtesan could, in the long run, adversely affect his earning power and creditworthiness.

When Ross asked that his nuptials be kept secret, it was not only to give Murray time to prove herself but also to ensure that 'some depend-ings and Expectations' which were due to him were not jeopardised. There were those, wrote Murray, who would be 'glad of any Excuse' to default on payments.[26]

She was right to be circumspect, for according to Ross, his marriage to Murray was still being used as the excuse for reneging on financial obligations several years later. On 5 March 1762, for example, Ross wrote to Lady Spencer to explain that his then straitened circumstances were in part owing to the fact that his relatives had shunned him following his marriage, and refused to support his benefit performance at the theatre, 'particularly Miss Ross of Conduit Street & many more glad I suppose of some Excuse since my marriage have withdrawn their friendship & usual favors at the Benefit'. The financial gains from Murray's annuity were, therefore, limited, while the idea that Ross married Murray for her money is too mercenary to fit with his gentlemanly and easy-going character.

Murray wrote to Captain Smith with news of Ross's acceptance shortly after her letter of thanks to Lord Spencer dated 20 December. She enclosed the letter, now lost, that she had received from Ross, giving his qualified consent to their marriage, and left it to Smith's discretion whether Ross's letter should be shown to Lord Spencer. Murray made it clear to Smith that if her new benefactor did not approve of the condi-tions Ross attached to their marriage, and the negotiations consequently fell through, she was willing to do whatever was required of her to prove her resolution to live respectably – 'I will goe in to the Country for some time if Mr Spencer likes of it,' wrote Murray, 'and where ever he pleases, and as he shall find by my behaviour, that I will doe everything he can ask or desire.'

Murray might even have pressed her suit at a private meeting with Lord Spencer. In her same letter to Smith, Murray urged him to arrange an interview with her benefactor so that she could convince him, face to face, of her determination to relinquish her former life. She added, as delicately as she could, that she would not be as destitute as she then was, had she not resolved to give up 'that', which word she had heavily underlined, and by which she meant prostitution:

> My intention was not to be any person Mistress, when he [Spencer] has been so good to enable me to Live without it, for I had a mine [mind] to be that, my Circumstance would not be in such a situation thay [sic] are in at present.

Details of their five-month courtship are vague, if only because of Ross's desire to keep the upcoming marriage secret. Since Ross had a weakness for 'the gratifications of the table', some of their meetings, during which they began to get to know one another, might have taken place over discreet late-night suppers after his performances at the theatre.[27] Other meetings might have been squeezed in between rehearsals, as Ross had a busy season while they were courting. On 16 January 1756 he played Young Bevil in *The Conscious Lovers* and again on 3 May.[28] Two weeks later, on 10 February, he was Osman in *The Tragedy of Zara* before taking the role of Egbert in a new play by John Brown entitled *Athelstan, A Tragedy*. Ross gave at least nine performances of *Athelstan* between the play's opening night on 27 February and its close on 18 March.

During April, Ross was even busier, playing Altamont in *The Fair Penitent*, Young Knowell in *Every Man in His Humour*, Rovewell in *The Fair Quaker of Deal*, Castalio in *The Orphan* and Lord George Brilliant, in *The Lady's Last Stake*. He also appeared in his own benefit performance of *The Tragedy of Jane Shore* which was advertised for 6 April with tickets available from Ross's house in Bow Street in Covent Garden.[29]

As the couple conducted their courtship in secret between Ross's rehearsals and performances, their affection grew and they settled into an easy and tender companionship with one another. Murray would have undoubtedly mounted a charm offensive to show herself off as beautiful and refined, yet also modest. Ross as 'a person finely form'd to please' would have matched her for charisma, handsomeness and elegance.[30] He would have undoubtedly wooed Murray with laughter, as Ross was a skilled raconteur and 'excelled in telling a humorous story', with the straightest of faces. Indeed, Taylor remarked that his friend's conversation 'more resembled the dialogue of Congreve's wits than that of any other person [he] ever knew'.[31] The intended marriage, based as it was on mutual affection and attraction, seemed set fair for success.

So, on the morning of Monday, 17 May 1756, Ross, one of Drury Lane's handsomest actors, married Murray, the most famous courtesan in England.[32] Her wedding day proved as unusual as the unique circumstances of her courtship. According to Taylor's recollections, 'the officiating priest', anxious at the prospect of joining Ross in holy matrimony to a woman of Murray's reputation, requested a private interview with her to satisfy himself of Murray's sincerity and fitness for marriage:

> Just before the marriage ceremony was performed, the officiating priest desired the bride to withdraw with him for a few minutes into the vestry-room. She consented, and he, delicately but solemnly alluding to her past life, told her that marriage was an awful and a sacred tie, and that unless she had determined to forsake all others and cleave only to her future husband, she would plunge herself into dreadful guilt by entering into the holy state. She appeared to be much affected at his doubts, but mildly assured him that it was her fixed resolution to lead a new life, and thereby endeavour to atone for former errors. The ceremony was then performed …[33]

The marriage was a quiet affair, in keeping with Ross's desire for secrecy, so that there might have been no one at the ceremony save the vicar and witnesses. Even when Ross bumped into one of his acquaintances, a Captain Hamilton, in the hours following his marriage, he remained tight-lipped about his nuptials.[34] There was no honeymoon, as Ross was back in the theatre on the evening of their wedding day, playing Captain Plume in a production of *The Recruiting Officer*.[35]

While the marriage remained secret, the couple probably kept up appearances by continuing to live separately – Murray at her house in New Palace Yard, and Ross in Covent Garden.[36] This arrangement might have continued for over a year, since one of Murray's letters to Lady Spencer showed that she was still paying rent on her lodgings in New Palace Yard in the summer of 1757. Their stratagem appears to have worked well, for the *Memoirs* (2:189) noted that, as late as 1759, 'the world are divided in their opinion, whether or no she is married'. Once the couple decided to make their marriage public, Murray probably left her New Palace Yard home to join Ross in Bow Street, and by 1762 the couple had moved to the nearby Little Piazza, south of Russell Street.[37]

On the morning following their marriage, Murray wrote to Lady Spencer with her wedding news and to remind her benefactors of the couple's desire for secrecy. To Murray's mind, this desire for discretion was less to do with financial expediency and more to do with giving her an opportunity to prove herself. Once she had 'behavd [sic] with prudence and Honor for some time to Mr Ross', wrote Murray rather poignantly, 'he need not then Blush to own me'. This was the first letter in which Murray signed herself as Fanny Ross and was a landmark moment in Murray's progress toward respectability. The last vestige of her old name and past life disappeared completely when she began to sign herself as F Ross and, sometime after 1757, as the altogether more reputable Frances Ross.

Even as Murray reported her nuptial felicity, she did not flinch from the delicate matter of asking Lady Spencer to intercede with Lord Spencer, on her behalf, for the outstanding monies he still owed on her rent arrears and small bills. In fact, there were a number of initial delays and teething troubles in settling Murray's debts and in organising the smooth running of the quarterly payments of her annuity.

It is telling that the new Murray was surprisingly assiduous in keeping track of her finances. She showed herself to be tactful and sensitive, yet firm and businesslike, in bringing her unpaid bills and overdue payments to the Spencers' attention, and she remained charmingly tenacious until unpaid accounts were settled. For example, Murray reminded Lady Spencer in a letter written in February 1756 that, as requested, she had sent her outstanding bills to Lord Spencer at Christmas 1755, but that she had heard nothing during the intervening two months, adding that the delay was 'a most Cruel Torment' and that 'the Tradesmen are Continualy Knocking at my Door and become rude and Troublsom'.

Murray was still pursuing the matter a year later. In a letter to Lady Spencer written in the early summer of 1757, Murray carefully acknowledged grateful receipt of two quarterly payments of her annuity, one of 30 guineas paid by Lord Spencer, and one of £30 from Lady Spencer, but she also reminded the Spencers that when the midsummer payment fell due, there would be a year's arrears payable on her annuity.[38] This was aside from the rent arrears on her house in New Palace Yard for which she paid £51 per annum.

Attaching a receipt dated 30 December 1755 for £38 5s 0d, as proof of payment to her landlord Robert Mathison, of three-quarters of the rent due, she once more respectfully reminded the Spencers that they had not made a quarterly payment on her rent since Lady's Day (25 March) 1756. Such delays and deferments were eventually ironed out, and the two remaining letters from Murray suggest that every New Year's Day, she sat down to write a letter in which she paid 'the tribute of a Gratefull Heart' to her benefactors in acknowledgement of the safe receipt, for another year, of her annuity.[39]

Details of Murray's annuity were widely, if erroneously, reported. It was a common mistake, one that had probably originated with the *Memoirs* (2:189), that the Spencers had settled £200 rather than £160 per annum upon her. Bubb Dodington made a joke about her annuity in a letter to Dr Thomas Thompson dated 27 March 1762. Referring to William Pitt's resignation as prime minister in October 1761, and the handsome pension of £3,000 per annum he had received, Bubb Dodington noted that he had done 'as Fanny Murray and others have done before him, his retiring from *Public Business* and living upon an annuity'.[40]

In 1781, the *Gazetteer and New Daily Advertiser* held up contemporaries of Murray, and Murray by association, as models of financial prudence for having accumulated sufficient funds to purchase annuities of £200 or £400 to assist them in old age. In reality, of course, Murray and her contemporaries had lived as recklessly as the next generation of *impures* for whom, said the *Gazetteer*, 'what is got on the Devil's belly, is spent on the back, and oeconomy takes no thought to chear the evening of their dirty day'.[41]

From the moment Ross placed a wedding band upon her finger, Murray proved a worthy recipient of the trust that had been placed in her by the Spencers and by Ross. The same could not be said of other former courtesans who had also given up the profession in order to marry. Nancy Parsons, for example, who had married Charles Maynard, 2nd Viscount Maynard in 1776, had become mistress to the 19-year-old Francis Russell, 5th Duke of Bedford by 1784. It was a similar story with Grace Dalrymple known as 'Dally the Tall', who married the physician John Eliot (or Elliot) (1737–87) in 1771. Eliot, who attended Murray in her final illness, divorced his wife in 1776 for her adultery with the Irish peer Lord Valentia.[42]

Murray, however, maintained an unassailable reputation throughout her marriage, and there was never a hint of impropriety in her manner or behaviour – in Taylor's words, 'her conduct was unimpeached, and probably unimpeachable'.[43] Edward Thompson in his poem *The Meretriciad* also paid tribute to Murray's marital virtue:

So *M----y* rose, but Lord how long ago?
When *Bath* was young, and *Nash* an infant Beau:
Soar'd from her basket to a Chariot Fame,
And lives this moment with the best good name.[44]

This good name was especially pleasing to Lady Spencer, as Murray had pledged to her, the day after her wedding, that she intended to 'come into the world with Grace and Reputation'.[45] It was, therefore, with evident satisfaction that Lady Spencer noted on the back of Murray's New Year's Day letter for 1777, which Murray had written from her lodgings in Tavistock Row in Covent Garden, that she had kept her promise of good behaviour, made at the time of her marriage to Ross '& lived with credit many years'.

Only Ross's friend Taylor had misgivings, but these centred on the couple's intellectual incompatibility rather than any concerns about Murray's previous immorality. He judged that Murray lacked sufficient mental agility to fully appreciate Ross's wit, sense of humour and skills as a raconteur.[46] Even so, Taylor readily conceded that 'there was nothing in [Murray's] manner or conversation that in the slightest degree indicated the free life from which she had been rescued by marriage' and he never doubted that his friend had married her 'from motives of real affection'.[47]

Ross described his tender feelings for Murray in a conversation with James Boswell on 9 January 1768, after they had been to the Theatre Royal in Edinburgh to see *The Suspicious Husband* and *The Citizen*. Back at Boswell's home, the two friends had 'supped and drank a cheerful glass' together before Ross confided 'all the history of his marriage'. Boswell did not record the details of their conversation, but Ross must have described his courtship and marriage in such an affecting way that it awakened in Boswell a desire for romance – '[Ross] put me into my old romantic frame,' wrote Boswell, 'I wished again for adventures, for proofs of my own address and of the generosity of charming women.'[48]

This portrait of Ross's marital harmony was challenged, however, by the report of his affair, around 1772, with the dancer Dolly Twist (d. 1774) which appeared in *Theatrical Biography* and which is discussed in chapter eleven. There were hints, too, of other liaisons. It would seem, therefore, that, like Boswell, Ross also wished for amorous adventure. Even so, the author of *Theatrical Biography* was surely wrong to suggest that Ross enjoyed extra-marital affairs at the theatre because 'his happiness was not at home' for there is no evidence of coldness between Murray and Ross in any of the personal recollections of their close friends.[49]

It must be acknowledged that in the wider world, Murray was still regarded as a symbol of immorality. Dr William Oliver, for example, a well-established physician from Murray's native Bath, cracked a joke in 'a long Shandean letter' to his Cornish clergyman cousin the Reverend William Borlase that depended for its humour on a shared recognition of Murray as promiscuous.[50] In this letter, written on 12 July 1760, Oliver ruminated on Laurence Sterne's *The Life and Opinions of Tristram Shandy*, the first two volumes of which had been published the year before. He remarked how Sterne was 'admired, beloved, not understood, and adored by all kinds of People, from the right Reverends down to Fanny Murray, Kitty Fisher, Lady Cov., and Mr. Whitfield'.[51] Oliver undoubtedly aimed at playful mischief by placing the Methodist preacher George Whitfield's name among women of uncertain reputation, but it is telling that, six years after she had withdrawn from prostitution, Oliver still thought of Murray as a courtesan at the lower end of his scale of virtue.

The year 1756 marked a watershed for Murray, as she turned her back on prostitution forever and began her new life as a respectably married woman. In so doing, she successfully transformed herself from a profligate spendthrift into a careful book-keeper, and from an enthusiastic prostitute into a decent and faithful wife. Murray did not marry into wealth, titles or political power, in the way that other celebrated courtesans such as Sophie Dubuchot, Elizabeth Armistead or Harriet Powell had done. Indeed, Murray's marital life would be a modest affair, punctuated by ups and downs, financial struggles and its fair share of disappointments. Nevertheless, and despite her husband's infidelities, theirs was a mutually supportive and affectionate marriage, and Murray's resolve to be an exemplary wife won her the respect of her benefactors, the Spencers, and the love of her husband, David Ross.

She never faltered from her chosen path, but throughout the trials and tribulations of her marriage she showed the strength of character and inner reserves that had been apparent from her early days in the brothels of London. She would need to garner these inner resources, for her marriage would be severely tested in the early 1760s as the media continued to capitalise on her former reputation as a courtesan, and she was engulfed by a major political scandal that sullied her hard-won good name. The political row, which embroiled former Medmenhamites, Lord Sandwich and John Wilkes, had a devastating effect on Murray as her name was dragged through the House of Lords, and she was ever afterward associated with 'the dirtiest poem in the English language'.[52]

Notes

1 *Woffington's Ghost. A Poem. In answer to The Meretriciad* (1761), p.15.
2 *Walpole Correspondence*, vol. 2, p.30. Letter to Horace Mann dated 20 June 1746.
3 Tobias Smollett, *The History of England from the Revolution to the Death of George the Second*, new ed., 5 vols (1796), vol. 3, p.143 (footnote).
4 Foreman, *Georgiana*, pp.6–7 (and footnote to p.6).
5 Harris, *Passion for Government*, p.349.
6 Although the Spencers were untitled before 1761, they are referred to throughout the text as Lord and Lady Spencer for purposes of clarification.
7 Lady Llanover (ed.), *Autobiography and Correspondence of Mary Granville, Mrs Delaney* (1861), vol. 3, p.340. Letter from Mrs Delaney to Mrs Dewes dated 3 March 1755; *Gentleman's Magazine and Historical Chronicle* (March 1814 issue), vol. 84, p.309.
8 Emily Jane Climenson (ed.), *Elizabeth Montagu, the Queen of the Bluestockings* ..., 2 vols (John Murray, 1906), vol. 2, p.148.
9 Castalia, Countess Granville (ed.), *Lord Granville Leveson Gower (First Earl Granville), Private Correspondence 1781 to 1821*, 2 vols (John Murray, 1917), vol. 1, p.312. Letter from Lady Stafford dated 30 November 1801.
10 Charlotte Barratt (ed.), *Diary and Letters of Madame D'Arblay* ..., 7 vols (Henry Colburn, 1842–46), vol. 5 (1843), p.250.
11 BL – Add MS 75714. Lady Spencer's charity letters are comprehensively analysed in Donna T. Andrew, 'Noblesse Oblige: Female Charity in an Age of Sentiment', in John Brewer and Susan Staves (eds), *Early Modern Conceptions of Property* (& New York: Routledge, 1995), pp.275–300.
12 Quoted in Andrew, 'Noblesse Oblige', p.276.
13 BL – Add MS 75714. Letter dated 28 March (after 1756).
14 Lady Spencer omitted to record that, aside from the annuity, her husband had also agreed to honour all of Murray's outstanding bills.
15 BL – Add MS 75714. Letter dated 18 May 1756.
16 Quoted in *Biographical Dictionary of Actors*, vol. 13 (1991), p.105. A detailed survey of Ross's theatrical career is to be found in vol. 13, pp.103–10.
17 *English Roscius*, p.109. See also, *Harris's List* (1761), p.39.

18 Thomas Davies, *Memoirs of the Life of David Garrick* ..., new ed., 2 vols (1780), vol. 1, p.160.

19 Taylor, *Records of My Life*, vol. 1, p.362.

20 BL – Add MS 75714. Letter dated 20 December 1755.

21 BL – Add MS 75714. Letter dated 18 May 1756.

22 *The Edinburgh Magazine: or, Literary Miscellany* (Edinburgh, 1790), vol. 12, p.151.

23 Taylor, *Records of My Life*, vol. 1, p.363.

24 William Maxwell Morison (ed.), *The Decisions of the Court of Session, From its Institution to the Present Time* ... (Edinburgh: 1804), vol. 17, pp.14948–49. In December 1769 Ross brought an action in the Scottish Court of Session and successfully contested his father's will. See Robert Hamilton, *Decisions of the Court of Session from November 1769 to January 1772* (Edinburgh: 1803), pp.71–74.

25 *Biographical Dictionary of Actors*, vol. 13, pp.105–06.

26 BL – Add MS 75714. Letter dated 18 May 1756.

27 Samuel Whyte, *A Collection of Poems, on Various Subjects, including the Theatre* ..., 2nd ed. (Dublin: 1792), p.292.

28 See *Public Advertiser* which publicised all theatrical events.

29 See, for example, *Public Advertiser*, 11 March 1756.

30 Hugh Kelly, *Thespis: or, a Critical Examination into the Merits of all the Principal Performers belonging to Covent Garden Theatre. Book the second* (1767), p.10.

31 Taylor, *Records of My Life*, vol. 1, p.363.

32 It has not been possible to locate their marriage certificate in parish registers held at WAC.

33 Taylor, *Records of My Life*, vol. 1, p.364.

34 BL – Add MS 75714. Letter dated 18 May 1756.

35 *Public Advertiser*, 17 May 1756.

36 Ross was lodging on the corner of the Great Piazza by March 1752, before he moved to Bow Street where he was a rate-paying resident between 1755 and 1760. See F.H.W. Sheppard (gen. ed.), *Survey of London, The Parish of St. Paul and Covent Garden* (The Athlone Press, 1970), vol. 36, pp.77 and 187–88.

37 *Public Advertiser*, 2 March 1762.

38 This would suggest that Murray's annuity amounted to just over £120 per annum rather than the £160 that Lady Spencer had recorded on the back of Murray's letter dated 20 December 1755. On the back of Murray's letter dated 1 January 1777, Lady Spencer had noted that Murray was in receipt of a 'Considerable annuity' of £150 per annum.

39 BL – Add MS 75714. New Year's Day letters are extant for 1777 and 1778.

40 Lloyd Sanders, *Patron and Place Hunter: A Study of George Bubb Dodington, Lord Melcombe* (John Lane, The Bodley Head & New York: John Lane Co., 1919), p.271.

41 *The Gazetteer and New Daily Advertiser*, 24 October 1781. A version of this also appeared in *The Amours of Carlo Khan* ... (1789), pp.182–83.

42 See Jo Manning, *My Lady Scandalous: The Amazing Life and Outrageous Times of Grace Dalrymple Elliot, Royal Courtesan* (& New York: Simon & Schuster, 2005).

43 Taylor, *Records of My Life*, vol. 1, p.364.

44 [Edward Thompson], *The Meretriciad*, 4th ed. (1763), p.34.

45 BL – Add MS 75714. Letter dated 18 May 1756.

46 Taylor, *Records of My Life*, vol. 1, p.51.

47 Taylor, *Records of My Life*, vol. 1, p.363.

48 Frank Brady and Frederick A. Pottle (eds), *Boswell in Search of a Wife 1766–1769* (& Melbourne & Toronto: William Heinemann Ltd, 1957), pp.123–24.

49 *Theatrical Biography: or, Memoirs of the Principal Performers* …, 2 vols (Dublin: 1772), vol. 2, pp.29–30.

50 Benjamin Boyce, *The Benevolent Man: A Life of Ralph Allen of Bath* (Cambridge Mass.: Harvard University Press, 1967), p.256.

51 William Copeland Borlase, *The Descent, Name and Arms of Borlase of Borlase in the County of Cornwall* … (George Bell & Sons and Exeter: William Pollard & Co., 1888), p.183. 'Lady Cov.' refers to Maria Gunning (1733–60) a society beauty who became Countess of Coventry on her marriage to George William (1722–1809), 6th Earl of Coventry.

52 Arthur H. Cash, *John Wilkes: The Scandalous Father of Civil Liberty* (& New Haven: Yale University Press, 2006), p.31.

9

'Awake my Fanny'

Awake, my Fanny, leave all meaner things,
This morn shall prove what raptures swiving brings.
Let us (since life can little more supply
Than just a few good Fucks and then we die)
Expatiate free o'er that lov'd scene of Man;
A mighty Maze! for mighty Pricks to scan.[1]

Fanny Murray described the pivotal moment of her transformation from courtesan to wife as a rebirth, but her renascence was not without its crises, challenges and disenchantments. For David Ross, too, marriage to a former courtesan, despite her exemplary conduct, brought its own peculiar stresses and strains. Putting aside his anxieties about the financial implications of marriage to a notoriously lewd woman, Ross was often too easily offended on Murray's behalf and overly protective in shielding her from perceived snubs, affronts or innuendos.

It was as well, therefore, that he did not hear of the actor Arthur Murphy's indirect attack on Murray, when Murphy described Ross as 'Fanny Murray's Cull'.[2] Cull, with its connotation of being duped by a cheat or prostitute, was a deliberately cutting reference to Murray's former life, her years of unblemished marriage notwithstanding.

As late as 1772, when Murray had been his wife for sixteen blameless years, Ross could still see snubs, borne of censure and disapproval, where perhaps none was intended. When, for example, George Colman, the acting manager of Covent Garden Theatre, failed to return Ross's visits, or to invite the Rosses to his home, Ross took it as a slight on Murray, and wrote to Colman to remind him of his manners and force a face-saving invitation for his wife:

> You are as unkind in the country as in town; for, though I have called several times at Bath House, [Colman's riverside home at Richmond] you have never been kind enough to look in upon us. Mrs Ross has often asked you, though you have never invited her to see your beautiful spot; she begs to be remembered to you.[3]

For the most part, however, adjusting to married life was more taxing for Murray. She might have been lonely, for example, for when plays were in production, Ross would have spent his days at the theatre in rehearsal and his evenings in performance. By the autumn of 1757, Ross had moved from Garrick's Drury Lane Theatre to join Covent Garden Theatre under the management of John Rich. Taking the lead role in *The Earl of Essex*, Ross made his debut there on 3 October 1757. The move to a new theatre company might have meant that Murray saw even less of her husband as he sought to make his mark by extending his repertoire and taking on more, and often leading, roles. There were to be further separations during the summers of 1762 and 1763 when Ross began to dabble in theatre management, and took companies of actors on tour to Manchester.[4]

This is not to say that Murray was completely without company, for Ross was gregarious by nature and friends and family were warmly welcomed to their home. Her days as a courtesan had made Murray an elegant and accomplished hostess, so that guests were treated to feasts of fine dining. Rare insights into their home life suggest that visitors tended to be Ross's male friends and family members, who came without female companions, and there is no record of any visits by Murray's own friends or family. John Taylor, for example, regularly came to play backgammon with Ross, and James Boswell sometimes joined the Rosses for supper after one of Ross's theatre performances.[5]

In his journal entry for 23 January 1768, for example, Boswell recalled dining at the Rosses in Edinburgh, in company with the actor John Sowdon and Robert Cullen, later Lord Cullen, after a performance of

Thomas Otway's *Venice Preserv'd*, in which Ross had played Jaffier.[6] Such evenings centred on male camaraderie but they might have also reflected a reluctance on the part of Ross's friends and acquaintances to introduce respectable ladies to a former courtesan, no matter how reformed. As their reminiscences revealed, when gentlemen friends called on the Rosses, they rarely saw beyond the woman who had once been Fanny Murray, to observe the then respectable Mrs Ross.

When, in November 1793, the writer known as Clytus recalled his invitations to the homes of the actors David Garrick, Ned Shuter and Ross, what he remembered was 'dining at the hospitable board of Ross (the celebrated FANNY MURRAY, then Mrs Ross, presiding)'.[7] Boswell, too, was fascinated by the courtesan rather than the wife. When he dined with the Rosses and Ross's nephew Walter Ross, a writer to the signet, on 15 April 1772, he was intrigued 'to see the celebrated Fanny Murray, as decent a Lady at her own table as any body'.[8] He was also charmed when, possibly on the same occasion, she made him 'a present of some very pretty straw mats for setting dishes on'.[9]

More testing than Murray's adjustment to the rhythms of married life was the realisation that her husband would neither fulfil his early theatrical promise nor provide the financial security she craved. Living with Ross taught Murray what theatre managers already knew – that while he was charming, witty and convivial, he was also unconscionably lazy and too much of a *bon viveur* to make a real success of his theatrical career. Ross's somniferous style of acting made him 'too apt to slumber over some scenes' and led to his reputation as 'a handsome piece of still life'.[10]

By the time Ross was performing at Covent Garden Theatre in the late 1750s, the actor/manager John Jackson had already determined that 'a natural inactivity, and the love of ease' were his 'great drawbacks'.[11] Indeed, Ross's self-indulgence led another actor/manager, Tate Wilkinson, to dub him the 'Prince of negligence'.[12] It was not only that Ross was lazy but, as Murray would discover, he easily lost heart if projects proved too daunting, or impinged too much on his enjoyment of life's other pleasures. As a result, the man who had had the potential to be a first-rate actor when he had courted Murray remained, throughout his life, a merely competent one in 'the second rank in tragedy and genteel comedy'.[13]

Away from the stage, Ross's 'love of ease' found particular expression in fine dining. The actor, Charles Lee Lewes (1740–1803), described

Ross's life as 'a comedy, where the whole business and plot was eating. Breakfast the Prologue, Dinner the Interlogue; Supper the Epilogue.'[14] When Ross's self-indulgence collapsed into gluttony and obesity, however, it proved, as Jackson had predicted, as great a threat to his career as his on-stage torpor had done. Excessive gourmandising compromised his acting skills to such an extent that, by 1758, Ross had become 'too plump-faced to shew off the distention or relaxation of the muscles, in exhibiting the passions'.[15]

As Ross's reputation for indolence began to cost him engagements, and his epicurean tastes outpaced his income, there was always a battle in the Ross household to make ends meet, and Ross gained a reputation as 'a very tardy paymaster'.[16] The effect on Murray should not be underestimated, for arrears of debt played on fears of impoverishment that had plagued her since childhood. Despite her annuity, Murray found that creditors were once more knocking at her door.

If Murray fretted about their financial situation; if she felt frustrated by her husband's indolence or his incessant gourmandising; if she were disappointed at his failure to fulfil his theatrical promise, her complaints are not recorded. Despite Ross's shortcomings, his onstage inertia and offstage self-indulgence, and even his increasing girth, Murray remained an affectionate and loyally supportive wife who bore her husband's foibles patiently and in dignified silence.

The stresses and strains that both Murray and Ross experienced as they adjusted to married life were compounded by the media's continued focus on Murray as courtesan. Her name, and its association with sex and desirability, remained immensely saleable well into the 1760s, and proved a lucrative money-spinner for hack-writers and engravers alike. As a result, Murray's marital status was no protection against unwarranted press intrusion from those keen to capitalise on the public's perpetual fascination with the former courtesan.

Although such intrusions were to be expected while Murray's marriage remained secret, they were nonetheless painful and distressing. Thus, just two months after her wedding, a 'Letter to F---y M----y', in which she was described as 'a famous courtesan in town', claimed that a naval officer on board the fleet in the Mediterranean was her lover. The 'letter' was a slight satire on the British navy's ill-fated defence of the island of Minorca, a British possession since 1708, as it came under attack from the French in 1756. Murray's supposed lover described briefly the fleet's naval engagements, but was more interested in telling Murray of her charms and how he longed to 'have an opportunity of clasping [Murray], [his] sweet honey suckle, once more in these arms'.[17]

By spring 1757, some months after Minorca had surrendered to the French, Murray featured in two versions of a satirical print that appeared following the court martial of Admiral John Byng (1704–57) who had been made a scapegoat by the British government for the humiliating loss of the island.[18] Found guilty of breaching the 12th Article of War by failing to do 'his utmost to take, seize and destroy the Ships of the *French* King', Byng was sentenced to death, the only verdict available under the Articles of War. The court, however, had been unanimous in recommending mercy since it was agreed that Byng's misconduct had arisen from neither cowardice nor disaffection but rather, an 'Error in Judgement'.[19] The court's recommendation was ignored and, according to sympathisers, Byng was sacrificed to political corruption and intrigue. On 14 March 1757, Byng faced a firing squad on the quarterdeck of his flagship, *The Monarch*, and became the only admiral ever to be executed by the Royal Navy. He was 52.

The two prints in which Murray featured were on the theme of a female court martial, and were among some eighty political prints alluding to Minorca that were produced between 1756 and 1757.[20] *Female Court Martial, Held upon the Conduct of an Admirable Lady*, by Louis Philippe Boitard was advertised for sale at sixpence in the *London Chronicle* on 12 March 1757, two days before Byng's execution.[21] Boitard's print was a more elaborate version of an anonymous print entitled *The Female Court Marshall* that had appeared the previous month. Both prints parodied Byng's trial, by imagining a young woman's court martial for adultery before a petticoat court of her peers. The defendant is fashionably dressed in a wide-panniered skirt and, in the Boitard print, she stands at one end of the table facing the judge advocate, named 'Miss Harsh Judge Advocate' in *The Female Court Marshall*, who is seated at the other. Eleven other fashionable members of the court martial, including Murray, are seated between the judge advocate and the defendant. Additional ladies crowd round the table and one to the left of the print holds a book entitled 'Cases of Adultery & Fornication'.[22]

Speech balloons emanate from the mouths of the female judges parodying observations that were made at Byng's trial, while military terms are sexually nuanced for added satiric effect. Thus, one balloon in the

Boitard print reads that the adulterous defendant had been 'forward to Engage' and another that she 'shew'd no fear in time of Action' – humorous double entendres that reprised the thirty-seventh resolution at Byng's trial which stated that he had shown neither cowardice nor disaffection. The legend beneath the print summarised the sentence of the court on the young adulteress by echoing the Byng verdict – she was found guilty 'as there is no alternative left to the discretion of the Court' under the law. As with Byng, however, the court concluded that her conduct was an 'error in Judgment' and recommended her 'as a proper Object of Mercy'.

Julia Banister has suggested that by identifying the trial of 'a failed military man' with the female prisoner, both prints aimed at censuring 'the confused manners and principle of the times' and at exposing Byng as a corruption of manliness:

> By praising the lady's willingness to enter a clandestine sexual liaison …, the female judges deliver an amoral verdict on a matter of female sexual behaviour and thus the image depicts the female prisoner as a masculinized counterpart to the effeminate Admiral Byng.[23]

Such political observations were, arguably, of less interest to the print-buying public than the fact that the twelve ladies of the court martial were represented by some of the most notorious women of the day – women such as Lady Caroline Harrington *née* Fitzroy, nicknamed 'the stable yard Messalina', the procuress Mrs Naylor, the actress Peg Woffington, and the adulteresses Frances, Lady Vane and Elizabeth Chudleigh, afterward Duchess of Kingston.

It was undoubtedly distressing to Murray, as she strove for respectability, to find herself once more in such promiscuous company and to discover that, despite her exemplary marital conduct, she was still being portrayed as a woman of ill repute. Although the members of the court martial were presented as stock female figures and no attempt was made to capture their individual likenesses, they were all readily identifiable from a list of their lightly disguised names which appeared immediately beneath the etching. In the Boitard print, the list appeared as a series of initials and dashes with Murray presented as 'Miss F.M—', while in *The Female Court Marshall* Murray was 'Fanny More-ha'.[24]

A year later, in 1758, Murray was once more in the spotlight when she was the dedicatee of an erotic novel entitled *The Scourge of Pleasure* –

'To the Bliss-Bestowing Fanny Murray, this Piece is Humbly Dedicated by her Amorous Humble Servant, the Author'. Thus, four years after her retirement from prostitution, Murray's name was still suggestive of superior exotic experiences which the author and his publishers hoped to cash in on. This exploitation of the Murray name found full expression in the same year with the publication of the *Memoirs*, which added further distress to the Rosses as the anonymous author raked over Murray's former life and lovers, wildly embellished true episodes from her past and invented false ones for the purposes of titillation.

Print-shops too, found that Murray was still an immensely saleable commodity. A new and particularly flattering mezzotint entitled *Miss Murray* which recalled Murray in her heyday appeared in print-shop windows, probably at the beginning of the 1760s. Murray was then in her early thirties, but the print represented her in all her youthful and desirable beauty, complete with her signature pendant pearl earrings and her chip hat worn over a lace cap.

The print is a three-quarter portrait, created by Richard Houston, in which Murray wears a sumptuous sack-backed open-robed dress with an expensive ruffled trim and three-quarter-length *engageante* sleeves. Her bodice is cut very deeply to reveal her pert bosoms and the areola of her left breast is clearly visible. Murray is placed against the backdrop of a manicured garden where a gardener, to her left, digs out a flower bed. The placing of Murray within a landscaped setting gives the print a sexual potency, since it has been argued that 'both women and landscape were continually being judged for their ability to titillate the imagination and satisfy the senses'.[25] Titillation of the imagination in this instance was achieved by means of a rose that Murray holds in her left hand and which she had just plucked from a potted plant that stands on a table beside her. The association of the plucked rose with lost virginity, combined with the seductive allure of Murray's smile, the coquettish turn of her neck, and the nakedness of her breasts all served to reinforce the sexual energy contained within the print.[26]

Miss Murray proved Murray's swan song, for she was rarely referred to again, either pictorially or in the ephemeral literature of the day, in terms that were quite so deferential to her beauty or sexual power. By the 1760s, a new tone was discernible, that either ridiculed Murray as a faded has-been or pointed to the usurpation of her premier position by younger, more beautiful rivals. Thus, Edward Thompson in *The Meretriciad* praised

Murray not for her own charms but for having introduced a rising star, the courtesan and actress, Ann Elliot (1743–69), to the town:

> Mur—y if e'er thy deeds, or Summer plays,
> Deserv'd encomiums, or the publick's praise,
> 'Tis now, for introducing to the light,
> The peerless *Elliot*, for the Town's delight.[27]

Only Kitty Fisher, however, was universally acknowledged as the rightful successor to Murray, and her ascendancy over her rival was first described in *The Juvenile Adventures of Miss Kitty F----r*, disparaged by the *Monthly Review* as 'miserable, lying, obscene trash'.[28]

Set in Madrid, this purported to be a translation of a Spanish original, but was simply London by another name. The thin veil of Spanish authenticity was for comic effect but also, of course, to avoid charges of libel. Thus, Fisher was born in 'Soholio', sent to school in 'Hammersmito' and later met a famous pimp called 'Don Harrisino'. In one of Fisher's escapades she visited a charlatan clairvoyant who predicted she would become 'the reigning toast of the first nobility in Spain' and that 'all the present triumphant beauties would be talked of no more. Miss Rocia, [Elizabeth Roach] miss Murrio [Fanny Murray], or miss Cupero's [Lucy Cooper] name no longer mentioned.'[29] The narrative also imagined a letter written by Murray to her rival in which she acknowledged that Fisher had 'supplanted [Murray] upon the polite theatre of gallantry' and urged Fisher to '*reform, and live virtuous*' before it was too late.[30]

This theme of Murray's eclipse was developed in 'A Humorous Poetical Dialogue, between the once celebrated Miss F---y M----y and the now famed Miss K---y F----r' which appeared in *The Droll Miscellany*, collected by the self-styled 'Professor of Drollery', Ferdinando Funny.[31] This too failed to impress the critics and was dismissed by the *Monthly Review* as having 'too little of either humour or poetry … to make it worth notice'.[32] In 'A Humorous Poetical Dialogue', an older and wiser Murray once again warned Fisher of the dangers of her reckless lifestyle. The poem imagined the two rivals meeting one afternoon near fashionable St James's, the scene of Fisher's recent 'merry accident', when her spectacular fall from a horse had excited a surge of publicity. The exquisite Fisher arrived for the meeting 'in morning negligé/ Artfully loose — tout degagée', all the while drawing admiring glances from the throng. By contrast, Murray, who was portrayed as past her prime and a shadow of her former self, passed through the crowds, unnoticed and unrecognised:

> F---y had hither bent her way:
> Lonely the well known spot she trod,
> Unnotic'd by the passing crowd:
> How chang'd from her, once light and gay,
> When coxcombs harbinger'd her way,
> Unrival'd beauty of the day.[33]

Such prints and ephemeral writings might have been hurtful to Murray's pride and vanity, but worse was to come in late 1763. The Rosses could have little imagined that the fallout from a political struggle over parliamentary rights and privileges which was being played out in parliament would find its way to their door and catch an unsuspecting Murray in its wake. Her hard-earned marital reputation was soon damaged as she was once more thrust into the limelight as the most notorious woman in England. On this occasion it was as the addressee of *An Essay on Woman*, an indecent and blasphemous parody of Alexander Pope's philosophical poem entitled *An Essay on Man* (1734).[34] Credited to John Wilkes, the scurrilous poem was at the centre of an infamous case for obscene libel and led to the self-imposed exile of Wilkes, then MP for Aylesbury, after his expulsion from the House of Commons in January 1764.

Once the poem became public in 1763, it was assumed that Wilkes was the sole author, an attribution he did nothing to deny. It has been suggested, however, that his good friend Thomas Potter (1718–59), the dissolute son of a former archbishop of Canterbury, was the principal author, and that Wilkes encouraged Potter with suggestions and criticisms.[35] According to this view, Wilkes's main contribution to the work was probably the wording and design of the textual surroundings – the obscene illustration for the title page, which included an inscription to 'Miss Fanny Murray', an advertisement by the editor, a notice of the design – as well as three shorter, lewd and blasphemous poems, which were to be included with the essay. These parodied Pope's 'Universal Prayer' and the hymn 'Veni Creator' which, in Wilkes's version, likened male genitalia to the Holy Trinity. A third poem, on premature ejaculation, was the eighteen line 'The Dying Lover to His Prick'. In this parody of Pope's 'The Dying Christian to His Soul', the writer called on Murray's masturbatory skills:

Fanny, your Murmur rings:
Lend, lend your Hand! I mount! I die!
O Prick, how great thy Victory!
O Pleasure! sweet thy Stings.[36]

Potter, it is argued, began work on *An Essay on Woman* around 1754. His motive was in part to mock the Reverend Dr William Warburton, Bishop of Gloucester, whom Potter detested for his high-minded pomposity, and with whose young wife, Gertrude, Potter had an affair. It was Warburton's friendship with Pope (he had edited Pope's works and produced a particularly scholarly commentary on *An Essay on Man*) that led Potter to choose Pope's poem and Warburton's annotations for parody. In Potter's version, Warburton was made the author of an obscene commentary on *An Essay on Woman* and credited with its authorship on the title page of the poem. Consequently Warburton's name appeared on the title page alongside an illustration, probably designed by Wilkes, representing a ten-inch phallus.[37]

Pope's poem, which was addressed to Henry St John, Viscount Bolingbroke, is made up of four epistles and extends to 1,304 lines. *An Essay on Woman* has survived as a ninety-four-line fragment, parodying Pope's first epistle, of 294 lines. Pope's aim in the first epistle had been to vindicate the ways of God to man by arguing that God had created a universe in which 'Whatever is, is RIGHT' (line 294). It was the pride of 'Presumptuous Man', argued Pope, which prevented him from comprehending, in its entirety, the divine ordering of God's creation. It was 'A mighty maze! but not without a plan' (line 6).

Reworking each alternate line of Pope's poem, to load it with sexually explicit imagery, Potter reduced the universal scope of Pope's argument to the world encompassed within a woman's body. The addressee of the poem was also changed for comic effect from Bolingbroke to Murray. It is possible that Murray's role within the poem was discussed in correspondence between Potter and Wilkes, as a letter from Potter dated 31 July 1755 queried Wilkes's mention of a certain Mrs M:

Who your Mrs M is with whom you rather wish me to copulate I am at a Loss to guess. I could reverse the Letter & attempt the Essay on Woman without even the Hope of having a commentator.[38]

Murray was, of course, an obvious choice as addressee, given the pornographic themes of the poem, and that she had been at the height of her sexual power and notoriety for several years by the time Potter started work on his parody, around 1754.[39] She was also the perfect sexually experienced woman with whom to discover the pleasures of the female form, and it was with Murray that the narrator:

The latent Tracts, the pleasing Depths explore,
And my Prick clapp'd where thousands were before'.[40]

Sometime after Potter's death in 1759, Wilkes began to edit and revise the work, and by September 1762, there were rumours that he had converted 'the whole essay on man into a bawdy poem'.[41] By May 1763 and with the four epistles, textual surroundings and his own shorter poems in manuscript form, Wilkes decided to have thirteen copies (some accounts suggest twelve) of the poem privately printed and bound.[42] This has given rise to speculation that the copies were destined for the twelve members of the inner circle, 'the apostles', at Medmenham (with one, perhaps, intended for the library), and that Potter and Wilkes might have amused fellow Medmenhamites with earlier versions of the poem.[43]

As Wilkes was aware, publishing pornography was a criminal offence, but he had reasonably assumed that printing copies of the poem for the private amusement of friends did not constitute publication and fell within the scope of the law. Thus, Wilkes instructed his printers to begin work on the poem, but, by the summer, he had redirected them to the reprinting of a second edition of the first forty-four issues of his weekly opposition periodical, the *North Briton*.[44] The infamous forty-fifth issue was added shortly afterward. Thus, only the first ninety-four lines of *An Essay on Woman* and Wilkes's shorter poems had reached proof stage.

Quite by chance, the poem had already come to the government's attention, when a controversial general warrant was used to arrest Wilkes on 30 April 1763 for seditious libel.[45] This followed his attack on George III's speech at the prorogation of Parliament and his denunciation of the king's ministers as 'the tools of despotism and corruption' in the forty-fifth issue of the *North Briton* which had been published on 23 April. Protected by parliamentary privilege, Wilkes was quickly released from imprisonment in the Tower of London, but not before government agents had ransacked his home in Great George Street and seized some of his papers, including the manuscript of *An Essay on Woman*. Having also seen a printed copy of the obscene title page, Wilkes's political enemies were eager for further evidence of his intention to print pornography – evidence that could be used in an obscene libel prosecution.

By July 1763, Wilkes's printing foreman, Michael Curry, had been bribed into handing over a set of proofs which were then passed to Lord Sandwich who had been appointed secretary of state for the Northern Department in August 1763, on the death of Lord Egremont. As secretary of state, Sandwich was responsible for all further proceedings against Wilkes, whom he pursued with an unexpected vigour and vindictiveness. This might have been prompted by personal animosity, a view dismissed by John Sainsbury in his study of Wilkes, or by intelligence that the forty-sixth issue of the *North Briton*, scheduled for 12 November 1763, contained a damning personal attack on Sandwich.[46]

It has also been suggested, though unconvincingly, that Sandwich's vindictiveness was caused by sexual jealousy over Murray. According to this view, Wilkes had written *An Essay on Woman* specifically for Murray's amusement when she was two-timing Sandwich with him.[47] The claim is inaccurate, if only because it ignores Potter's involvement with the poem and the fact that Sandwich's liaison with Murray dated from around 1745, almost twenty years before the political scandal broke. Moreover, there is no evidence that Murray was ever Wilkes's lover.[48] The idea of a love triangle has persisted, however, and Dan Cruickshank, in his recent study of Georgian London, painted a lively, if unsubstantiated, picture of Sandwich catching Wilkes and Murray together and being 'reduced to a pistol-waving but ultimately impotent rage'.[49]

With proof of the existence of *An Essay on Woman* in printed form, Sandwich orchestrated a meticulous and simultaneous two-pronged attack against Wilkes at the opening of the new session of Parliament on 15 November 1763. The House of Commons moved to deprive Wilkes of his parliamentary privilege, so that he could then be prosecuted for seditious libel for his publication of the *North Briton*. At the same time, the House of Lords charged Wilkes with obscene libel for publishing *An Essay on Woman* and libelling Warburton.

When Sandwich rose to his feet in the House of Lords, he announced to the unsuspecting members in the chamber that he had certain grave communications to impart. He then proceeded to read aloud extracts from the poem and commentary, including the inscription on the title page to 'Miss Fanny Murray'.[50] As Sandwich read from the poem which began 'Awake, my Fanny', the House sensed the hypocrisy of hearing the former friend of Wilkes and enthusiastic member of the Order of St Francis, sanctimoniously reading out a poem that was inscribed to his former lover. Even his good friend Dashwood, then Lord Le Despencer, was surprised at Sandwich's self-righteousness, and murmured that this was the first time he had heard Satan preach against sin.[51]

By Christmas Day 1763 Wilkes had escaped to France, and then to Paris, and he remained in self-imposed exile for four years, refusing to return to attend either parliament or the Court of King's Bench for his trial. He did not take up permanent residence in England again until December 1767. Wilkes was expelled from parliament as an unworthy member on 19 January 1764, and on 21 February he was convicted *in absentia*, at the Court of Kings Bench, of publishing seditious and obscene libels in the form of the *North Briton* and *An Essay on Woman*. Failing to respond to five summonses to appear before parliament, Wilkes was outlawed on 1 November 1764.

As the case against Wilkes for obscene libel was being prepared, Murray might have heard distressing rumours that she too was to be summoned to appear in court. Charles Churchill had been 'much entertained' by the story he had heard of 'the Trial of the Conspirators relative to Miss Fanny' and gossiped about it in a letter to Wilkes dated 13 July 1762. In the event, Murray was not called, but Churchill's wry account suggests that she would have received little sympathy from the court and have been exposed to yet further public humiliation. 'They proposed to bring the Girl into Court', wrote Churchill but the judge, probably Lord Chief Justice Mansfield who presided over the trial, decided against it. He did so, suggested Churchill, for the lewdest of reasons:

> Applying his hand to [that] part of the body where Fools they say are better provided than Men of Sense, significantly declared that he [the judge] would advise them not to bring her in, for, quoth my Lord, I find I shall certainly be at her.[52]

An Essay on Woman, and Murray's part in it, was the talk of Westminster. One of the notes in the commentary attributed to Warburton, which compared Murray to the Virgin Mary, was singled out for special comment – 'our Virgin Fanny in this ought to take the wall of our Virgin Mary; for the *first never had a Child*, nor I truly believe did she ever conceive'.[53] Walpole, who had witnessed Sandwich's performance in the House of Lords, made a particular reference to this in a letter to his friend, Horace Mann. The poem, wrote Walpole, was 'dedicated to Fanny Murray, whom it prefers to the Virgin Mary from never having had a child'.[54] In similar terms, George Dempster, MP for the Perth Burghs, gossiped about the affair to Boswell in a letter dated 19 November, commenting that 'the work was inscribed to Fanny Murray, and consisted chiefly of a parallel between that courtesan and the Blessed Virgin, much in favour of the former'.[55]

The poem soon escaped beyond the tight circle of printers, government agents and members of the House of Lords who had been concerned in Wilkes's prosecution. Indeed, Wilkes noted the irony that it was the government, not he, that had first published the pornographic poem. According to Wilkes, after Sandwich had finished reading *An Essay on Woman* in the House of Lords, it was 'ordered to lie on the table, for the clerks of the House to copy, and to *publish* through the nation'.[56]

Donald McCormick has suggested that once Murray was rumoured to be the heroine of the poem, it was this that led 'rapscallion pornographic pamphleteers' to attempt to cash in on *An Essay on Women* by hawking about 'absolutely authenticated quotations from the Amours of Fanny Murray and her Monkish Friends at Mednam'.[57] While it has not proved possible to authenticate this, it is true that '*spurious copies soon after sold as genuine* – some with a few genuine passages, probably copied from the Bill of Indictment, worked into them, and others *without one genuine line*'.[58] According to Louise Kaplan, 'within a week there were at least fourteen fraudulent copies of *Essay on Woman* on the London book market, some of them far more prurient than the original and others so mild that customers demanded their money back'.[59]

Murray's association with *An Essay on Woman* might have indeed led to the surge of interest in the poem, but in published editions she was no longer the addressee and only mentioned *en passant*, if at all. For example, *An Essay on Woman in Three Epistles* [1763], which included a French translation, was addressed to 'C----' while the addressee of a 1764 version of the poem, printed by E. Sumpter, was 'Celia'. Sumpter's edition also included additional poems, including one entitled 'Fanny's Charms'.[60] Another edition, this time addressed to Sandwich, was printed by George Richards and appeared in 1769. This version borrowed some of the exact phrasings from the government editions of the poem and added the well-trodden theme of Murray's eclipse by Fisher:

> The latent tracts, the secret cause explore
> Of each who is, or longs to be a whore;
> Eye woman's walks, from earth unto the skies,
> A MURRAY fallen, or a FISHER rise;
> Weep where we must, but laugh where'er we can,
> And prove that woman, still is fond of man.[61]

If the humiliation of being known as the original addressee of a pornographic poem was not enough, Murray was also the subject of two hurtful woodcuts that were probably released in 1764. The woodcuts, which were printed on the same sheet of paper, featured on the left, *Miss Fanny Murray, The Fair and Reigning Toast, in her Primitive Innocence* and, on the right, *The Careless Maid: or, the Charms of the Garter. With some Reflections on the Folly of the Modern Dresses of the Ladies.*[62] As previously noted, *Miss Fanny Murray* was repurposed from a print, first published in 1754, by the engraver and music seller Richard Bennet. This was repurposed again, at a later date, as a portrait of Kitty Fisher. In the print, Murray is fashionably but modestly dressed and holds a sheet of music in her right hand. By contrast, in the companion piece, *The Careless Maid*, Murray is portrayed after the loss of 'her Primitive Innocence' as a common prostitute. Her dress is low cut and she knowingly meets the viewer's gaze as she exposes her leg to her thigh in order to adjust her garter.[63] This representation of Murray as a prostitute was undoubtedly mortifying to the Rosses as they attempted to live in quiet respectability. Equally wounding were the verses that accompanied *Miss Fanny Murray* which, once again, rehearsed themes of Murray's lost beauty and her desertion by former admirers in favour of the latest toasts of the town:

> Paint, Powder, washes are apply'd –
> No Arts the sad Disgrace can hide:

The Fops forsake, the Wits deride
Their once-lov'd, charming *Fanny*.

Murray's usurpation by younger, more desirable rivals was revisited the
following year in a song to the tune of 'Lucy Cooper'. The song, which
was included in a miscellaneous collection of comic pieces, described
how Murray and her contemporary Cooper had been overshadowed by
another new toast, Polly Russel:

No more shall Fanny Murray boast,
Nor swain inspiring Cooper,
No longer they shall rule the roost,
But far behind must troop sir,
Superiour grace, demands the place,
And makes a mighty bustle
Each nymph shall fly, with envious eye,
The charms of Polly Russel.[64]

By 1765, when this song appeared, the worst of the furore over *An Essay
on Woman* had passed. Murray was then 36 and had been married for
nine years. During this time, she had maintained a stainless reputation
as a faithful and dutiful wife, and this in the face of a publicity mill that
refused to allow the scandalous indiscretions of her former life to be
forgotten. The numerous publications that featured Murray in the years
following her marriage were proof of a continued public interest in the
former courtesan, and of the profits that were still to be made from her
name. When she no longer sold good copy as beautiful and promiscuous
there was still money to be made by ridiculing her as old and faded.

The publication of her *Memoirs*, and especially *An Essay on Woman*,
brought Murray to a national and international prominence that she
was powerless to escape.[65] This prurient interest in her former life was
undoubtedly humiliating, and the cause of deep distress to both Murray
and Ross as they attempted to live together in private respectability. Had
she Fisher's temperament, then Murray might have complained to the
newspapers, as Fisher had done, of 'the Baseness of little Scribblers and
scurvy Malevolence' of those who exploited her name.[66] This was not
Murray's way – while she would have undoubtedly shared her sense of
humiliation with her husband, she remained silent to the outside world

and made no public protest against the arbitrary and unwarranted intrusion into her private life. For a second time in her life, Murray might have wished to escape the world that had closed in on her. It was perhaps time to begin life afresh once more.

Notes

1 Quoted in Cash, *Essay on Woman*, p.97.
2 David Garrick, *The Private Correspondence of David Garrick …*, 2 vols (Henry Colburn & Richard Bentley, 1831–32), vol. 2 (1832), p.335. The letter to Garrick is undated.
3 Richard Brinsley Peake (ed.), *Memoirs of the Colman Family …*, 2 vols (Richard Bentley, 1841), vol. 1, p.264. Letter dated August 1772.
4 Richard Wright Procter, *Manchester in Holiday Dress* (Simpkin, Marshall & Co. and Manchester: Abel Heywood & Son, 1866), pp.18–20.
5 Taylor, *Records of My Life*, vol. 1, p.363.
6 Brady and Pottle (eds), *Boswell in Search of a Wife*, p.130.
7 *Sporting Magazine* (November 1793 issue, 1794), vol. 3, p.61.
8 Geoffrey Scott & Frederick A. Pottle (eds), *Private Papers of James Boswell from Malahide Castle …*, 18 vols (privately printed, 1930), vol. 9, p.86.
9 Charles Rogers (ed.), *Boswelliana: The Common Place Book of James Boswell with a Memoir and Annotations …* (Houlston & Sons, 1876), p.269.
10 Taylor, *Records of My Life*, vol. 1, p.365; *Monthly Mirror* (Vernor & Hood, April 1799 issue), vol. 7, p.253. See also, Walley Chamberlain Oulton, *The History of the Theatres of London …*, 2 vols (1796), vol. 2, pp.75–78.
11 John Jackson, *The History of the Scottish Stage …* (Edinburgh: 1793), p.73.
12 Tate Wilkinson, *The Wandering Patentee; or, a History of the Yorkshire Theatres …*, 4 vols (York: 1795), vol. 1, p.261.
13 *Gentleman's Magazine: and Historical Chronicle* (September 1790 issue) vol. 60, part 2, p.865.
14 Charles Lee Lewes, *Memoirs of Charles Lee Lewes …*, 4 vols (1805), vol. 3, p.194.
15 *Monthly Mirror* (Vernor & Hood, April 1799 issue), vol. 7, p.253.
16 Taylor, *Records of My Life*, vol. 1, p.365.
17 'Letter to F---y M----y', in *The Literary Magazine: or, Universal Review, for the Year 1756*, 3 vols (1756–58), vol. 1 (1756), p.123. This is mispaginated and should be p.131.
18 For studies of Byng, see, for example, Chris Ware, *Admiral Byng: His Rise and Execution* (Barnsley: Pen & Sword Maritime, 2009); M. John Cardwell, *Arts and Arms: Literature, Politics and Patriotism during the Seven Years War* (Manchester & New York: Manchester University Press, 2004), pp.46–102; Charles Fearne (ed.), *The Trial of the Honourable Admiral John Byng, at a Court Martial …* (1757).
19 Fearne (ed.), *Trial of the Honourable Admiral John Byng*, pp.130 and 126.
20 Cardwell, *Art and Arms*, p.68.

21 *The London Chronicle: or, Universal Evening Post*, 10–12 March 1757.

22 For further information on the two Byng satires, see http://www. britishmuseum.org/collection. See also, Stephens (ed.), *Catalogue of Prints and Drawings in the British Museum*, vol. 3 part 2, p.1117–18; 'The Crying Consort. With a View of the Court Martial', in *The Gentleman's and London Magazine* … (December 1784 issue), pp.721–22.

23 Julia Banister, 'The Court Martial of Admiral John Byng: Politeness and the Military Man in the Mid-Eighteenth Century', in Heather Ellis and Jessica Meyer (eds), *Masculinity and the Other: Historical Perspectives* (Cambridge: Cambridge Scholars Publishing, 2009), p.246; Cardwell, *Art and Arms*, pp.61–62.

24 See also, a satiric leaflet entitled *The Female Court-Martial* [1757] where Murray appeared as 'Fanny M----y'.

25 Carole Fabricant, 'Binding and Dressing Nature's Loose Tresses: The Ideology of Augustan Landscape Design', in Roseann Runte (ed.), *Studies in Eighteenth-Century Culture* (Madison: The University of Wisconsin Press, 1979), vol. 8, p.111.

26 The plucked rose as a metaphor for lost virginity finds resonance in *Harris's Lists* for 1793 (p.79) and 1789 (p.47) where reference is made to virgin roses.

27 Edward Thompson, *The Meretriciad* (1761), p.19. Elliot was, at one time, mistress to Ross's friend, the playwright Arthur Murphy (1727–1805).

28 *Monthly Review* (March 1759 issue), vol. 20, p.276. See also, *Critical Review* (August 1759 issue), vol. 8, p.176.

29 *Juvenile Adventures*, vol. 1, p.117.

30 *Juvenile Adventures*, vol. 2, pp.169 and 171.

31 'A Humorous Poetical Dialogue, between the once celebrated Miss F---y M----y and the now famed Miss K---y F----r', in Ferdinando Funny, *The Droll Miscellany* … (Dublin: 1760), pp.76–79.

32 *Monthly Review* (May 1760 issue) vol. 22, p.439.

33 'Humorous Poetical Dialogue', p.76.

34 This discussion of *An Essay on Woman* draws particularly on Cash, *Essay on Woman*. See also, Cash, *Wilkes*, pp.96–164; Sainsbury, *Wilkes*, pp.146–62.

35 See, for example, Bradshaw, *Thomas Bradshaw*, p.33 (footnote 13); Cash, *Essay on Woman*, pp.139–52; Cash, *Wilkes*, pp.31–32; *N&Q*, 2 Ser. 81 (18 July 1857), p.42. This view is challenged by Peter D.G. Thomas in *John Wilkes, A Friend to Liberty* (Oxford: Clarendon Press, 1996), p.4; Paulson, *Hogarth's Harlot*, p.383 (endnote 52); Sainsbury, *Wilkes*, p.146 and appendix pp.249–52.

36 Cash, *Essay on Woman*, p.125.

37 For a reconstruction of how the title page might have looked, see Cash, *Essay on Woman*, p.85.

38 BL – Add MS 30880 B f. 3; Horace Bleackley, *Life of John Wilkes* (John Lane, The Bodley Head, 1917), pp.37 and 441; Raymond Postgate, 'That Devil Wilkes' (Constable & Co. Ltd, 1930), p.80.

39 Cash, *Essay on Woman*, p.33. Cash described Murray as an illogical choice, since the addressee of the poem becomes male after a few lines.

40 Cash, *Essay on Woman*, p.101.

41 Quoted in Sainsbury, *Wilkes*, p.152.

42 See, for example, Sainsbury, *Wilkes*, p.146 (footnote 58); Cash, *Essay on Woman*, p.56.

43 Thomas, *Wilkes*, p.4.

44 See also, *N&Q*, 11 Ser. IX (7 March 1914), pp.183–85.

45 General warrants gave the authorities indiscriminate powers to arrest any person or persons, who did not need to be named, and to conduct unlimited searches of persons and property.

46 Sainsbury, *Wilkes*, p.154, Rodger, *Insatiable Earl*, p.102.

47 See Mannix, *Hell-fire Club*, p.81.

48 Burford (ed.), *Bawdy Verse, A Pleasant Collection*, p.272.

49 Cruickshank, *Secret History of Georgian London*, p.409.

50 Cash, *Essay on Woman*, pp.69–76, in his reconstruction of Wilkes's lost poem, argued that the poem read by Sandwich to the House of Lords was not Wilkes's original. He suggested that John Kidgell, a defrocked clergyman, who was involved in appropriating a set of proofs, had added forged lines to Wilkes's manuscript. Until recently, the only known extant copy of the poem was held in the Dyce collection at the National Art Library at the Victoria and Albert Museum. Cash has since discovered two more copies of the poem – one at Southern Illinois University at Carbondale, and one in the Bibliothèque Nationale, Paris. He argues that these newly discovered copies are second editions of the five copies which were presented in the House of Lords by Sandwich on 15 November 1763, and that 'the Dyce copy is a late-eighteenth or early-nineteenth-century print-facsimile' (p.76).

51 Martelli, *Jemmy Twitcher*, p.62.

52 BL – Add MS 30878 f.3; Postgate, '*That Devil Wilkes*,' pp.97–98.

53 Cash, *Essay on Woman*, p.99 (verse 8). Cash explains (p.131, note 34) that 'take the wall' refers to walking close to a wall, the safest and cleanest part of a thoroughfare, away from the emptying of chamber pots overhead.

54 Quoted in *N&Q*, 10 Ser. IX (6 June 1908), p.443.

55 Frederick A. Pottle (ed.), *Boswell in Holland, 1763–1764* ... (& Melbourne & Toronto: William Heinemann Ltd, 1952), p.71.

56 *Letters between the Duke of Grafton ... and John Wilkes*, vol. 1, p.212.

57 McCormick, *Hell-Fire Club*, p.146.

58 *N&Q*, 2 Ser. 79 (4 July 1857), p.2 and reproduced in Dilke, *Papers of a Critic*, p.267.

59 Louise J. Kaplan, *The Family Romance of the Impostor-Poet, Thomas Chatterton* (New York: Atheneum, 1988), p.149.

60 *An Essay on Woman* (1764), p.28.

61 An *Essay on Woman* (1769), p.2.

62 McCreery, *Satirical Gaze*, p.83 (footnote 9).

63 Moira Goff et al., *Georgians Revealed: Life, Style and the Making of Modern Britain* (The British Library, 2013), p.103.

64 Oddibus, *Collection of Original Comic Songs*, p.27.

65 A German edition of the *Memoirs* appeared in 1768 entitled *Geschichte der berühmten Miss Fanny Murray* ... (Nuremberg: 1768). See also, *Les Amours and les Aventures du Lord Fox* (Geneva, 1786), p.167.

66 *Public Advertiser*, 24 March 1759.

10

'Auld Reekie'

But you have seen the King of Denmark, and possibly may have got a ticket for the masquerade without costing you thirty guineas.[1]

For two or three years before 1767, Ross had been contemplating a change in direction that would represent the most ambitious undertaking of his theatrical career. After ten years with Covent Garden Theatre, and despite administrative experience that had been mainly limited to summer tours to Manchester, Ross decided to try his hand at managing his own theatre. The theatre he had fixed upon was a small playhouse in Edinburgh known as the Canongate Concert Hall which offered 'a concert of musick, with a play "between the acts"'.[2] The theatre's name and programme of entertainments were designed to circumvent the fact that, despite being the city's principal theatre for the previous twenty years, the Canongate operated illegally without a royal patent. The unlicensed playhouse was only a stepping stone, however, in Ross's more grandiose scheme of building a brand new theatre for Edinburgh, one to rival the playhouses of London and Dublin.[3]

The seed for Ross's theatrical ambitions was probably planted in 1765 while he was at the Canongate for the summer season and all talk was of the monumental new development which was soon to be constructed along a low ridge of land to the north of the Old Town. Indeed, even before building plans had been agreed, work had begun in 1765 on the

202

North Bridge over the Nor Loch which would serve as the main artery, linking the Old and projected New Town. As Ross witnessed the early stages of its construction, the north end of the bridge might have struck Ross, even then, as the perfect location for his theatre. Situated on the edge of the new development, Ross's proposed theatre would be within easy reach of Old Town audiences as well as their more affluent counterparts in the new development.

Ross returned to London and Murray in the summer of 1765, excited by the opportunities that a city on the cusp of great change afforded a man of theatrical ambition. Murray might have been apprehensive about Ross's plans to uproot her from London and transplant her to cold northern climes 400 miles away where she knew no one. At the same time, however, she might have been glad to escape the city where hack writers continually intruded upon her privacy and where the publication of *An Essay on Woman* had brought her renewed and painful notoriety. She might have had equally mixed emotions about the project itself and whether it would prove too much for a man of Ross's well-attested indolence.

Any pride she felt in the upward mobility that her husband's new role in theatre management represented, might have been tempered by anxiety over the vast sums Ross's scheme would cost, and the financial consequences should it all go wrong. Whatever her misgivings, sometime after 22 May 1767, when Ross had appeared as Don Philip in *She Wou'd and She Wou'd Not; or, The Kind Impostor*, in possibly his last performance of the season on the Covent Garden stage, Murray and Ross set off on the twelve-day journey to a new life in Edinburgh.[4]

Dominated by its dramatic and imposing castle built on the craggy outcrop of an extinct volcano, Edinburgh Old Town clung to the steep sides of a narrow ridge that ran north–south from the castle to Holyrood House at its lower end. Along the length of the main thoroughfare, named Market Street, a rabbit warren of short streets, closes, wynds (lanes) and courtyards spurred off on either side and, in Murray's time, chairmen did brisk business carrying weary pedestrians in their sedan chairs up and down the town's unforgiving inclines.

Murray and Ross took lodgings at the top of the Old Town, in one of the looming tenement houses, known as 'lands', in the narrowest part of Market Street, at Castle Hill. Situated just below the castle, it was a strenuous climb to their lodgings, but the castle esplanade rewarded them with a grandstand view of the emerging New Town, on a site where open fields and the marshy Nor Loch had once been.

Living conditions in Edinburgh Old Town were a far cry from the sophistications that Murray had enjoyed in New Palace Yard, being over-crowded, noisome and insanitary. Indeed it was the smoke from burning wood and coal, as it billowed from the city's chimney pots which cre-ated the suffocating smell that gave the Old Town its sobriquet of 'auld reekie'. When the diarist and author Mrs Piozzi visited in July 1789 she was appalled by the absence of 'privies' and the custom, known col-loquially as 'gardyloo' from the French *gardez l'eau*, of emptying human waste each evening from tenement windows.[5]

The tall, narrow lands, where Ross and Murray lived, are reputed to be among the first high-rise buildings in Europe. Designed for high-density living, each 'land' was up to twelve storeys (or houses) high, and each 'house' was occupied by a family sharing a communal stair-case. It was little wonder that Edward Topham, a young English visitor to Edinburgh between 1774 and 1775, thought that 'the High street in Edinburgh [was] inhabited by a greater number of persons than any street in Europe'.[6] Indeed, by the 1750s more than 60,000 people were crammed into Edinburgh's congested streets and insanitary tenements.[7]

A year before Murray and Ross arrived in Edinburgh, the City Corporation, keen to relieve pressure on the Old Town and 'enlarge and improve this city, to adorn it with public buildings, which may be a national benefit' had launched a competition to find the best design for a new development.[8] The winning submission came from an unknown 26-year-old mason named James Craig, whose elegant, neo-classical vision centred upon three grand and impressive streets built in solid sandstone, which stretched for over a mile in an east–west direction, the patriotically named George, Queen and Princes Streets.

Craig's development came at an opportune moment for the proprie-tors of the Canongate as they entered into private negotiations with Ross to take over the management of the theatre. Following a riot in January 1767 over their refusal to reinstate George Stayley, a popular comic actor, the proprietors had decided to put their theatre on a proper legal footing by applying to parliament for a royal patent.[9] Their request coincided with the passing of an act of parliament to extend the bound-ary of the royal burgh to include the proposed New Town. It was a relatively straightforward matter, therefore, to insert a clause into the Act empowering the Crown to grant a royal patent. This meant that, for the first time since the introduction of the Licensing Act of 1737, Scotland had a fully licensed and lawfully established theatre.

As negotiations progressed, Ross set about raising the necessary funds, including the £1,100 required by the Canongate proprietors to cover their costs in obtaining the royal patent, as well as an additional £400 for the annual rental charges.[10] According to the actor Charles Lee Lewes, Ross borrowed £1,600 from James Bland, whom Ross then made a quarter partner in the Canongate. Bland was to have a long-term relationship with the theatre as its treasurer, and later as co-manager with the Irish actor/manager West Digges.

Lewes claimed that Ross also borrowed money from Murray, saying that it was 'by means of a considerable lift from Bland and his lovely companion, the celebrated Fanny Murray, [that Ross] became sole patentee'.[11] Lewes's claim is interesting in that he described Murray as a companion of independent means, rather than a wife whose funds, such as they were, belonged, in law, to her husband. Putting these finer points aside, Lewes's observations suggest that Murray offered loyal support to Ross, and that her annuity from the Spencers was instrumental in financing her husband's scheme.

Ross's appointment as patentee, in the autumn of 1767, did not go unopposed. Objectors, including the previous managers, John Lee and the actor, Stayley, regarded Ross as an 'Improper Person' to run the theatre and a 'fierce paper warfare' ensued. A mock playbill for a performance of *The Double Dealers*, for example, described Ross as 'Mr Opium' to make fun of his leaden style of acting and his ability to send audiences to sleep.[12] The playbill also listed 'the celebrated Miss Fanny' as one of the actors in the play in order to expose the supporting role she had played in her husband's theatrical ambitions.[13] More vicious was the attempt to discredit Ross by referencing Murray's former profession in a poetic attack on Ross entitled 'To the Friends of Virtue and Liberty'. In this poem, Murray was vilified as 'sneering Vice':

SEE sacred Virtue, with indignant mien,
Eyes the profaner of the tragic scene.
While sneering Vice, in form like R—s's spouse,
Leads on a wanton band to fill the house.[14]

The furore eventually died down and, with its royal patent and Ross as theatre manager, the Canongate reopened as the Theatre Royal on 9 December 1767. Ross chose *The Earl of Essex* written by the bricklayer-turned-playwright Henry Jones as the first play to be performed legally upon a Scottish stage. It was the play in which Ross had made his debut at Covent Garden Theatre on 3 October 1757, and he reprised the lead role for his opening night. In a historic moment, Ross spoke the first words on his newly licensed stage when he recited the prologue he had commissioned from James Boswell to celebrate his theatre's royal patent.[15] The commission marked the beginning of a lifelong friendship between the two men, and ever afterward Boswell referred to his friend affectionately as 'Royal Ross' in acknowledgement of his theatrical achievement.

Ross's first season as an actor/manager went well, and during the second season Ross showed drive and entrepreneurial flair as he began work on plans for the construction, and financing, of his new Theatre Royal.[16] Ross estimated the overall cost of his theatre at £2,500 and he succeeded in raising the necessary capital through subscription. By 1 March 1768, Ross had published a set of building proposals and two weeks later, on 16 March, he proudly laid the foundation stone of his new theatre.[17]

Ross's ambitious plans were coming to fruition and his star was very much in the ascendant. His management of the Canongate had begun well, and Ross had earned a special place in theatrical history by becoming the first patentee of a licensed theatre in Scotland. It also spoke of Ross's enterprise and vision that his playhouse was one of the first buildings erected in Craig's spectacular New Town. Success seemed assured, but those who knew Ross well suspected his staying power. David Garrick wrote to Boswell on 8 March 1768, a week before the foundation stone was laid, to say that he felt sure Ross 'must Succeed if he will not be too lazy'.[18]

The controversy over the royal patent aside, Murray, now aged 39, lived a quieter, domestic existence as Ross's wife, yet she was to have one last moment in the limelight. On Monday 10 October 1768, she attended a magnificent masquerade ball at the Opera House in the Haymarket, hosted by the 19-year-old King Christian VII of Denmark and Norway (1749–1808).[19] It was the society event of the year and was attended by 'the greatest number of nobility and gentry ever assembled together upon any occasion of the like nature'.[20] Murray would shine as brightly that evening as she had done in her heyday.

The Danish king's masquerade was to reciprocate the hospitality he had received during his two-month visit to England as the guest of his cousin and brother-in-law George III (1738–1820).[21] Christian had married George's 15-year-old sister, Princess Caroline Matilda (1751–75) two years previously, in 1766. The marriage was already doomed, however, by the time of Christian's visit to England for he was, as Mary Wollstonecraft described him some thirty years later, 'a notorious debauchee, and an idiot into the bargain'.[22] Christian's mental instability, which was probably 'a form of progressive dementia', combined with a dissolute and debauched personality made him unfit as both husband and king.[23] It was said that he 'roamed the streets at night, broke windows and lamps, and [that] he spent his days in wild rioting' with his mistress, the prostitute Anne Cathrine Benthagen, better known as 'Milady' or Støvlet-Cathrine.[24]

Such night-time sallies were also rumoured to have been a feature of Christian's royal progress through England. It was said that, accompanied by his court favourite/lover, the handsome 23-year-old Count Conrad Holcke, Master of the King's Wardrobe, the Danish king spent most nights in:

> the most disgusting debauchery, and these rambles were generally commenced after midnight. The king opened the ball at Sion House with his sister-in-law, the Queen of Great Britain; he danced with the Princess of Saxe-Gotha and the Duchess of Ancaster; and, within an hour after quitting these scenes of royal grandeur, he would throw off his gorgeous dress, disguise himself as a sailor, and haunt the lowest purlieus of St. Giles's.[25]

Given Christian VII's dissolute nature, it was not surprising that he had chosen to thank his royal hosts and all those who had offered him hospitality by lavishing £3,000 (about £326,000 today) on an extravagant entertainment with a reputation for licentiousness. Masquerades were widely regarded as immoral. In contrast to fancy dress, where costume did not conceal identity, the act of masking was believed to put female honour at risk by removing social and sexual constraint, and enabling women, unchaperoned and incognito, to embrace sexual freedom and intrigue.[26] Elizabeth Chudleigh epitomised the immorality of the masquerade when she appeared bare-breasted in the character of Iphigenia at a masked ball in 1749. The bluestocking Mrs Montagu famously remarked that 'Miss Chudleigh's dress, or rather undress, was remarkable; she was Iphigenia for the sacrifice, but so naked, the high priest might easily inspect the entrails of the victim'.[27]

In her career as a courtesan, Murray would have frequented numerous masked balls, and her appearance at a masquerade in 1748 as a member of the Duke of Cumberland's party has already been noted.[28] Murray's identification with the masquerade and its loose morals is most clearly seen in a mezzotint by Thomas Johnson (fl. *c.* 1763–*c.* 1770) entitled *The Celebrated Miss Murray*.[29] As Sheila O' Connell has shown, even the strands of hair that escaped from Murray's hat and fell across her forehead acted as a visual code within the portrait to suggest Murray's moral laxity.[30] The portrait was commissioned sometime in the early 1750s and reflected the then rage for costumes in the style of Helena Fourment, the second wife and muse of Peter Paul Rubens.[31] In the three-quarter portrait, Murray is seated against a rural backdrop in a rich dress of heavy velvet and silk with a tight bejewelled bodice and starched ruff. Her costume is finished off with a straw hat decorated with Fourment's signature ostrich feathers and a mask which she holds in her left hand. The print appears to have sold well so that by 1775 it was described in one print-seller's catalogue as 'extremely fine and rare'.[32]

The *Memoirs* (1:83–5) also associated Murray with the sexual mischief and immorality of masquerades by setting two of its anecdotes within the context of the masked ball. The first took place shortly after Murray had become mistress to the foul-breathed Mr F and while she was still working for the bawd, Mrs Softing. According to the *Memoirs*, a handsome admirer duped Murray into spending the night with him by disguising himself in an exact copy of her elderly lover's costume. Mr F's gouty leg and halitosis notwithstanding, Murray was completely taken in by the young man's costume, voice and gesture and it was not until they were in bed together that Murray discovered, to her infinite pleasure, that her lover was not the aged Mr F but the vigorous Captain N.

In another, equally fanciful, masked ball escapade, the *Memoirs* (2:176–81) described how Murray agreed to swap costumes with a lady and to impersonate her for the remainder of the evening. This was to enable the lady in question to spend the evening with her lover in Haddock's bagnio without arousing the suspicions of her colonel husband.

Although tickets were selling for as much as 35 guineas each, equating to over £3,000 today, between 2,500 and 3,000 revellers, including 500 unmasked spectators who were seated in the gallery, attended the ball.[33] The politician and pamphleteer Sir Philip Francis, writing to his private secretary and brother-in-law Alexander Macrabie, captured the mood of heightened agitation as competition for tickets intensified:

> We are all raving mad about the king of Denmark's masquerade, which is to be given next Monday. The tickets bear a higher premium than those in the lottery. I have got one, and expect two more, to the grief of my friends and the astonishment of my enemies.[34]

At such prices, Murray could have only attended the ball if Ross had managed to get a complimentary ticket for her through his theatre connections, or former friends had lobbied the impressionable Danish monarch to issue her with a personal invitation.[35] It is always possible, of course, that the dissolute young king required no such prompting but was himself eager to meet the former courtesan who had enthralled London so many years before and who was the notorious addressee of *An Essay on Woman*. However she came by it, Murray was in possession of one of the hottest tickets in London.

The day of the much anticipated ball was one of intense activity and the streets near Covent Garden and especially 'Tavistock-street [were] thronged with Coaches and Attendants of the Nobility and Gentry buying Masquerade Dresses'. It was reported that over £10,000 exchanged hands for mask dresses during the course of the day.[36] The evening witnessed the same undignified crush as hundreds of coaches converged on the Opera House from Pall Mall and the Haymarket, and crowds of curious spectators thronged the streets to witness the spectacle of so many of the nobility glittering in their finery. The grandeur of the guests was matched, in breathtaking fashion, by that of the Opera House itself. King Christian had ordered lavish decorations so that every part of the theatre was illuminated by rows of elegant lamps that hung from the galleries and the stage was extravagantly lined with crimson velvet.[37]

The running order for the evening was precise: the doors of the Opera House opened at 7 p.m. to allow spectators to take up their seats in the gallery, and masqueraders were permitted entry from 9 p.m.[38] The Danish king, who wore 'a domino of gold and silver stuff, a black hat and white feather', arrived between 10 p.m. and 11 p.m. in the company of Count Holcke.[39] Revellers were to unmask at midnight although, in the event, the crowded rooms and oppressive heat forced many to unmask much earlier.[40] At midnight the Supper Rooms were opened and 400 waiters served at tables that were 'covered with all imaginable Elegance, both of Wines and Eatables'. The desserts, some of which were moulded into 'stately Palaces, and beautiful Landschapes [sic]', were thought 'beyond Description'.[41] At 2 a.m. the ball was opened by King Christian who led the dancing with Mary, Duchess of Ancaster who was dressed in a Sultana costume 'of purple sattin bordered with ermine, and flowing on the ground in all the pomp and state of Eastern magnificence'.[42] The dancing went on until 6 a.m. although from 4 a.m. 'the company began to go away, but the house was not totally clear till past eight'.[43]

The precise order of the evening was offset by the astounding variety and richness of costumes, which were described in great detail in all the London and provincial newspapers and periodicals. Perhaps following King Christian's lead, there was a preponderance of domino costumes among the male masqueraders, and oriental themes were also popular. Other costumes showed a mixture of inventiveness, originality and humour. There was everything from 'the conjurer, the black, and the old woman' (who was Horace Walpole's friend Henry Seymour Conway) to 'a methodist preacher, a chimney sweeper, with his bag, shovel, and scraper, and a boar with a bull's head'.[44]

The costumes aside, there was also the dazzling spectacle of £2 million worth of jewels (about £217 million today) on display that evening. Lady Spencer's costume was deemed by Lady Cowper, to be one of the finest – Murray's benefactress had borrowed from Lady Cowper, a 'diamond stomacher, which, added to her own jewels, made her very brilliant'.[45] Among the merchant classes the show was even greater. The wife of one 'eminent merchant had her dress ornamented with jewels to the amount of £30,000' (over £3 million) while:

an East-India Director was dressed in the real habit of a Chinese Mandarin, ornamented with diamonds, particularly the collar, which was entirely covered with diamonds, to an immense value, which greatly attracted the notice of his Danish majesty, who viewed the same for a considerable time.[46]

Murray could not have possibly competed with such shows of wealth, yet her costume was chosen from the thousands on display for special mention in nearly all the newspapers and journals that reported on the masquerade. Indeed, in an illustration of the ball published in the *Gentleman's Magazine*, she was the most prominent figure, just right of centre, her dark outfit contrasting noticeably with all those around her. In the same publication, Murray was first to be named 'among the characters of more humour but less opulence' – in other words, among those with more wit than diamonds. Disguised 'in the character of Night' Murray was said to have displayed 'much fancy in the choice of her dress; it was a thin black silk, studded with stars, and fastened to the head by a moon very happily executed'.[47] She was also described in flattering terms in 'The Masquerade', a poem described by the *Political Register* as 'below mediocrity':

> *Night* ventur'd there, but she had come too soon,
> Did not the stars around her, from their moon,
> Borrow such lustre, that it banish'd fear,
> Since *Night* in our possession glitter'd here.[48]

After her attendance at the King of Denmark's masquerade ball, Murray slipped almost completely from public view. She was nearing 40, a fact not overlooked in some of the poetic descriptions of the masquerade evening. For example, in the satiric 'A Sailor's Description of the Masquerade as Played before the King of Denmark', which appeared in a number of periodicals for October 1768, gentle reference was made to Murray's faded beauty:

> Mild Night too, who long shone the sun of this shore,
> But set in the fair Mrs Ross.[49]

Only the *Annual Register* desisted from also printing the more unforgiving 'Epigram on Mrs Ross's performing *Night*, at the Masquerade':

> Behold, in character of *Night*,
> All clad in dark array,
> *Fanny* appears! – the thought how right!
> *Fanny* has had her Day.[50]

Notes

1 *The Manuscripts of Captain Howard Vicente Knox,* Historical Manuscripts Commission, Report on Manuscripts in Various Collections (Dublin: 1909), vol. 6, p.102. Letter from Lord Clare to William Knox dated 10 October 1768.

2 Hugo Arnot, *The History of Edinburgh* … (Edinburgh: 1779), p.370.

3 *The Edinburgh Literary Journal: or, Weekly Register of Criticism and Belles Lettres* (Edinburgh: Constable and Co., 1829), no. 3, p.40 (for 29 November 1828).

4 *Public Advertiser,* 14 May 1767.

5 Edward A. Bloom & Lillian D. Bloom, *The Piozzi Letters: Correspondence of Hester Lynch Piozzi (1784–1821) (formerly Mrs Thrale),* 6 vols (Newark: University of Delaware Press, 1989–2002), vol. 1 (1989), p.306.

6 Edward Topham, *Letters from Edinburgh; Written in the Years 1774 and 1775* …, 2 vols (Dublin: [1780]), vol. 1, p.43.

7 John Montgomery, *The New Wealth of Cities: City Dynamics and the Fifth Wave* (Aldershot & Burlington, Vermont: Ashgate Publishing, 2008), p.121.

8 [Lord Gilbert Elliot Minto], *Proposals for Carrying on Certain Public Works in the City of Edinburgh* [1752], p.9.

9 *Gentleman's and London Magazine* (March 1767 issue), pp.190–91; Joseph Donohue (ed.), *The Cambridge History of British Theatre,* 3 vols (Cambridge: Cambridge University Press, 2004), vol. 2, p.172.

10 Bill Findlay (ed.), *A History of Scottish Theatre* (Edinburgh: Polygon, 1998), p.113; *Biographical Dictionary of Actors,* vol. 13, p.107.

11 Lewes, *Memoirs of Charles Lee Lewes,* vol. 3, p.71.

12 *Biographical Dictionary of Actors,* vol. 13, p.107.

13 James C. Dibdin, *The Annals of the Edinburgh Stage* … (Edinburgh: Richard Cameron, 1888), pp.146–47.

14 'To The Friends of Virtue and Liberty' [1767], http://digital.nls.uk/74894047.

15 *The Annual Register --- for the Year 1767* (1768), pp.238–39 (poetry section).

16 The royal patent would transfer to the Theatre Royal.

17 *The Scots Magazine* (Edinburgh: March 1768 issue), vol. 30, p.162.

18 David Mason Little & George Morrow Kahrl (eds), *The Letters of David Garrick,* 3 vols (Oxford University Press, 1963), vol. 2, p.601.

19 See *Walpole Correspondence,* vol. 5, pp.118–25; Aileen Ribeiro, 'The King of Denmark's Masquerade', in *History Today* (June 1977), vol. 26, no. 6, pp.385–89.

20 *The Annual Register … for the Year 1768* (1768), p.177.

21 Tillyard, *Royal Affair,* pp.105–13

22 Mary Wollstonecraft, *Letters Written during a Short Residence in Sweden, Norway, and Denmark* (1796), p.205.

23 Paul Langford, *A Polite and Commercial People: England 1727–1783* (Oxford: Clarendon Press, 1998), p.579. Other commentators have described the king's illness as schizophrenia. See for example, Michael Bregnsbo, 'Danish Absolutism and Queenship: Louisa, Caroline Matilda and Juliana Maria', in

Clarissa Campbell Orr (ed.), *Queenship in Europe 1660–1815: The Role of the Consort* (Cambridge: Cambridge University Press, 2004), p.350.

24 Theo. B. Hyslop, *The Great Abnormals* (Philip Allan & Co., 1925), p.55. See also, Wraxall, *Life and Times of Her Majesty Caroline Matilda*, vol. 1, pp.112–13.

25 Wraxall, *Life and Times of Her Majesty Caroline Matilda*, vol. 1, p.152.

26 Gillian Russell, *Women, Sociability and Theatre in Georgian London* (Cambridge: Cambridge University Press, 2007), pp.39–41. See also, Terry Castle, *Masquerade and Civilization: The Carnivalesque in Eighteenth-Century English Culture and Fiction* (Methuen & Co. Ltd, 1986), pp.84 and 96.

27 Montagu (ed.), *Letters of Mrs Elizabeth Montagu*, vol. 3 (1813), p.158. Letter to her sister dated 8 May 1751.

28 See Ch. 5, above, pp.111–12.

29 The identity of the original artist is unclear – http://www.britishmuseum. org/collection names him as Thomas Ross, and states that he was active in the late 1730s, which was before Murray was famous. *A catalogue of a most valuable and curious collection of prints, drawings, pictures, and books of prints …* (Magazin Des Estampes, [1775]), p.107, suggests the artist was Page, and lists the print as 'Miss Fanny Murray in a masquerade dress, after Page by Johnston'. See also, Smith, *British Mezzotinto Portraits*, 2nd part (1879), p.731.

30 O' Connell, *London 1753*, p.141.

31 See Celina Fox and Aileen Ribeiro, *Masquerade* (Museum of London, 1983), p.10. See also, Aileen Ribeiro, *The Dress Worn at Masquerades in England, 1730 to 1790 …* (& New York: Garland Publishing Inc., 1984), pp.144–46. O' Connell, *London 1753*, p.141, described it as a fashion for the 'Van Dyck Dress' – Rubens's portrait of Fourment was often attributed to Van Dyck in the eighteenth century.

32 *Catalogue of a most valuable and curious collection of prints*, p.107.

33 *Gazetteer and New Daily Advertiser*, 12 October 1768. Newspaper advertisements appeared offering tickets for sale: see *Lloyd's Evening Post*, 5–7 October 1768.

34 Herman Merivale (ed.), *Memoirs of Sir Philip Francis …*, 2 vols (Longmans, Green & Co., 1867), vol. 1, p.217. Letter dated 3 October 1768.

35 Bradshaw, *Thomas Bradshaw*, p.33 (footnote 14).

36 *St James's Chronicle: or, the British Evening Post*, 11–13 October 1768.

37 *The Political Register, and Impartial Review of New Books for 1768* (November 1768 issue), vol. 3, no. 20, p.319; *Gazetteer and New Daily Advertiser*, 12 October 1768.

38 *The London Journal*, 15 October 1768.

39 *Political Register* (November 1768 issue), vol. 3, no. 20, p.318.

40 Lady Llanover (ed.), *The Autobiography and Correspondence of Mary Granville, Mrs Delaney …*, 2nd series, 3 vols (Richard Bentley, 1862), vol. 1, p.189. Letter from Countess Cowper to Miss Dewes dated 21 November 1768.

41 *London Journal*, 15 October 1768.

42 *Political Register* (November 1768 issue), vol. 3, no. 20, p.319.

43 *The Oxford Magazine: or, University Museum* ... (October 1768 issue), vol. 1, p.161.

44 *Annual Register ... for the Year 1768*, p.177.

45 Lady Llanover (ed.), *Autobiography and Correspondence of Mary Granville*, 2nd series (1862), vol. 1, p.186. Letter from Countess Cowper to Miss Dewes dated 16 October 1768.

46 *Oxford Magazine* (October 1768 issue), p.160.

47 *Gentleman's Magazine and Historical Chronicle* (October 1768 issue), vol. 38, p.450.

48 *Political Register* (December 1768 issue), vol. 3, no. 21, p.384; 'The Masquerade; A Poem. Inscribed to the King of Denmark' (1768), p.19.

49 *London Magazine* (October 1768 issue), vol. 37, p.552; *Annual Register ... for the year 1768*, p.240 (poetry section).

50 *London Magazine* (October 1768 issue), vol. 37, p.552; *Political Register* (November 1768 issue), vol. 3, no. 20, p.320; *Scots Magazine* (Edinburgh: October 1768 issue), vol. 30, p.538.

II

The Final Years

At length, with fruitless Hope worn out,
She quits the giddy youthful Rout,
And turns so monstrously devout,
No Saint was e'er like Fanny.[1]

After the headiness of the King of Denmark's glittering masquerade, Murray returned to Edinburgh and an increasingly
dispirited Ross. Despite his considerable achievements in
spearheading a brand new patented theatre for Edinburgh, there had
been problems with his ambitious theatrical enterprise from the outset.
Lacking sufficient financial experience, Ross had grossly underestimated
the capital sums required to bankroll his theatre. Calculations made by
John Jackson, the actor/manager who bought the theatre from Ross in
1781, showed that there was a shortfall of £4,400 in Ross's estimations
and that the true cost of his theatre was closer to £6,900 rather than the
£2,500 that Ross had projected.[2]

There were other miscalculations too. It soon emerged, for example,
that Ross's new theatre, with its capacity of 1,500, was too small ever to
recoup his investment.[3] Even after Ross had increased ticket prices for
the boxes, pit and galleries, the maximum return he could expect from
a full house was £140.[4] In reality, however, takings were always going to
be considerably less, since it was well known that 'Edinburgh [did] not

give encouragement to the stage proportionable to the populousness of the city'.[5]

A further blow was dealt to the success of the theatre when, on 3 August 1769 the partly completed North Bridge collapsed, killing five people, after vaults on the southern side gave way. As the only direct link from the Old Town to the theatre, the bridge was the new theatre's lifeline. Without it, theatre-goers were discouragingly diverted through the steep and narrow alleyways of Leith, and Halkerston's Wynds. Thus, on the bitterly cold winter nights of Ross's opening season, when ice impacted on the steep inclines, these treacherous passageways were all but impassable. The bridge remained closed until 1772 and did not open to carriages until 1778:

> Awake my Muse, exert your skill,
> Of Roscius sing, and Play-house hill,
> For you by flight may reach the place,
> Which coach, or chairman cannot face.[6]

These challenges were all proving too much for a man who valued a life of ease and indolence above hard work and steady application. Indeed, the actor Charles Lee Lewes commented that from the moment Ross arrived in Edinburgh he had taken 'more delight in frequenting the fish-market (the cheapness of which pleased him much) than in attending his business at the theatre'.[7]

By the time the North Bridge collapsed, and only four months before the opening of his new theatre, Ross had lost heart and was looking for a way back to London for himself and Murray. Ross's way was greatly eased by the fact that about this time he had successfully contested his father's will, in which he had been disinherited, and was awarded £6,000 by a decision of the House of Lords.[8] Thus, at a time when preparations for the new theatre required his full attention, Ross absented himself for a few weeks as he devised an exit strategy.

Taking Murray with him, Ross travelled to Stratford-upon-Avon for the first national celebration of William Shakespeare, on the 200th anniversary of his birth in 1564 – the Stratford Jubilee was five years late. As Ross contemplated his return to the London stage, his motives for going to Stratford were less to do with honouring the Bard and more to do with re-establishing connections with influential friends and acquaintances as the theatrical world descended on the Warwickshire market town.[9] Indeed, it might have been while at Stratford that Ross negotiated with Samuel Foote a three-year lease on his Edinburgh theatre at 500 guineas per annum, to begin in the summer of 1770.

With the three-day event beginning on Wednesday 6 September, the couple probably left Edinburgh toward the end of August 1769. Before they set off, and with the collapse of the North Bridge something of a last straw, Ross wrote to George Colman, the acting manager of Covent Garden Theatre, to negotiate with him a return to the London stage. This letter is now lost, but its main tenets can be constructed from another letter to Colman, written by Ross on 9 September as he journeyed back to Edinburgh at the close of the celebrations. In high-handed manner, Ross restated his willingness to return to Covent Garden Theatre, on condition that Colman agreed to his terms. These included 'an article for five years, this and four more, four hundred pounds for the season, and the parts [he] played at the theatre when [he] left it, if [he] choose to perform them'.[10]

The Stratford Jubilee has been remembered for two main reasons; 'firstly, that torrential rain stopped play; and secondly, that there was no play to be stopped'.[11] The rain-soaked event included every imaginable entertainment from fireworks to masquerades and concerts to horse racing – everything, in fact, except a performance of a Shakespeare play. The celebrations began early on Wednesday morning with a canon salute, followed by a public breakfast. In Edward Thompson's satirical poem *Trinculo's Trip to the Jubilee*, Murray was imagined as dashing from the breakfast to Holy Trinity Church to hear a performance of Arne's oratoria *Judith*, sung by the beautiful Sophia Baddeley:

Breakfast over, hurry-scurry,
Lady RODNEY, FANNY MURRAY,
To the church repair;
Where music divine,
Inspir'd by the NINE,
Inchants the wond'ring earth, and floats along the air.[12]

The first day of festivities also included a procession, with musical accompaniment, to a riverside amphitheatre which had been purpose-built for the occasion. Foote, in sarcastic mode, described it as 'a gingerbread amphitheatre, which, like a house of cards, tumbled to pieces as soon as it was finished'.[13] A dinner was served there at three in the afternoon followed by a musical entertainment provided by David Garrick, who sang a selection of songs especially written for the occasion. Murray and Ross found time during this busy first day to drink tea with their friend James Boswell, who was also in town for the celebrations. In a rare example of Murray's acceptance in mixed company, the three friends made a convivial afternoon party with the Drury Lane comedian Thomas King and his wife, the dancer and actress Mary Baker.[14]

The focus of the second day of festivities was Garrick's performance of his 'Ode to Shakespeare'. Garrick had specially composed this poem for the dedication of both the newly built town hall and a statue of Shakespeare, given by Garrick to the corporation, which was to be erected inside.[15] Thursday's other highlight was a midnight masquerade ball which was held in the new amphitheatre and 'crowded to an extravagance' with over 1,000 attendees.[16] Boswell claimed that it was 'one of the best that has been in Britain'.[17] Having attended the King of Denmark's ball the year before, Murray might have smiled at the presumption.

Before the ball, Ross, King and Boswell dined together 'quietly and comfortably' and then Ross, Boswell and Murray accompanied the London bookseller Richard Baldwin to his lodgings where they all drank tea. Murray once again found acceptance in mixed company when she was introduced to the very respectable Mrs Baldwin, whom Boswell described as a 'grave, sensible, well-behaved woman' and to the Baldwins's daughter, whom Boswell was disappointed to note 'took after her mother'.[18]

Given her recent success at the King of Denmark's masked ball and her love of masquerades, Murray was probably more than willing to brave the torrential rains that had fallen throughout the second day to attend the Jubilee masquerade. Yet, there is no mention of her in any of the numerous reports of the ball. The evening belonged to Boswell who, in deference to his friend Pasquale Paoli, the Corsican independence fighter, went as 'an armed Corsican Chief'.[19] It also belonged to three young women – Lady Elizabeth Pembroke, Mrs Harriet Bouverie of Delapre Abbey in Northamptonshire, and Mrs Frances Anne Crewe – who were disguised as the three witches from *Macbeth*. Feting them as the 'three handsomest faces in England', they were teasingly held accountable for the dreadful weather with their 'when shall we three meet again, in thunder, lightning or in rain' speech.[20] The beautiful Mrs Crewe was just 21, and Murray might have felt the march of time as she watched her hold court that evening. More than twenty years before, Murray and Mrs Crewe's mother, the poetess Frances Greville, *née* Macartney, had been youthful rivals for a place in *The Beauties*, Horace Walpole's poetic shortlist of female lovelies.

The lashing rains continued into Friday, making the last day of the Jubilee a washout. The pageant in which Shakespeare's main characters were to walk in 'grand procession' had to be abandoned, although the Jubilee Cup went ahead, with the horses racing knee-deep in water.[21] A rather damp closing Grand Ball, which was held in the town hall, also went ahead, but the incessant rains had already prompted the start of a chaotic mass exodus from Stratford. As Boswell noted in his journal, 'after the joy of the Jubilee came the uneasy reflection that I was in a little village in wet weather and knew not how to get away, for all the post-chaises were bespoke'.[22] Ross and Murray had more luck than Boswell, for they had secured places on a northbound coach and so began a sodden journey back to Edinburgh.

The following day (Saturday, 9 September) they had completed the first leg of the journey and had reached the Swan coaching inn, in Birmingham. It was there that Ross replied to the letter that Colman had sent to him at Stratford regarding his re-engagement at Covent Garden Theatre. Ross apologised for replying to Colman 'on bad paper' from the inn but was otherwise overbearingly arrogant as he restated that a five-year contract and £400 a season were the only terms he was willing to accept. 'I have fixed my resolution,' insisted Ross, 'and nothing but these terms can induce me to quit my own little farm.'

Unmoved by Ross's imperious demands, Colman offered him three years at the theatre, but on his old terms. Ross accepted.[23] Thus, during the summer of 1769 and at least four months before 'his own little farm' was due to open, Ross had decided to throw in the towel and aimed to be back in London with Murray by April 1770.

The newly built Theatre Royal opened on 9 December 1769 with a performance of Richard Steele's *The Conscious Lovers*, two years to the day since the Canongate had reopened under Ross's management. Initial reactions to the new theatre were positive – its plain, unaffected exterior was thought to contrast elegantly with the fine curve of the auditorium and the expensive and tasteful furnishings of the candlelit interior. Audiences were far less favourable, however, about the lacklustre theatre company that Ross had assembled for the opening season.

In an effort to recoup his losses, Ross had presented an indifferent company, with no big (and expensive) names to tempt theatre audiences, and gambled that his investment in the interior decorations of the theatre, its scenery and costumes would carry the day. It was a serious miscalculation, as Ross's mediocre company failed to answer the challenges of bad weather, a broken-down bridge, a theatre that stood forlornly alone amidst an unfinished town and the natural disinclination of Edinburgh audiences to attend the theatre regularly.

Future managers learned from Ross's mistake. Samuel Foote, for example, in an unprecedented step, brought his entire London company from the Haymarket Theatre to Edinburgh for his opening season in 1770.[24] John Jackson netted the greater prize, however, by presenting the famous tragedian Mrs Sarah Siddons in 1784. 'Siddons fever' swept the city so that in one day there were 2,557 applications for 630 seats.[25]

In January 1770, a month after the Theatre Royal had opened, a six-penny poem entitled *A New Rosciad* made a vitriolic attack on Ross, his abilities as an actor/manager and on the calibre of actors – 'a worthless tribe, of no degree' – he had assembled for the season. Predictably, Ross's size and soporific style of acting came in for particular ridicule from the anonymous poet:

Like BEHEMOTH, he rolls along,
The mightiest monster of the throng!
Conceal'd in flesh his features lie,
And microscopic search defy.[26]

In his memoirs, Lewes claimed that Murray, in loyal defence of her husband, offered 20 guineas to anyone in Edinburgh who would reveal the poet's identity. Although no one came forward, Ross always suspected that the poem had been written by his business partner, James Bland, who had been in dispute with Ross over a loan.[27]

By the time *A New Rosciad* was published, Ross knew that he only had to sit it out in Edinburgh for two more months. As Ross counted down the days until his return to London his lack of interest in his Theatre Royal became palpable. An undated anecdote, recounted by Lewes, gives an indication of the level of Ross's managerial laziness. According to Lewes, Ross had ill-advisedly engaged a stocking weaver-cum-actor to play Hastings in *The Tragedy of Jane Shore*. On the night of the performance, the player, who had a broad Scottish brogue and limited acting ability, was promptly hissed off the stage. The actor fled the theatre and a messenger, possibly one of 'the fraternity of Cadies' who acted as guides and errand boys through the nooks and crannies of the Old Town, was sent immediately to fetch Ross from his lodgings on Castle Hill.[28] Ross, however, resolutely refused to return to the theatre to take over the part that he knew so well:

> But rather than quit his bottle, he sent word to the prompter to cut out all of Hastings's act, and begin with the following one, which was accordingly done, and it passed off that night almost imperceptibly; but the censure that ensued upon talking of it next day rendered Ross unpopular as a manager ever after.[29]

The Rosses returned to London in time for Ross to join Foote's company at the Haymarket for the summer season. He then transferred to Covent Garden Theatre to take up his three-year contract with Colman, and made 'his 1st Appearance on this Stage these 4 Years' on 10 October 1770 as the lead in *The Earl of Essex*.[30] Ross had made this role his own and had also played it on other landmark occasions in his life. It was as Essex that Ross had made his debut at Covent Garden Theatre on 3 October 1757 and at the Canongate when it had reopened on 9 December 1767 as the first patented theatre in Scotland. It was also as Essex that Murray first confronted Ross over his affair with the dancer Dolly Twist.[31]

Twist, who was about ten years Murray's junior, had spent most of her stage career at Covent Garden Theatre and might have received regular billing there from 1757 until her death in 1774.[32] Some years later a poem 'To the Memory of Miss Dolly Twist' immortalised the 'cherry lip' that Ross had enjoyed and imagined an afterlife for her in which she 'dance[d] under golden trees'.[33] According to the author of *Theatrical Biography*, which was published in 1772, around the time of the affair, Ross 'carried on so open a commerce [with Twist], as to reach the knowledge of the lowest retainers to the house'.[34] Murray, so the author of *Theatrical Biography* claimed, bore her husband's infidelity with dignity: 'instead of reproaching, she has, at all times, endeavoured to reclaim him by the most gentle and *exemplary* behaviour.'[35]

Some fifty years later, however, *The Drama; or, Theatrical Pocket Magazine* gave a rather different version of Murray's response to the affair, which was startlingly violent and showed a flash of the fiery Murray of old. According to this magazine, Murray only found out about her rival when she happened to be backstage at a performance of *The Earl of Essex* and saw Ross 'toying' with Twist:

> She ran to him, and scratched his face with so much violence, that four red rivulets ran copiously down it; and as Ross could not re-appear before the audience in such a condition, an apology was made for him on the plea of sudden illness.[36]

It is unknown whether their contretemps prompted Ross to give up Twist, or whether the liaison continued until Twist's death in 1774. What both versions of the discovery of the affair demonstrate, however, is the depth of Murray's feeling for her husband and the hurt he caused her by his infidelity.

Colman did not re-engage Ross when his three-year contract expired, and his final performance of the season was as Lear on 8 May 1773. It was another four years before Ross returned to the Covent Garden stage. In the intervening years, he performed in Edinburgh during the 1773–74 and 1775–76 seasons, and in Dublin and Cork in the spring and summer of 1775.[37] The actor/manager Tate Wilkinson engaged Ross to play at York, where he opened on the 22 February 1777, once more in the role of Essex. The season was not a success, and according to Wilkinson, Ross 'could not please in any characters' so that 'the York Theatre was deserted'.[38]

Ross's failure to engage his audiences was in part due to his style of acting, but also to his declining health. He had missed part of the 1773 season at Covent Garden Theatre due to a severe attack of gout and sometime after 1776, 'in a very infirm state of health', he had gone to Lyme Regis in Dorset, presumably with Murray, to recuperate.[39] When he appeared at York in the role of Sir Charles Easy in *The Careless Husband*, on 4 March 1777, Wilkinson noted that he looked 'gouty' and was 'grown pursy [short-winded and overweight] in person' so that 'the audience shrunk from him'.[40]

Ross returned to Covent Garden Theatre on 6 October 1777, where he reprised the role of Lear. Again, Ross failed to please. The theatre critic for the *Morning Post* described his performance as 'irregular as ever' and reminded readers of the 'coldness and insensibility' that Ross generally brought to his roles.[41] Audiences had grown tired of Ross, and with his career in steep decline, his last appearance at Covent Garden Theatre was on 17 February 1778, once more in the role of Sir Charles Easy.

Ross had more pressing preoccupations than his failing theatrical career as he performed on stage that February evening. Murray, at the age of 49, was dying. She might have been declining for some years, and had certainly aged less well than some of her contemporaries. When Charlotte Hayes turned 40, for example, she was described as 'fair as ten years past, with little paint'.[42] At about the same age, Murray had 'pleasing features and an agreeable countenance', but she was greatly altered and her former beauty 'was more than on the wane'. John Taylor recalled an occasion, presumably during an evening of backgammon with Ross, when Murray had shown him a portrait of herself from her former years:

> I remember her showing me a miniature, representing a lady of exquisite beauty, painted, I believe, in enamel. She asked if I knew the original of that portrait; and though her face must have undergone much alteration, yet I could trace the resemblance, and she seemed to be much gratified in finding that I knew it to be a portrait of herself.[43]

Despite her faded looks, it had been anticipating events somewhat when Murray had read her own obituary notice in one of the newspapers some years before. Her death had been erroneously reported on 26 November 1751 when the *London Daily Advertiser* made the brief announcement that 'a few Days since died the celebrated Miss Fanny Murray'. Such misreporting was not an unusual occurrence. The supposed death of the courtesan Margaret Caroline Rudd, who was involved in the Perreau forgery case, was reported several times. Indeed the *Morning Post* for 29 November 1786 noted that 'the celebrated Mrs Rudd, who has been so often killed by the newspapers, was on Monday night at Covent Garden theatre'.[44] Just a few months previously in July 1786, the same newspaper had reported the death, in Paris, of Mary 'Perdita' Robinson.[45] Her denial was published three weeks later on 5 August, when she announced that 'so far from being *dead*, I am in the most perfect state of health; except a trifling lameness'.[46] Unlike Robinson, however, Murray did not seek additional publicity by writing to the newspapers to inform them of their mistake or to demand a retraction. Rather, the false report was put to rights, without her interference, the following week with an equally brief announcement: 'we hear that Fanny Murray is not dead, as mentioned in one of the Papers.'[47]

Murray died at her home in Cecil Street on the south side of the Strand, where she and Ross had been living since at least January 1777. The exact date of her death is unclear. Some newspapers reported that she had died on the night of Tuesday 31 March 1778, others on Wednesday 1 April and still others on Thursday 2 April.[48] The cause of her death is unknown, but it is possible that aggressive cures for venereal disease during her youth had compromised her constitution. No expense was spared to save her, and the Rosses called on two of the most respected physicians in London to attend her, both of whom lived in Cecil Street. Dr William Heberden the Elder (1710–1801) was 'one of the most distinguished clinicians of his day': he was a Fellow of the Royal Society and, in 1778, was elected to the Royal Society of Medicine at Paris. Equally distinguished but far more fashionable was Sir John Eliot, who was noted for being 'one of the most conspicuous and busy town-doctors' then working in London.[49] He had been knighted in 1776, was physician to the Prince of Wales and received a baronetcy in the year of Murray's death. He also had something of a reputation as 'a merry eccentric little being' and did not think it at all off-putting to his patients that had a coach with 'a death's head painted on the pannel of his carriage'.[50] As previously noted, he too was no stranger to scandal, having divorced the courtesan Grace Dalrymple in 1776 for her adultery with Lord Valentia two years earlier.[51]

Eliot's practice made him a wealthy man, and he earned between £4,000 and £5,000 a year in professional fees. It is unclear, therefore, how Ross afforded Murray's medical treatment during her last illness, especially as there seemed to be nothing left of the £6,000 inheritance that Ross had been awarded at the beginning of the 1770s. Indeed, in her deathbed letter to the Spencers, Murray stated that her husband had 'but little and must save something for his old age'.[52] Eliot and Heberden might well have waived their charges, for it was said of Eliot that while 'he did not spare the wealthy, his practice was gratuitous to the poor'. Although the two physicians were unable to save Murray, they would have made her last weeks as comfortable as possible. Heberden was known for his 'great sweetness of manners' and it was said of Eliot that 'in address and manner, particularly to women, [he] excelled' so that he was very much a favourite with his female patients who responded positively to his cheery and kindly bedside manner.[53]

When Murray realised that her case was hopeless, she rallied herself, with the help of her sister, Mrs Brown, whose husband had been killed in the war with America, to perform one final act of benevolence. On 29 March, just days before her death, with her sister acting as her amanuensis, Murray wrote to Lord and Lady Spencer to bid a final farewell to her benefactors, and to thank them for their support. It was a poignant letter and filled with a genuine affection for the Spencers:

> I am now lying on a sick Bed and have been for six weeks past attended by Sir John Elliott [sic] and Doctor Heberdine [sic] and am now past all hopes they can do no more for me I fear my time is but of short date. Your generous Benevolences for twenty years back is near my Heart and I own I long to see you and my Lord my best and dearest friends.

In her last moments her thoughts were not for herself but with provision for her aged father. In her deathbed letter, she revealed that since first receiving her annuity, she had given £50 a year for her father's support. Murray's concern for the welfare of her father speaks strongly of her own benevolence, but also of Ross's 'love and tenderness' toward his wife and of his own generous and honourable nature. Despite their own financial difficulties, according to Murray, Ross had 'most cheerfully payd' this annual sum to his father-in-law.

The Spencers were out of town when Murray's letter arrived at Spencer House, their magnificent home at 27 St James's Place, and they did not return until midnight on 31 March. The Spencers' response was immediate. They were not only 'sincerely concern'd to hear [Murray] is so ill' but were also touched by her plea in her deathbed letter that 'it would be a Comfort to my Heart and a Relief to my mind and a noble addition to your generous Bounty if when I am no more you would think of [her father]'. Knowing that time was of the essence, the Spencers moved quickly. Fearing that, so close to death, a personal visit from her benefactors 'could do her no good', Lady Spencer rushed off a letter that was delivered to Cecil Street between midnight and one o'clock.[54] The letter was to reassure her 'that Lord Spencer Consents to allow Mrs Ross's Father the fifty pounds a year she requests' along with their hopes that her illness 'may take a favourable turn'. On the back of this letter, which was somehow returned to the family, Lady Spencer added a note confirming that the letter 'got there in time to give it her before her Death at which she [Murray] expressed the greatest gratitude & satisfaction'.[55]

The news that 'Mrs Ross (the late celebrated Miss Fanny Murray) wife of Mr Ross, the comedian' had died was carried in all the London and provincial newspapers, and in numerous magazines and journals.[56] The simple announcement made no mention of her past life as a courtesan beyond that contained within the discreet phrase 'the late celebrated Fanny Murray'. There were exceptions such as the *General Evening Post* which made a tasteless punned reference to Murray's promiscuous past in its announcement: 'Mrs Ross, (formerly Fanny Murray) though from her early starting in public life, known for a succession of years to all ranks of people.'[57] The *Morning Chronicle and London Advertiser* was rare in carrying an affecting obituary notice which was clearly written by someone intimately acquainted with Murray, perhaps Ross himself. The words are tender and affectionate, and her loss heartfelt:

> On Tuesday night died, universally lamented by all who had the happiness of her acquaintance, Mrs Ross, wife of David Ross, Esq; of Cecil-street, in the Strand, who in the course of twenty years proved herself a most amiable and affectionate wife, the best of children, by a dutiful and tender care of an aged parent, and who brought up and set forward in the world many brothers and sisters; it may be truly said of this lady, that she had a tear for pity, and a hand open as day for melting charity.[58]

At the age of 49, the most dazzling courtesan of her day was dead. She was laid to rest in a coffin that bore no embellishments other than a simple acknowledgement of her age.[59]

Notes

1 *Miss Fanny Murray, the Fair and Reigning Toast, in her Primitive Innocence* (*c.* 1764).

2 See Jackson, *History of the Scottish Stage*, pp.73–76. Hugo Arnot estimated the total cost of the theatre, wardrobe and scenery at £5,000. See Arnot, *History of Edinburgh*, p.372.

3 *The Encyclopaedia Britannica* ..., 8th ed., 22 vols (Edinburgh: Adam & Charles Black, 1853–60), vol. 8 (1855), p.406.

4 *Scots Magazine* (Edinburgh: March 1768 issue), vol. 30, p.163; Thomas Gilliland, *The Dramatic Mirror: Containing the History of the Stage* ..., 2 vols (1808), vol. 1,

p.249; Topham estimated £130 in 1774. See Topham, *Letters from Edinburgh*, vol. 1, p.125.

5 Arnot, *History of Edinburgh*, p.372.

6 *A New Rosciad* ... (Edinburgh: 1770), p.3.

7 Lewes, *Memoirs of Charles Lee Lewes*, vol. 4, p.197. See also, *The English Chronicle: or, Universal Evening Post*, 25–28 September 1790.

8 *Scots Magazine* (September 1790 issue) p.465; Rogers (ed.), *Boswelliana*, p.18.

9 John Chippendall Montesquieu Bellew, *Shakespere's* [sic] *Home at New Place, Stratford upon Avon* ... (Virtue Brothers & Co., 1863), pp.323–25.

10 Peake, *Memoirs of the Colman Family*, vol. 1, p.240.

11 Kate Rumbold, 'Shakespeare and the Stratford Jubilee', in Fiona Ritchie and Peter Sabor (eds), *Shakespeare in the Eighteenth Century* (Cambridge: Cambridge University Press, 2012), p.254. For other descriptions of the Jubilee celebrations see Christian Deelman, *The Great Shakespeare Jubilee* (Michael Joseph, 1964); Johanne Magdalen Stochholm, *Garrick's Folly: The Shakespeare Jubilee of 1769 at Stratford and Drury Lane* (Methuen & Co. Ltd, 1964); 'The Great Stratford Jubilee of 1769', in *Dublin University Magazine* ... (Dublin: George Herbert, June 1865 issue), vol. 65, no. 390, pp.603–25; *Prolegomena to the Works of Shakspeare* [sic] ... (Sherwood & Co., 1825), pp.lxiv–lxv; *The Literary Register: or, Weekly Miscellany* ... (Newcastle: 1769), vol. 1, p.220–22.

12 [Edward Thompson], *Trinculo's Trip to the Jubilee* ... (1769), p.13.

13 *The Annual Register* ... *for the Year 1769* (1770), p.129.

14 Stochholm, *Garrick's Folly*, pp.63 and 94; Brady and Pottle (eds), *Boswell in Search of a Wife*, p.299.

15 R. Chambers (ed.), *The Book of Days. A Miscellany of Popular Antiquities* ..., 2 vols (& Edinburgh: W. & R. Chambers, 1864), vol. 2, pp.318–19.

16 *T&C* (September 1769 issue), p.475.

17 James Boswell, 'A Letter from James Boswell, Esq; on Shakespeare's Jubilee at Stratford-upon-Avon', in *London Magazine* (September 1769 issue), vol. 38, p.454.

18 Brady and Pottle (eds), *Boswell in Search of a Wife*, p.300.

19 'An Account of the Armed Corsican Chief at the Masquerade, at Shakespeare's Jubilee, at Stratford-upon-Avon, September 1769', in *London Magazine* (September 1769 issue), vol. 38, p.455.

20 James Boaden (ed.), *Memoirs of Mrs Siddons* ..., 2 vols (Henry Colburn, 1827), vol. 2, p.191; George Colman, *Prose on Several Occasions* ..., 3 vols (1787), vol. 2, p.318.

21 *Annual Register* ... *for the Year 1769*, p.129.

22 Brady and Pottle (eds), *Boswell in Search of a Wife*, p.301.

23 Peake, *Memoirs of the Colman Family*, vol. 1, pp.240–42.

24 Foote made a 1,000-guinea profit by the end of the first season from his superior theatrical company. Finding even these returns insufficient, Foote sold his lease, at a loss, to West Digges and Ross's former partner, John Bland in spring 1771. The lease still had two years to run, and in 1773/74 Digges

negotiated a seven-year lease with Ross at 300 guineas per annum. See *The Edinburgh Literary Journal* ... (Edinburgh: Constable & Co., 1829), no. 4, pp.52–3 (for 6 December 1828).

25 *Sketch of the History of the Edinburgh Theatre-Royal Prepared for this Evening of its Final Closing May 25, 1859* (Edinburgh: Wood and Co., 1859), pp.8–9.

26 *New Rosciad*, pp.13 and 4.

27 According to Lewes, in *Memoirs of Charles Lee Lewes*, vol. 4, p.195, Bland 'bore Ross a grudge for his intention after the first year of throwing the £700 he had lent him for the purchase of the patent back again, without giving him any other consideration for his fourth share'.

28 Topham, *Letters from Edinburgh*, vol. 1, p.106.

29 Lewes, *Memoirs of Charles Lee Lewes*, vol. 4, pp.197–98.

30 *Public Advertiser*, 10 October 1770.

31 See *Theatrical Biography*, vol. 2, pp.29–30.

32 See *Biographical Dictionary of Actors*, vol. 15 (1993), pp.69–72.

33 'To the Memory of Miss Dolly Twist', in *The Muse's Mirrour: Being a Collection of Poems* ..., 2nd ed., 2 vols (1783), vol. 1, pp.50–51.

34 *Theatrical Biography*, vol. 2, p.30.

35 *Theatrical Biography*, vol. 2, p.30.

36 *The Drama: or, Theatrical Pocket Magazine* ... (T. & J. Elvey, July 1823 issue), vol. 4, no. 7, p.328.

37 *Biographical Dictionary of Actors*, vol. 13, p.108; 'Memoirs of David Ross Esq; Patentee of the Theatre at Edinburgh, and now performing at the Theatre-Royal, in Smock-Alley ...', in *Hibernian Magazine* (Dublin: March 1775 issue), vol. 5, pp.129–30.

38 Wilkinson, *Wandering Patentee*, vol. 1, p.246.

39 *Biographical Dictionary of Actors*, vol. 13, p.108; Samuel William Ryley, *The Itinerant: or, Memoirs of an Actor* ..., 3 vols (1808), vol. 2, p.214.

40 Wilkinson, *Wandering Patentee*, vol. 1, p.248.

41 *The Morning Post and Daily Advertiser*, 7 October 1777.

42 Thompson, *Meretriciad*, 3rd ed. (1761), p.26.

43 Taylor, *Records of My Life*, vol. 1, p.363.

44 Quoted in Bakewell, *Smart: The True Story of Margaret Caroline Rudd*, p.281.

45 *Morning Post and Daily Advertiser*, 14 July 1786.

46 *Morning Post and Daily Advertiser*, 5 August 1786.

47 *Whitehall Evening Post*, 23–26 November 1751.

48 Until quite recently, the date of Murray's death was thought to be 1770. See for example, *N&Q*, 7 Ser. XII (12 December 1891), p.470; 10 Ser. XI (12 June 1909), p.466; Postgate, '*That Devil Wilkes*', p.80; Sheila O'Connell, *The Popular Print in England* (British Museum, 1999), p.58; Lewis Melville, *Bath under Beau Nash*, p.266. *The Morning Chronicle and London Advertiser*, 2 April 1778, gave the date of her death as Tuesday, 31 March. *The Gazetteer and New Daily Advertiser*, 3 April 1778 and *The General Advertiser and Morning Intelligencer*, 3 April 1778, gave the date as 1 April. *The Scots Magazine*, vol. 40 (Edinburgh:

April 1778 issue) p.221 gave the date as 2 April. *Adams's Weekly Courant,* 7 April 1778 gave the date as 6 April. This is possibly because the editor simply copied verbatim news of Murray's death from a publication that had come out earlier in the week and which stated 'yesterday died, at their House ...'

49 Ernest Heberden, 'William Heberden the Elder (1710–1801): Aspects of his London Practice', in *Medical History* (1986), vol. 30, pp.303–21; 'Anecdotes of the Late Sir John Eliott', in *European Magazine and London Review* ... (February 1787 issue), vol. 2, p.68. See also, J.R. Partington & Douglas McKie, 'Sir John Eliot, Bart. (1736–86), and John Elliot (1747–87)', in *Annals of Science* (1950), vol. 6, no. 3, pp.262–63.

50 [Forbes Winslow], *Physic and Physicians* ..., 2 vols (Longman, Orme, Brown & Co., 1839), vol. 1, pp.74 and 76.

51 In later years she became a royal courtesan, mistress to both George, Prince of Wales and the Duc d'Orleans. See Manning, *My Lady Scandalous*, pp.61–102; *T&C* (August 1774 issue), pp.401–3; *N&Q*, 3 Ser. X (1 September 1866), pp.161–62.

52 BL – Add MS 75714. Letter to Lord and Lady Spencer dated 29 March 1778.

53 Thomas Joseph Pettigrew, *Biographical Memoirs of the Most Celebrated Physicians, Surgeons, etc., etc.* ... (Whittaker & Co., 1839), p.8 (of Heberden chapter); 'Anecdotes of the Late Sir John Eliott', p.68.

54 BL – Add MS 75714. This was noted on the back of the letter from Lord and Lady Spencer dated 31 March 1778.

55 BL – Add MS 75714. Letter from Lord and Lady Spencer dated 31 March 1778.

56 Comedian was a generic term for actors. See, for example, *London Evening Post*, 31 March–2 April 1778; *London Chronicle*, 2–4 April 1778; *T&C* (April 1778 issue) p.223; *Lady's Magazine* (April 1778 issue), p.223.

57 *General Evening Post*, 9–11 April 1778. See also, *Gazetteer and New Daily Advertiser*, 10 April 1778.

58 *Morning Chronicle and London Advertiser*, 2 April 1778.

59 *General Evening Post*, 9–11 April 1778.

Epilogue

By the time of her death in 1778, Murray had outlived nearly all her close Cyprian friends and rivals. Only Charlotte Hayes, who died in her mid-eighties in 1813, survived her.

The one-eyed Betsy Wemyss died in straitened circumstances in February 1760, and her bones were interred at Fulham. It was Wemyss who, some years before, had seduced Richard Atkins away from Murray after an evening at the Shakespear's Head Tavern. Another rival, 'the once gay and beautiful' Lucy Cooper, died on 18 October 1772, also in penurious circumstances.[1] Hers was a long, lingering illness, the result of excessive 'venery, disorders and drinking' that finally 'tore away those beauties she was once admired for'.[2] She was 42.

Murray also outlived Kitty Fisher who had died at Bath, en route to Bristol, on 10 March 1767 at the age of 28. Opinion is divided on whether smallpox, consumption or lead poisoning from the cosmetics she used had caused her death. Before her body was removed for burial in the family vault at Benenden Church in Kent, her husband of six months, John Norris, MP for Rye, gave instructions for her to be laid out in Bath. She was placed, not in a shroud but 'in her costliest finery, with satin ribbons and sparkling jewels', and the people of Bath were invited to pay their last respects to her beauty.[3] An elegy entitled 'On Kitty Fisher lying in State at Bath', which was composed around 1780 by Henry Harington (1727–1816), later mayor of Bath, reinforced the idea of Fisher's quasi-regal status in death.

By contrast, Murray's funeral would have been a modest affair and, as at the interment of the former prostitute Sally M---t, the parson probably preached a funeral sermon that 'concealed her failings, and exaggerated her virtues'.[4] It is likely that Murray's remains were placed in an unmarked grave, for Ross could have ill afforded the expense of a stone memorial. Ross's own 'plain private funeral' in 1790, which was paid for by his friends, cost £15 3s 3d, (about £1,400 today), a sum that was well beyond Ross's means.[5] Murray's exact burial place is unknown but she might lie in the churchyard of either St Martin-in-the-Fields or St Clement Danes, as Cecil Street, where she died, lay within these parish boundaries.[6]

Ross was grief-stricken by Murray's death. James Boswell met him a fortnight later on 18 April, and wrote in his journal how Ross had 'cried for the death of his wife, and embraced me cordially, and I promised to call on him in Cecil Street, and expressed a wish to do all in my power to divert his affliction'. The staunch Boswell was as good as his word and called on Ross within the week on 24 April.[7] Ross had little time to grieve, however, as the need to find work obliged him to take a week's engagement at the Theatre Royal in Liverpool towards the end of July, where he appeared alongside the actors John Henderson and Charles Lee Lewes.[8] He also performed at the Manchester playhouse in the months following Murray's death.[9]

The last vestiges of the life Murray shared with Ross would have soon disappeared. Ross probably gave up their Cecil Street home shortly before he left for Liverpool, being too poor to maintain a London home while also paying for lodgings in Liverpool and Manchester. As well as parting with the home he had shared with Murray, Ross also had to dispose of Murray's personal effects – her trinkets, clothes and perhaps the three little paintings of Roman antiquities she had once bought from the painter Arthur Pond. An itinerant actor had little room for sentiment as he moved from place to place, his possessions contained within a travelling portmanteau. Even so, perhaps like Boswell, on the death of his wife Margaret Montgomerie (d. 1789), Ross had 'carefully preserved her purse, a lock of her hair, [and] her wedding-ring'.[10]

In this dismantling of Murray's life with Ross, only one of her possessions is known to have survived. This is a miniature by Wolfgang William Claret (d. 1706) of Charles II's French mistress Louise de Kéroualle (or Kérouaille) (1649–1734), Duchess of Portsmouth, which is now in the

Spencer family collection at Althorp. Known as that 'Jezebel of Malice and Pride', the duchess had been gifted to Charles II by Louis XIV. Legend has it that when another of Charles's mistresses, the famous orange seller Nell Gwyn, was mistaken for the duchess in the street, she shouted to the assembled crowds, 'Nay, good people, I am the Protestant whore'.

Ross sent the miniature to the Spencers, possibly at Murray's behest, shortly after her death. In an accompanying letter, dated 27 April, and addressed to Lady Spencer, Ross noted that the miniature was 'the only thing among her trifles that I find worthy of your Ladyships Cabinet' and he asked the countess to accept it 'as a mark of a grateful heart'.

The portrait was not the only gift that Murray had made to her benefactors, for Ross's letter makes reference to a miniature of Bishop Gore that Murray had presented to Lady Spencer some years previously. Although Claret's initials are clearly visible on the Kéroualle miniature, in his letter to Lady Spencer, Ross mistakenly attributed the portrait to the influential seventeenth-century miniaturist Samuel Cooper (1608–72). It is a pleasing portrait and the French duchess stares seductively from a simple, brass frame wearing 'a bluish décolleté dress trimmed with white, and a blue scarf on her left shoulder'. Her eyes are half-closed and her famous baby-faced features are framed by an abundance of dark curls that fall sensuously over each shoulder.[11]

Ross survived his wife by twelve years, dying suddenly on 14 September 1790 at Thatched House Court in St James's Street. The intervening years were marked by hardship during which Ross suffered further ill-health and extremes of poverty. At the time of Murray's death, his long-standing financial worries were exacerbated by the fact that Murray's annuity from the Spencers had died with her. As letters to and from the actor/managers George Colman and David Garrick demonstrated, Ross was a forthright negotiator when it came to money, so he might have wasted little time in petitioning the Spencers to transfer Murray's annuity to him. Certainly, Ross's friend John Taylor was sure that he 'represented his situation to the head of that family, and was allowed a moiety of the annuity for the remainder of his life'.[12]

In 1781, Ross sold his theatre and its patent to the actor/manager John Jackson for an undisclosed sum which included all 'debts and incumberances' and a lifetime annuity of £150, to be paid annually.[13] It was widely reported at the time of Ross's death, however, that the annuity had been paid so irregularly that it 'served rather to tantalize than to relieve'.[14]

Ross's financial situation became all the more acute as theatrical work all but dried up. Apart from performing at the Smock Alley Theatre in Dublin for the 1783–4 season, Ross had few engagements during the 1780s. Taylor laid the cause of his friend's under-employment squarely at his own door believing that Ross 'ate himself into so unseemly a shape, that he could not procure a situation on the London boards'.[15] In 1787, a badly broken leg finally put paid to his stage career and 'deprive[d] [him] of the use of [his] Limb to walk'.[16]

Ross was not without female company during his widowhood and, according to Boswell, he was living with 'a low-bred, obliging girl whom he called Mrs Ross' at the time of his death.[17] From Boswell's phrasing, it seems unlikely that Ross had remarried, but rather that the woman was his live-in companion and mistress. Nothing else is known of the second Mrs Ross, other than that she paled into insignificance next to the incomparable Fanny Murray. She might have been with Ross at the onset of his final illness which came on overnight – death followed so suddenly that Boswell, though sent for, did not arrive in time.

Ross's funeral took place on 17 September, but so many of his friends were out of town that day, that only a 'select few', including Boswell as chief mourner, met together at Ross's lodgings to accompany his remains to St James's Church in Piccadilly.[18]

Boswell wrote an affectionate tribute to his old friend in a letter to the Reverend William Temple, dated 15 September 1790. 'Poor Ross,' penned Boswell, 'was an unfortunate man in some respects. But he was a true *bon vivant*, a most social man, and never was without good eating and drinking, and hearty companions.'[19] Ross was, of course, much more than this – most significantly, he made a lasting contribution to the theatrical life of Scotland by laying the foundation for a Scottish national theatre. His playhouse, when it opened in 1769, was not only 'the principal focal point of theatrical entertainment in Scotland for the next 90 years' but also did much to awaken Scottish cultural pride.[20] In its heyday, Ross's theatre was regarded as 'one of the neatest and most elegant theatres in Europe', one that did 'honour to the country, and to his taste'.[21]

By the time Ross was laid to rest, his late wife, the once beautiful and adored Murray had slipped almost completely from public memory. If she were remembered at all, it was not as a faithful wife of twenty years standing, but as a symbol of promiscuity and immorality.

Indeed, within two years of her death, she had been reduced to a straw effigy in a 'skimmington ride' that was said to have taken place in a village on the outskirts of London. Such rides, whereby local communities meted out their own justice to wayward neighbours, or voiced moral censure, through rituals of public humiliation, had a long history within popular culture.[22] The *Morning Post* for November 1780 carried a somewhat facetious report by 'a Traveller' who claimed to have witnessed a rowdy protest by female villagers against a recent publication by a cleric in favour of polygamy, probably *Thelyphthora* (1780) by the Reverend Martin Madan. The women, it was claimed, decided to hang the minister in effigy for his offence. To heighten the sexual and irreverent nature of the mockery, the figure of the cleric was placed on a goat between effigies of Murray, and her famous predecessor, Sally Salisbury:

> In a few minutes an effigy of the delinquent was brought forward mounted upon an he goat, a figure of a woman placed before, and another behind him; these I found upon enquiry to be the intended representatives of Fanny Murray and Sally Salisbury – and was informed that the books, one of which he held out in each hand, were Rochester's poems and the Woman of Pleasure.[23]

Other references to Murray following her death also carried sexual overtones. For example, and as previously noted, she was associated in verse, in 1784, with the dissipations of Medmenham, when she was represented as weeping over the body of the Order's founder, Sir Francis Dashwood.[24] Elsewhere, her name, along with those of other long-dead courtesans, was appropriated by homosexuals, such as the mollies who frequented the White Swan on Vere Street around 1810. In 1789, just before Ross's death, *Harris's List* reiterated the old claim that the successful careers of women like Murray and Fisher had 'debauched more girls than all the officers of the guards', by persuading young women that prostitution could offer them similar wealth and fame.[25]

It was only with Ross's death in September 1790 that Murray was once more restored to public memory as a wife of unimpeachable reputation. This was in large part thanks to Boswell who was the probable author of Ross's obituary that first appeared in the *Gentleman's Magazine* and the *London Chronicle*. His praise for Murray as a model wife was the standard by which she was judged thereafter in numerous magazines and journals that carried news of Ross's death:

> [Ross's] domestic life was marked by his marriage with the once celebrated Fanny Murray, who, whatever her former indiscretions were, conducted herself as a wife with exemplary prudence and discretion.[26]

With the dawning of the nineteenth century, Murray finally achieved the anonymity she had craved, at least from the time of her marriage to Ross. As the young men who had followed Murray's fortunes grew old and died, she was no longer spoken of. Where once there had been thousands of prints of her, these were all but lost, repurposed or simply pulped. Indeed, her portraits became so scarce that Robert Henry Fryar, a private publisher in Bath, wrote into *Notes & Queries* in 1891 in the hope that readers might be able to help him track down her likeness. The details of Murray's life had already become so sketchy that Fryar mistakenly described her as 'a Bath beauty about 1735', when she would have been 6 years old.[27]

There were only occasional reminders of Murray, as when a copy of the *Memoirs* or a mezzotint of her portrait appeared in a catalogue advertising an upcoming sale of books and prints. These might well have come from the private libraries of her former admirers when their deceased estates were broken up and their personal effects, including their libraries, were sold off at auction. It was then that among their worthy histories and works of literature, and their respectable portraits of royals, military men and politicians that their collection of racy biographies and portraits of courtesans and actresses from a previous age came to light. For example, when the library of the actor, John Philip Kemble, was broken up a couple of years before his death in 1823, it included among portraits of royalty, nobility and actors, prints of Murray, Peg Woffington and Nancy Dawson.[28] Similarly, when the immense library of Charles Burney, father to the novelist Fanny Burney, was sold to the British Museum in 1818, it contained two prints of Murray by Richard Corbutt.[29]

Murray's anonymity would not last long – her famed beauty, the anecdote of the banknote sandwich, and her connections to some of the most famous men of the eighteenth century would soon rekindle interest in her for a new generation of admirers. For a short while, however, there were those who knew little of her beyond her name. By 1888, a contributor to *Notes & Queries* could pose a question that would have been unthinkable a century before:

> Can any correspondent well acquainted with the *ana* of the last century give a clue to where aught may be found referring to a certain Fanny Murray …?[30]

Fanny Murray was a phenomenon in her own time and for eight years she was the supremely successful courtesan of her day. Her notoriety, exceptional beauty and style captivated and enthralled men and women from all walks of life. As the very personification of glamour and excess, she fuelled a generation of male sexual fantasies and female dreams of fame, fortune and desirability. Retrieved from the *Memoirs'* monopolistic hold over the telling of her story, the life of the real Fanny Murray contributes an intriguing chapter to the study of eighteenth-century courtesans.

Hers was a life of opposing tensions and during her heyday the dazzling splendour of her public life often belied the tawdriness of her private existence. Murray's remarkable career was built on a succession of unsavoury liaisons with men who enjoyed, and then discarded her; men such as John Spencer, the dissolute serial seducer and the thuggish Edward Strode. Even in marriage she found that she was replaceable, as Ross took at least one mistress and after Murray's death set himself up with a second Mrs Ross. It is apposite, therefore, that the story of Murray's fame and fortune should have been told in second-rate literature, in poor doggerel verse and 'miserable catchpenny book[s]' penned, in large part, by jobbing hack-writers.

Fanny Murray still manages to engender feelings of admiration and affection, possibly because of the mix of vulnerability and courage she displayed as she fought to overcome the many adversities in her life. She was a born survivor and after a career that made her the most celebrated woman of her age, she ended her days with quiet dignity, having secured a place for herself, and those she loved, in an often hostile world.

Notes

1 *T&C* (October 1772 issue), p.560.
2 Taylor, *Records of My Life*, vol. 1, p.52. See also, Wilkinson, *Memoirs of his own Life*, vol. 2, p.89; *General Evening Post*, 17–20 October 1772.

3 Bleackley, *Ladies Fair and Frail*, p.94.

4 *Humours of Fleet-Street*, Part II, p.104.

5 Marion S. Pottle, Claude Colleer Abbott, Frederick A. Pottle (eds), *Catalogue of the Papers of James Boswell at Yale University*, 3 vols (& Edinburgh & New Haven: Edinburgh & Yale University Press, 1993), vol. 1, p.358. See also, vol. 3, p.1118.

6 It has not been possible to locate Murray in the parish burial records for Westminster held at WAC.

7 Charles McC. Weis and Frederick A. Pottle (eds), *Boswell in Extremes, 1776–1778* (Heinemann, 1971), pp.299 and 309. See also, Stone, *The Family, Sex and Marriage* (1977), p.250.

8 *Williamson's Liverpool Advertiser and Mercantile Chronicle*, 24 July 1778.

9 Proctor, *Manchester in Holiday Dress*, p.19.

10 Stone, *Family, Sex and Marriage*, p.584.

11 See Basil S. Long, *British Miniaturists* (Geoffrey Bles, 1929), p.71; Charles Wheeler, *The Age of Charles II, Royal Academy of Arts Winter Exhibition, 1960–61* (Royal Academy of Arts, 1961), p.175.

12 Taylor, *Records of My Life*, vol. 1, p.363.

13 Jackson, *History of the Scottish Stage*, p.76. See also, p.179. Lewes gave a different version of the sale of the Theatre Royal in Lewes, *Memoirs of Charles Lee Lewes*, vol. 3, pp.81–83.

14 *Gentleman's Magazine: and Historical Chronicle* (September 1790 issue), vol. 60, Part 2, p.865.

15 Taylor, *Records of My Life*, vol. 1, p.362.

16 BL – Add Ms 75714. Letter from Ross to Lady Spencer dated 13 November 1787.

17 Marlies K. Danziger and Frank Brady (eds), *Boswell: The Great Biographer 1789–1795* (Heinemann, 1989), p.106.

18 *London Chronicle*, 18–21 September 1790.

19 Chauncey Brewster Tinker (ed.), *Letters of James Boswell …*, 2 vols (Oxford: Clarendon Press, 1924), vol. 2, p.401.

20 Donald Mackenzie, *Scotland's First National Theatre* (Edinburgh: The Stanley Press, 1963), p.9. See also, Donald Campbell, *Playing for Scotland: A History of the Scottish Stage 1715–1965* (Edinburgh: Mercat Press, 1996), p.19.

21 Quoted in *Edinburgh Literary Journal* (Edinburgh: Constable and Co., 1829), p.40 (for 29 November 1828). Ross's theatre stood for ninety years before being substantially rebuilt in 1830 and finally demolished in 1859 to make way for the new General Post Office. Tastes had changed, and instead of being praised for its simplicity and neatness, it was loathed as 'one of the plainest public buildings in Edinburgh' and its few embellishments regarded as 'offensive to good taste'. See John Marius Wilson, *The Imperial Gazetteer of Scotland ---*, 2 vols (Edinburgh: A. Fullerton & Co., 1854–57), vol. 1 (1854), p.530.

22 See, for example, Martin Ingram, 'Ridings, Rough Music and Mocking Rhymes in Early Modern England', in Barry Reay (ed.), *Popular Culture in Seventeenth-Century England* (& Sydney: Croom Helm, 1985), pp.166–97.

23 *Morning Post and Daily Advertiser*, 21 November 1780.

24 *Public Advertiser*, 27 September 1784.

25 *Harris's List* (1789), p.58.

26 *Gentleman's Magazine: and Historical Chronicle* (September 1790 issue), vol. 60, part 2, p.865. See, for example, *London Chronicle*, 18–21 September 1790.

27 *N&Q*, 7 Ser. XII (17 October 1891), p.307.

28 *A Catalogue of the Valuable and Extensive Miscellaneous Library … of John Philip Kemble …* (1821), p.58.

29 Burney's library was sold to the British Museum for £13,500.

30 *N&Q*, 7 Ser. V (19 May 1888), p.389.

Select Bibliography

Manuscript Sources and Archival Materials

Bath Record Office
103/1/2/1 – Minute Book of the Blue Coat Charity School 1711–73.

Bath Central Library
B.352.0422 – Bath Council Book, vol. 2 (1684–1751), no.5 (1728–38)
B.352.0422 – Bath Council Book, vol. 3 (1751–83), no. 7 (From 21 November 1751–16 March 1761).
B.942.38 – City of Bath Rate Books, vol. 1 (1766–73).
Jewers, Arthur J. (ed.), The Registers of the Abbey Church of SS Peter and Paul, Bath, 2 vols (The Harleian Society (vols 27–28) 1900–01).
B929.3 SAI – The Register of St James's, Bath, 4 vols. (n/d).
L929.3 BAT – 'The Register Book of the Parish of Wolley [sic]', in Parish Registers – Bathwick, Wooley, (sic) Englishcombe.

British Library
Add MS 75714 – Lady Spencer's Collection of Manuscript Letters.
Add MS 23724 – Arthur Pond's Journal of Receipts and Expenses, 1734–50. Entry for 15 July 1748.
Egerton MS 3736 f.139 – Correspondence of George Scott of Woolston Hall. Letter to Thomas Wilson dated 11 June 1761.
Add MS 30880 B f.3 – Correspondence of John Wilkes, chiefly with ladies.

Add MS 30878 f.3 – Correspondence of John Wilkes with Charles Churchill.

Caird Library at the National Maritime Museum
SAN/V/113 – *Al Koran* of the Divan Club (microfilm).

The City of Westminster Archive Centre
St James's Piccadilly (microfilm no. 22 – burials 1754–1812) – The Register
    Book for Burials in the Parish of St James in Westminster in the County of
    Middlesex begun 1 May 1754, vol. 4.

Library of the Royal College of Surgeons of England
MS0022/1/3 Series No 1 – Lock Hospital General Court Book (July 1746–May
    1762).
Williams, David Innes, *The London Lock: A Charitable Hospital for Venereal Disease*
    1746–1952 (& New York: Royal Society of Medicine Press Ltd, 1995).

London Metropolitan Archives
DL/C/0173 (Microfilm X079/091) – Allegations, Libels and Sentence Book, July
    1754–June 1759.
DL/C/0553/149–51 – Divorce papers relating to Lucy Naomi Strode *née*
    Gough.

The National Archives Public Record Office
Prob/11/823/487 – Sir Richard Atkins's will.

National Art Library at the Victoria and Albert Museum
Dyce Collection – Dyce S 8vo 10598 – *An Essay on Woman* (*c.* 1764).
Dyce Collection – Dyce S 12mo 10559 – *An Essay on Woman* (between 1780 and
    1799).

National Library of Scotland
Harris's List of Covent Garden Ladies: or, New Atalantis for the Year 1761 (1761).
'To The Friends of Virtue and Liberty' [1767], http://digital.nls.uk/74894047.

Woodhorn – Northumberland Archives
2DE/42/3/1–8 – Papers relating to Elizabeth Roach.

Unpublished Theses
Bourque, Kevin Jordan, 'Blind Items: Anonymity, Notoriety, and the Making of
    Eighteenth-Century Celebrity' (unpublished doctoral thesis: University of
    Texas at Austin, 2012).
James, Kenneth Edward, 'Concert Life in Eighteenth-Century Bath' (unpublished
    doctoral thesis: University of London, 1987).

MacInnes, Iain I., 'The Highland Bagpipe: The Impact of The Highland Societies of London and Scotland 1781–1844' (unpublished M. Litt. thesis: University of Edinburgh, 1988).

Printed Sources

Primary Source Materials (Including Modern Editions)

The Adulteress (1773).

Almon, John (ed.), *The New Foundling Hospital for Wit ... Part of the Third* (1769).

Ambross, Miss [E.], *The Life and Memoirs of the Late Miss Ann Catley, the Celebrated Actress ...* [1789].

The Amours of Carlo Khan: Interspersed with Curious Anecdotes and Bon Mots of Many Distinguished Personages ... (1789).

Aspinall-Oglander, Cecil, *Admiral's Wife: Being the Life and Letters of The Hon. Mrs Edward Boscawen from 1719 to 1761* (& New York & Toronto: Longmans, Green & Co., 1940).

Atkyns, John Tracy (ed.), *Reports of Cases Argued and Determined in the High Court of Chancery in the time of Chancellor Hardwicke ...* (1765).

Ben Johnson's Jests: or, the Wit's Pocket Companion ..., 3rd ed. (1755).

Boswell, James, *Boswelliana: The Common Place Book of James Boswell with a Memoir and Annotations*, edited by Charles Rogers (Houlston & Sons, 1876).

Boswell, James, *Boswell in Extremes, 1776–1778*, edited by Charles McC. Weis and Frederick A. Pottle (Heinemann, 1971).

Boswell, James, *Boswell in Holland, 1763–1764 ...*, edited by Frederick A. Pottle (& Melbourne & Toronto: William Heinemann Ltd, 1952).

Boswell, James, *Boswell in Search of a Wife, 1766–1769*, edited by Frank Brady and Frederick A. Pottle (& Melbourne & Toronto: William Heinemann Ltd, 1957).

Boswell, James, *Boswell's London Journal 1762–1763*, edited by Frederick A. Pottle (& New Haven: Yale University Press, 1992).

Boswell, James, *The Correspondence of James Boswell and William Johnson Temple, 1756–1795*, edited by Thomas Crawford (Edinburgh & New Haven: Edinburgh & Yale University Presses, 1997) 2 vols.

Boswell, James, *Private Papers of James Boswell from Malahide Castle*, edited by Geoffrey Scott and Frederick A. Pottle (privately printed, 1930), 18 vols, vol. 9.

Boyce, William, 'While Some, in Never Dying Verse: a Song Wrote by Mr Boyce' (BL Music Collection G.313. (205)).

The British Letter-writer: or Letter-writer's Complete Instructor ... (c. 1765).

British Worthies: or, Characters of the Age. A Panegyrico-Satirical Poem with notes variorum ... (1758).

Carswell, John, and Lewis Arnold Dralle (eds), *The Political Journal of George Bubb Dodington* (Oxford: Clarendon Press, 1965).

Casanova, Giacomo, Chevalier de Seingalt, *History of My Life*, translated by William R. Trask, abridged by Peter Washington and introduction by John Julius Norwich (& New York & Toronto: Alfred A. Knopf, 2006).

Catalogue of a most valuable and curious collection of prints, drawings, pictures, and books of prints ... (Magazin Des Estampes, [1775]).

Chandler, Mary, *A Description of Bath: A Poem. Humbly Inscribed to Her Royal Highness the Princess Amelia* (1734).

Characters of the Present Most Celebrated Courtezans ... (1780).

Charnock, John, *Biographia Navalis: or, Impartial Memoirs of the Lives and Characters of Officers of the Navy of Great Britain* ..., 6 vols (1794–98).

Cheny, John, *An Historical List of Horse-Matches Run, and of Plates and Prizes, Run for in Great Britain in 1750* ... (1751).

Churchill, Charles, *The Candidate. A Poem (1764)*.

Clarke, W., *The Authentic and Impartial Life of Mrs Mary Anne Clarke ---*, 2nd ed. (T. Kelly, 1809), p.7.

Cleland, John, *Memoirs of a Woman of Pleasure*, 2 vols (1749).

Clio and Euterpe: or, British Harmony: A collection of celebrated songs and cantatas ..., 3 vols (1762).

Coke, Lady Jane, *Letters from Lady Jane Coke to her Friend Mrs Eyre of Derby, 1747–1758*, edited by Mrs Ambrose Rathborne (Swan Sonnenschein & Co. Ltd, 1899).

The Complete Letter-Writer ..., 2nd ed. (1756).

A Congratulatory Epistle from a Reformed Rake to John F----G, Esq, Upon the New Scheme of Reclaiming Prostitutes (c. 1758).

'The Connoisseur', no. 47 (for 19 December 1754) in Alexander Chalmers (ed.), *The British Essayists*, vol. 31 (1807).

Cooksey, Richard, *Essay on the Life and Character of John Lord Somers, Baron of Evesham: also Sketches of an Essay on the Life and Character of Philip Earl of Hardwicke* ... (Worcester: 1791).

Derrick, Samuel, *Letters written from Leverpoole, Chester, Corke, The Lake of Killarney, Dublin, Tunbridge-Wells, and Bath*, 2 vols (Dublin: 1767).

Dilke, Charles Wentworth (ed.), *The Papers of a Critic. Selected from the Writings of the Late Charles Wentworth Dilke* ..., 2 vols (John Murray, 1875).

Dodd, William, *The Sisters: or, the History of Lucy and Caroline Sanson, Entrusted to a False Friend*, 2 vols (1754).

The Drama: or, Theatrical Pocket Magazine ... (T. & J. Elvey, July 1823 issue).

The English Roscius: Garrick's Jests, or, Genius in High Glee ... [1785].

The Fool: Being a Collection of Essays and Epistles, Moral, Political, Humourous, and Entertaining. Published in the Daily Gazetteer ..., 2 vols (1748).

Garrick, David, *The Private Correspondence of David Garrick* ..., 2 vols (Henry Colburn & Richard Bentley, (1831–32).

Goldsmith, Oliver, *The Life of Richard Nash, of Bath, Esq* ... (1762).

[Goudar, Ange], *The Chinese Spy: or, emissary from the court of Pekin, commissioned to examine into the present state of Europe. Translated from the Chinese*, 6 vols (1765).

Granville, Mary, *The Autobiography and Correspondence of Mary Granville, Mrs Delaney*, edited by Lady Llanover, 3 vols (Richard Bentley, 1861) and 2nd series, 3 vols (Richard Bentley, 1862).

Harris, Jack (pseud.), *Harris's List of Covent Garden Ladies* ... (1761, 1773, 1789 and 1793).

Haywood, Eliza Fowler, *The Invisible Spy by Exploralibus*, 4 vols (1755).

Heath, Robert, *The Gentleman and Lady's Palladium for the Year of Our Lord 1751* ... [1751].

Heber, Reginald, *An Historical List of Horse-Matches Run ... in the Year 1759* ... (1760).

Hill, John, *The Inspector*, 2 vols (1753).

[Holloway, Robert], *The Phoenix of Sodom: or, the Vere Street Coterie* (J. Cook, 1813).

'A Humorous Poetical Dialogue, between the once celebrated Miss F---y M----y and the now famed Miss K---y F---r', in Ferdinando Funny, *The Droll Miscellany: or, Book of Fun* ... (Dublin: 1760).

The Humours of Fleet-Street: and the Strand; being the Lives and Adventures of the Most Noted Ladies of Pleasure ... By an Old Sportsman (1749).

Jackson, John, *The History of the Scottish Stage* ... (Edinburgh: 1793).

The Jests of Beau Nash, Late Master of the Ceremonies at Bath ... (1763).

Joe Miller's Jests ..., 7th ed. (1744).

The Juvenile Adventures of Miss Kitty Fisher, 2 vols (1759).

Kelly, Hugh, *Thespis: or, a Critical Examination into the Merits of all the Principal Performers belonging to Covent Garden Theatre. Book the second* (1767).

Letters between the Duke of Grafton---and John Wilkes Esq ... 2 vols (1769).

'Letter to F---y M----y', in *The Literary Magazine: or, Universal Review, for the Year 1756*, 3 vols (1756–58).

Lewes, Charles Lee, *Memoirs of Charles Lee Lewes: containing anecdotes, historical and Biographical of the English and Scottish Stages, during a period of forty years*, 4 vols (1805).

Little, David Mason, & George Morrow Kahrl (eds), *The Letters of David Garrick*, 3 vols (Oxford University Press, 1963).

Mallet, David, 'The Reward: or, Apollo's Acknowledgements to Charles Stanhope' (written 1757), and 'Cupid and Hymen: or, The Wedding-Day', in Samuel Johnson, *The Works of the English Poets. With Prefaces, Biographical and Critical* (1779), vol. 53.

'The Masquerade: A Poem. Inscribed to the King of Denmark' (1768).

Memoirs and Interesting Adventures of an Embroidered Waistcoat. Part II. In which is introduced, 'The Episode of a Petticoat' (1751).

Memoirs of the Celebrated Miss Fanny M-----, 2nd ed. (J. Scott and M. Thrush, 1759), vol. 1, and *Memoirs of the Celebrated Miss Fanny M-----* (M. Thrush, 1759), vol. 2.

Miss Fanny Murray, the Fair and Reigning Toast, in her Primitive Innocence ... (c. 1764).

The Modern Courtezan, an Heroic Poem. Inscrib'd to Miss F---y M----y ... [1750].

A New Rosciad ... (Edinburgh: 1770).

Nocturnal Revels: or, the History of King's-Place and other Modern Nunneries... By a Monk of the Order of Saint Francis, 2nd ed., 2 vols (1779).

Oddibus, Funnybus, *A Collection of Original Comic Songs and Others* ... [1765].

Peake, Richard Brinsley (ed.), *Memoirs of the Colman Family* ..., 2 vols (Richard Bentley, 1841).

Pick, William, *Authentic Historical Racing Calendar of all the Plates, Sweepstakes, Matches, &c. Run for at York* ... [York: 1785].

Robert Sayer's New and Enlarged Catalogue for the Year 1774 ... [1774].

Russell, John, *Correspondence of John, Fourth Duke of Bedford selected from the Originals at Woburn Abbey with an Introduction by Lord John Russell*, 3 vols (Longman, Brown, Green & Longmans, 1842–46).

Satan's Harvest Home: or, the Present State of Whorecraft ... Collected from the Memoirs of an Intimate Comrade of the Hon. Jack S--n---r, and Concern'd with him in many of his Adventures ... (1749).

The Scourge of Pleasure. (1758).

Smollett, Tobias, *The Expedition of Humphry Clinker*, edited with an introduction by Angus Ross (Harmondsworth: Penguin Classics, 1967, repr. 1985).

Stanhope, Philip Dormer, *The Letters of Philip Dormer Stanhope, Earl of Chesterfield* ... edited by Lord Mahon, 4 vols (1845).

Steele, Elizabeth, *The Memoirs of Mrs Sophia Baddeley* ..., 6 vols (1787).

Stevens, George Alexander, *The History of Tom Fool*, 2 vols (1760).

Taylor, John, *Records of My Life* ..., 2 vols (Edward Bull, 1832).

Theatrical Biography: or, Memoirs of the Principal Performers ..., 2 vols (Dublin: 1772).

Thompson, Edward, *The Meretriciad* (1761); 3rd ed. (1763); 6th ed. (1765).

Thompson, Edward, *Trinculo's Trip to the Jubilee* (1769).

Thomson, [James], 'An Ode on Miss Fanny Murray', in *A New-Years Miscellany* ... (1747).

'To the Memory of Miss Dolly Twist' in *The Muse's Mirrour: Being a Collection of Poems* ......, 2nd ed., 2 vols (1783).

Topham, Edward, *Letters from Edinburgh; Written in the Years 1774 and 1775* ..., 2 vols (Dublin: [1780]).

Verney, Lady Margaret Maria (ed.), *Verney Letters of the Eighteenth Century from the MSS. at Claydon House*, 2 vols (Ernest Benn Ltd, 1930).

The Vis-à-Vis of Berkley-Square: or, A Wheel off Mrs W-t--n's Carriage. Inscribed to Florizel (1783).

Walpole, Horace, *The Beauties: An Epistle to Mr Eckhardt, the Painter* (1746).

Walpole, Horace, *Journals of Visits to Country Seats, etc.* (Oxford: Oxford University Press, 1928), vol. 16 of *The Walpole Society*.

Walpole, Horace, *The Letters of Horace Walpole, Earl of Orford*, edited by Peter Cunningham, 8 vols (Richard Bentley, 1857).

Ward, Edward, *A Step to the Bath: with a Character of the Place* (1700).

Wilkinson, Tate, *Memoirs of his Own Life* ..., 4 vols (York: 1790).

Wilkinson, Tate, *The Wandering Patentee; or, a History of the Yorkshire Theatres …*, 4 vols (York: 1795).

The Witling: Being a Compleat Collection of the most Celebrated Conundrums Now in Vogue Among People of High Taste (1749) and *A Key to the Witling: Being Proper Answers to a Compleat Collection of the most Celebrated Conundrums Now in Vogue Among People of High Taste* (1750).

Woffington's Ghost. A Poem. In answer to The Meretriciad (1761).

Wood, John, *A Description of Bath …* (1765), (Facsimile edition, Bath: Kingsmead Reprints, 1969).

Yorick's Jests: or, Wit's Common-Place Book … (1790).

Newspapers and Periodicals

Adams's Weekly Courant.

The Annual Register … for the Year …

The Bath Journal.

The Caledonian Mercury.

The Centinel.

Chambers' Journal of Popular Literature, Science and Arts.

The Crab-Tree.

The Critical Review: or, Annals of Literature.

The Derby Mercury.

The Drama: or, Theatrical Pocket Magazine.

The Dublin University Magazine.

The Edinburgh Literary Journal: or, Weekly Register of Criticism and Belles Lettres.

The Edinburgh Magazine: or, Literary Miscellany.

The English Chronicle: or, Universal Evening Post.

The European Magazine and London Review

The Gazetteer and New Daily Advertiser.

The General Advertiser and Morning Intelligencer.

The General Evening Post.

The Gentleman's and London Magazine.

The Gentleman's Magazine and Historical Chronicle.

The Gentleman's Magazine: or, Monthly Intelligencer.

The Hibernian Magazine: or, Compendium of Entertaining Knowledge.

Jackson's Oxford Journal.

The Lady's Magazine: or, Entertaining Companion for the Fair Sex.

The Leeds Intelligencer.

The Literary Magazine: or, Universal Review.

The Literary Register: or, Weekly Miscellany.

Lloyd's Evening Post and British Chronicle.

The London Chronicle: or, Universal Evening Post.

The London Evening Post.

The London Journal.
The London Magazine: or, Gentleman's Monthly Intelligencer.
The Monthly Mirror Reflecting Men and Manners.
The Monthly Review: or, Literary Journal.
The Morning Chronicle and London Advertiser.
The Morning Herald.
The Morning Post and Daily Advertiser.
The Newcastle Courant.
Notes & Queries.
The Oxford Magazine: or, University Museum.
The Political Register and Impartial Review of New Books.
The Public Advertiser.
Ranger's Repository: or, Annual Packet, of Mirth, Whim and Humour for the year 1796.
Read's Weekly Journal: or, British Gazetteer.
St James's Chronicle: or, the British Evening Post.
The Scots Magazine.
The Sporting Magazine: or, Monthly Calendar.
The Town and Country Magazine.
The Universal Magazine of Knowledge and Pleasure.
The Westminster Magazine: or, the Pantheon of Taste.
The Whitehall Evening Post: or, London Intelligencer.
Williamson's Liverpool Advertiser and Mercantile Chronicle.

Printed Secondary Sources

Andrew, Donna T., 'Noblesse Oblige: Female Charity in the Age of Sentiment', in John Brewer and Susan Staves (eds), *Early Modern Conceptions of Property* (& New York: Routledge, 1995), pp.275–300.

Ashe, Geoffrey, *Do What You Will: A History of Anti-Morality* (& New York: W.H. Allen, 1974).

Askham, Francis, *The Gay Delavals* (Jonathan Cape, 1955).

Banister, Julia, 'The Court Martial of Admiral John Byng: Politeness and the Military Man in the Mid-Eighteenth Century', in Heather Ellis and Jessica Meyer (eds), *Masculinity and the Other: Historical Perspectives* (Cambridge: Cambridge Scholars Publishing, 2009).

Bassermann, Lujo, *The Oldest Profession: A History of Prostitution*, translated from the German by James Cleugh (Arthur Barker Ltd, 1967).

Battestin, Martin C., 'Fielding and "Master Punch" in Panton Street', in *Philological Quarterly* (1966), vol. 45, no.1, pp.191–208.

Battestin, Martin C. with Ruthe R. Battestin, *Henry Fielding, a Life* (& New York: Routledge, 1989).

Blanch, Lesley (ed.), *Harriette Wilson's Memoirs: The Greatest Courtesan of her Age* (Phoenix, 2003).

Bleackley, Horace, *Ladies Fair and Frail: Sketches of the Demi-Monde during the Eighteenth Century* (John Lane, The Bodley Head, 1909).

Borlase, William Copeland, *The Descent, Name and Arms of Borlase of Borlase in the County of Cornwall* (George Bell & Sons, & Exeter: William Pollard & Co., 1888).

Boyce, Benjamin, *The Benevolent Man: A Life of Ralph Allen of Bath* (Cambridge, Mass.: Harvard University Press 1967).

Bradshaw, Richard Lee, *Thomas Bradshaw 1733–1774: A Georgian Politician in the Time of the American Revolution* (Bloomington, Indiana: Xlibris, 2011).

Brewer, John, *Sentimental Murder: Love and Madness in the Eighteenth Century* (HarperCollins, 2004).

Burford, E.J. (ed.), *Bawdy Verse: A Pleasant Collection* (Harmondsworth: Penguin, 1982).

Burford, E.J. and Joy Wotton, *Private Vices–Public Virtues: Bawdry in London from Elizabethan Times to the Regency* (Robert Hale, 1995).

Burford, E.J., *Royal St James's: Being a Story of Kings, Clubmen, and Courtesans* (Robert Hale, 1988).

Burford, E.J., *Wits, Wenchers and Wantons, London's Low Life: Covent Garden in the Eighteenth Century* (Robert Hale, 1990).

Byrne, Paula, *Perdita, the Life of Mary Robinson,* (Harper Perennial, 2005).

Campbell, Lord John, *The Lives of the Lord Chancellors of England and Keepers of the Great Seal of England …*, 2nd series, 8 vols (John Murray, 1846–69).

Cardwell, M. John, *Arts and Arms: Literature, Politics and Patriotism during the Seven Years War* (Manchester & New York: Manchester University Press, 2004).

Cash, Arthur H., *An Essay on Woman by John Wilkes and Thomas Potter. A Reconstruction of a Lost Book with a Historical Essay on the Writing, Printing, and Suppressing of this 'Blasphemous and Obscene Work'* (New York: AMS Press Inc., 2000).

Cash, Arthur H., *John Wilkes: The Scandalous Father of Civil Liberty* (& New Haven: Yale University Press, 2006).

Connely, Willard, *Beau Nash: Monarch of Bath and Tunbridge Wells* (Werner Laurie, 1955).

Cruickshank, Dan, *The Secret History of Georgian London* (Windmill Books, 2010).

Dabhoiwala, Faramerz, *The Origins of Sex: A History of the First Sexual Revolution* (Allen Lane, 2012).

Dashwood, Sir Francis, *The Dashwoods of West Wycombe* (Aurem Press, 1987).

De Barri, Kinsman, *The Bucks and Bawds of London Town* (Leslie Frewin, 1974).

Eglin, John, *The Imaginary Autocrat, Beau Nash and the Invention of Bath* (Profile Books, 2005).

Finnegan, Rachel, 'The Divan Club, 1744–46', in *Electronic Journal of Oriental Studies*, IX (2006), no. 9, pp. 1–86.

Foss, Edward, *The Judges of England; with Sketches of their Lives …*, 9 vols (John Murray, 1848–64).

Franklin, Michael J., *Orientalist Jones, Sir William Jones, Poet, Lawyer and Linguist, 1746–1794* (Oxford: Oxford University Press, 2011).

Frith, Wendy, 'Sexuality and Politics in the Gardens of West Wycombe and Medmenham Abbey', in Michel Conan (ed.), *Bourgeois and Aristocratic Cultural Encounters in Garden Art, 1550–1850* (Washington DC: Dumbarton Oaks, 2002).

Fuller, Ronald, *Hell-Fire Francis* (Chatto & Windus, 1939).

Gatrell, Vic, *The First Bohemians: Life and Art in London's Golden Age* (Allen Lane, 2013).

Goff, Moira et al., *Georgians Revealed: Life, Style and the Making of Modern Britain* (The British Library, 2013).

Griffin, Susan, *The Book of the Courtesans: A Catalogue of their Virtues* (Macmillan, 2002).

Hamilton, Robert (ed.), *Decisions of the Court of Session from November 1769 to January 1772* (Edinburgh: 1803).

Harris, Frances, *A Passion for Government: The Life of Sarah, Duchess of Marlborough* (Oxford: Clarendon Press, 1991).

Harris, George, *The Life of Lord Chancellor Hardwick with Selections from his Correspondence, Diaries, Speeches and Judgements*, 3 vols (Edward Moxon, 1847).

Harris, John, *The Artist and the Country House: A History of Country House and Garden View Painting in Britain, 1540–1870* (Philip Wilson Publishers Ltd, 1979).

Hickman, Katie, *Courtesans* (HarperCollins, 2003).

Highfill, Philip Halman, A. Burnim & Edward A. Langhans (eds), *A Biographical Dictionary of Actors, Actresses, Musicians, Dancers, Managers and other Stage Personnel in London, 1660–1800*, 13 vols (Carbondale & Edwardsville: Southern Illinois University Press, 1973–93).

Hilton, Lisa, *Mistress Peachum's Pleasure: The Life of Lavinia, Duchess of Bolton* (Weidenfeld & Nicolson, 2005).

Hinde, Thomas, *Tales from the Pump Room. Nine Hundred Years of Bath: the Place, its People, and its Gossip* (Victor Gollancz, 1988).

Ingram, Martin, 'Ridings, Rough Music and Mocking Rhymes in Early Modern England', in Barry Reay (ed.), *Popular Culture in Seventeenth-Century England* (& Sydney: Croom Helm, 1985).

Jones, Louis Clark, *The Clubs of the Georgian Rakes* (New York: Columbia University Press, 1942).

Linnane, Fergus, *The Lives of the English Rakes* (Piatkus, 2010).

Linnane, Fergus, *London, the Wicked City: A Thousand Years of Vice in the Capital* (Robson Books, 2007).

Linnane, Fergus, *Madams, Bawds & Brothel-Keepers of London* (Stroud: The History Press, 2005).

Lord, Evelyn, *The Hell-Fire Clubs: Sex, Satanism and Secret Societies* (& New Haven: Yale University Press, 2008).

Low, Donald A., 'An Eighteenth-Century Imitation of Donne's First Satire', in *The Review of English Studies* (August 1965), vol. 16, no. 63.

McCormick Donald, *The Hell-Fire Club: The Story of the Amorous Knights of Wycombe* (Jarrolds, 1958).

McCreery, Cindy, 'Keeping up with the *Bon Ton*: the *Tête à Tête* series in the *Town and Country Magazine*', in Hannah Barker and Elaine Chalus (eds),

Gender in Eighteenth-Century England: Roles, Representations and Responsibilities (New York: Longman, 1997) pp.207–29.

McCreery, Cindy, *The Satirical Gaze: Prints of Women in Late Eighteenth-Century England* (Oxford: Oxford University Press, 2004).

Mackenzie, Donald, *Scotland's First National Theatre* … (Edinburgh: The Stanley Press, 1963).

Manning, Jo, *My Lady Scandalous: The Amazing Life and Outrageous Times of Grace Dalrymple Elliot, Royal Courtesan* (& New York: Simon & Schuster, 2005).

Mannix, Daniel P., *The Hell-Fire Club* (New English Library, 1970).

Martelli, George, *Jemmy Twitcher: A Life of John Montagu, 4th Earl of Sandwich 1718–1792* (Jonathan Cape, 1962).

Melville, Lewis, *Bath Under Beau Nash* (Eveleigh Nash, 1907).

Merians, Linda E., 'The London Lock Hospital and the Lock Asylum for Women', in Linda E. Merians (ed.), *The Secret Malady: Venereal Disease in Eighteenth-Century Britain and France* (Kentucky: University Press of Kentucky, 1996).

Miller, Daniel A., *Sir Joseph Yorke and Anglo-Dutch Relations, 1774–1780* (The Hague & Paris: Mouton, 1970).

Morison, William Maxwell (ed.), *The Decisions of the Court of Session, From its Institution to the Present Time* … (Edinburgh: 1804), vol. 17.

Neale, R.S., *Bath, A Social History, 1680–1850, or A Valley of Pleasure, yet a Sink of Iniquity* (Routledge & Kegan Paul, 1981).

Norton, Rictor, *Mother Clap's Molly House: The Gay Subculture in England 1700–1830*, 2nd ed. (Stroud: The Chalford Press, 2006).

O'Connell, Sheila, *London 1753* (The British Museum Press, 2003).

O'Connell, Sheila, *Popular Print in England* (British Museum, 1999).

Peace, Mary, '"On the soft beds of luxury most Kingdoms have expired": 1759 and the Lives of Prostitutes', in Shaun Regan (ed.), *Reading 1759: Literary Culture in Mid-Eighteenth-Century Britain and France* (Lewisburg: Bucknell University Press, 2013).

Peakman, Julie, *Lascivious Bodies: A Sexual History of the Eighteenth Century* (Atlantic Books, 2004).

Peakman, Julie (ed.), *Whore Biographies, 1700–1825*, 8 vols (Pickering & Chatto, 2006–07).

Pearson, John, *Blood Royal: The Story of the Spencers and the Royals* (HarperCollins, 1999).

Poole, Keith B., *The Two Beaux* (East Ardsley: E.P. Publishing, 1976).

Pooll, A.H. Batten, *A West Country Potpourri* (Bath: published privately, 1969).

Postgate, Raymond, '*That Devil Wilkes*' (Constable & Co. Ltd, 1930).

Procter, Richard Wright, *Manchester in Holiday Dress* (Simpkin, Marshall & Co., and Manchester: Abel Heywood & Son, 1866).

Richardson, Joanna, *The Courtesans: The Demi-Monde in 19th-Century France* (Phoenix Press, 2000).

Rodger, N.A.M., *The Insatiable Earl: A Life of John Montagu, 4th Earl of Sandwich 1718–1792* (& New York: W.W. Norton & Co., 1994).

Rosenthal, Laura J., *Infamous Commerce, Prostitution in Eighteenth-Century British Literature and Culture* (& Ithaca: Cornell University Press, 2006).

Rosenthal, Laura J. (ed.), *Nightwalkers: Prostitute Narratives from the Eighteenth Century* (Peterborough, Ontario: Broadview Press, 2008).

Rubenhold, Hallie, *The Covent Garden Ladies: Pimp General Jack & the Extraordinary Story of Harris's List* (Stroud: Tempus, 2005).

Sainsbury, John, *John Wilkes, The Lives of a Libertine* (Aldershot & Burlington, Vermont: Ashgate Publishing, 2006).

Sanders, Lloyd, *Patron and Place Hunter: A Study of George Bubb Dodington Lord Melcombe* (John Lane, The Bodley Head & New York: John Lane Co., 1919).

Smyth, Amelia Gillespie (ed.), *Memoirs and Correspondence (Official and Familiar) of Sir Robert Murray Keith …*, 2 vols (Henry Colburn, 1849).

Spencer, Charles, *The Spencer Family* (Harmondsworth: Penguin, 2000).

Stephens, Frederic G. (ed.), *Catalogue of Prints and Drawings in the British Museum. Division 1. Political and Personal Satires*, 4 vols (1870–83).

Stochholm, Johanne Magdalen, *Garrick's Folly: The Shakespeare Jubilee of 1769 at Stratford and Drury Lane* (Methuen & Co. Ltd, 1964).

Suster, Gerald, *The Hell-Fire Friars* (Robson Books, 2000).

Tillyard, Stella, *A Royal Affair: George III and his Troublesome Siblings* (Chatto & Windus, 2006).

Tillyard, Stella, '"Paths of Glory": Fame and the Public in Eighteenth-Century London', in Martin Postle (ed.), *Joshua Reynolds: The Creation of Celebrity* (Tate Publishing, 2005).

Towers, Eric, *Dashwood the Man and the Myth: The Life and Times of the Hell Fire Club's Founder* (Crucible, 1986).

Trumbach, Randolph, *Sex and the Gender Revolution: Volume One, Heterosexuality and the Third Gender in Enlightenment London* (Chicago: University of Chicago Press, 1998).

Walters, John, *Splendour and Scandal: The Reign of Beau Nash* (Jarrolds, 1968).

Walters, John, *The Royal Griffin: Frederick Prince of Wales 1707–51* (Jarrolds, 1972).

Ware, Mrs Mary Clementina Hibbert, *The King of Bath: or, Life at a Spa in the Eighteenth Century. A Picture of the Life and Times of Beau Nash*, 2nd ed., 2 vols (Charles J. Skeet, 1879).

Wheeler, Charles, *The Age of Charles II, Royal Academy of Arts Winter Exhibition, 1960–61* (Royal Academy of Arts, 1961).

Williamson, Audrey, *Wilkes 'A Friend to Liberty'* (George Allen & Unwin Ltd, 1974).

Wraxall, C.F. Lascelles, *Life and Times of Her Majesty Queen Matilda …*, 3 vols (W.H. Allen & Co., 1864).

Index

If you enjoyed this book, you may also be interested in ...

Naval Wives and Mistresses
MARGARETTE LINCOLN

A fascinating social history that draws on rare sources, which illuminates all aspects of society. Illustrated with images from the National Maritime Museum's extensive collection of oil paintings, prints and drawings.

978 0 7524 6091 8

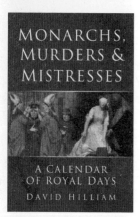

Mysterious Mistress
MARGARET CROSLAND

Jane Shore often gets just a byline in history. She was the mistress of a king. But where did she come from? And how was it that having been mistress to the most powerful man in the land, she ended her years in prison and poverty? This work draws on literary, historical and artistic sources to explore Jane's life.

978 0 7509 3851 8

Monarchs, Murders & Mistresses
DAVID HILLIAM

An entertaining record of the scandals that have plagued the royal family throughout the decades. *Monarchs, Murders & Mistresses* presents a royal event for each day of the calendar year in vivid detail, with close-ups of the personalities involved.

978 0 7524 5235 7